**Constructing the
Socialist Way of Life**
Mass Housing and Urbanism
in North Korea

Constructing the
Socialist Way of Life
Mass Housing and Urbanism
in North Korea

Edited by Inha Jung

*With contributions by Inha Jung, Kim Young-cheol,
Kim Jong-yeon, Shin Gun-soo, and Kim Mina*

목차

★ **Foreword** 6

★ **Chapter 1**
The Reconstruction of Two Cities: Pyongyang and Hamhŭng 11

★ **Chapter 2**
Piotr Zaremba and the Urban Planning of Chongjin 45

★ **Chapter 3**
The Creation of Kim Il-sung Square in Pyongyang 69

★ **Chapter 4**
The Emergence of Mass Housing in Post-war North Korea 93

★ **Chapter 5**
The Microdistrict-based Approach to Site Planning 113

★ **Chapter 6**
Socialising Rural Space in North Korea 139

★ **Chapter 7**
The Planning of Gwangbok Street New Town in Pyongyang 163

★ **Chapter 8**
The Development of the Housing Market and its Influence on Apartment Unit Plans 201

★ **Annex**
Bibliography 231

Foreword

Inha Jung

North Korea is one of a few countries that retained its socialist system following the collapse of the Soviet Union in 1991. While most socialist countries introduced a market economy and moved toward globalisation, North Korea opted to preserve its own closed system in defiance of the trend. North Korea is also the only socialist country to have implemented hereditary succession – over three generations. Indeed, the Juche ideology (*Juche* roughly translates as 'self-reliance') was invented to legitimise this type of succession and justify North Korea's transition from a socialist state to a despotic nation. Meanwhile, the country has continued its pursuit of nuclear armament, prompting the United Nations to impose harsh economic sanctions. Since the 1990s, international sanctions have virtually paralysed North Korea's food distribution system, creating severe food shortages among citizens. This extraordinary situation prompts us to ask why the North Korean system is still working despite such economic hardships. North Korea's political forces and ideologies have been accused of brainwashing its people. However, the testimonies of many North Korean defectors reveal such interpretations to be derivative and superficial; a wider spectrum of approaches to North Korean reality is required.

Unlike political and economic approaches to North Korean issues, this book focuses on housing and urban planning, areas which constitute a key element of North Korea's material foundation. In the post-war era, the country attempted to socialise all types of living space, from small apartment rooms to urban settings, on the basis of political ideology. Exploring North Korean domestic culture and daily life, this book aims to capture the actual lives of North Koreans, who have largely supported this unique political system. This is no easy task, given the diversity of perspectives on North Korean life. Much of this confusion is rooted in two contrasting approaches – intrinsic and extrinsic – to North Korean society that offer competing, and often entirely contradictory, interpretations of society and events. The intrinsic approach requires us to take the North Korean system for what it is and understand it in terms of its own structure. It explains various phenomena in North Korean society by reference to this society's autonomous framework. Scholars who take this approach believe that North Koreans are leading their lives in extremely restricted conditions, and that the North Korean regime is struggling to secure its own means of survival. By contrast, the extrinsic approach takes a critical attitude to North Korea and attempts to evaluate the country's perceived wrongdoings in accordance with universal human values. This approach gained popularity with the intensified interest in the North Korean regime in the late 1990s, when the country officially revealed its intention to develop nuclear weapons.

These contrasting approaches significantly affect our understandings and expectations of North Korea. Adoption of the extrinsic approach makes it difficult to anticipate what will happen in North Korea. For instance, many experts predicted that North Korea would collapse after the death of Kim Il-sung and Kim Jong-il. Instead, the regimes that followed in each case reinforced their totalitarian rule. This dilemma demonstrates how difficult it is for us to understand North Korean society in a normal context. More optimistic commentators now believe that the North Korean regime will abandon its strategy of nuclear armament if the US and other world powers pressure it to do so; however,

Kim Jong-un has in fact merely intensified his pursuit of this strategy. Thus, attempts to understand North Korea must be based on two perspectives: on one hand, only the intrinsic approach can give us insight into how North Koreans actually live; on the other hand, a critical stance is needed to prevent our analysis from veering offtrack. Selecting the correct stance and approach thus poses a challenge in studies on North Korea.

This book toes the line between the intrinsic and extrinsic viewpoints. This necessitates a careful, delicately nuanced approach to the data and literature on the theme. Primary data are essential for ensuring the accuracy of our discussion. The quality of research on North Korean society undoubtedly often depends on how it is accessed and used. Without trustworthy inside information, our discussions are inevitably limited, potentially paving the way for subjective assumptions and judgments. Wary of such dangers, this book deliberately omits unidentified areas of study, leaving us with a kind of vacuum that can be filled when new facts are discovered. Even if primary data are available, their interpretation constitutes another major problem. Official historical literature on North Korea's housing and urban planning has already been published, such as *The History of Joseon Architecture 1* and *2* (1989) and *The Entire History of Pyongyang Construction* (1997). These works typically include many detailed descriptions of housing and urban planning because the North Korean regime has promoted the advantages of the socialist system in dealing with these subjects. However, the literature has also been distorted by strict censorship; content deemed ill-suited to the regime's propaganda has been excised. For example, to emphasise the regime's self-reliance, the literature contains little information on aid provided by other socialist countries during the reconstruction period. In reality, the aid provided by these countries made a significant contribution to the formation of urban spaces in North Korea. Moreover, as all final results were ascribed to the greatness of the country's political leaders, the role played by individual architects and planners in projects was very difficult to make out from the outside. The excessive domination of politics over expertise makes it difficult to arrive at a more realistic understanding.

To address such limitations, this book utilises visual materials such as drawings, maps, and diagrams obtained from various archives. While these are neutral forms of communication, they also convey the actual intentions of North Korean architects and planners that are hidden behind the claims of the political leader. Sources used in this book include documents relating to the urban planning of Pyongyang held by the National Archives of the US and the National Diet Library of Japan; material on Hamhŭng, predominantly from the collection of the Bauhaus Dessau Foundation and the Bundesarchiv in Berlin; Kim Jeong-hui's PhD dissertation, sourced from the State Archives of Russia; and material on Chongjin at the State Archives of Szczecin. Finally, this book would not have been possible without the aid of a group of researchers from Hanyang University's Modern Architecture Laboratory. In particular, credit for Chapter 1 is largely owed to Kim Young-cheol, for Chapter 2 to Kim Jong-yeon, for Chapters 4 and 6 to Shin Gun-soo, and for Chapters 5 and 7 to Kim Mina. I would like to express my sincere gratitude to these researchers for their assistance and support. I would also like to thank the National Research Foundation of Korea for funding this endeavour since 2013.

Façades of two residential buildings in Pyonyang.
Source: dreamstime/Boggy

Façade of a residential building in Pyonyang.
Source: dreamstime/Boggy

하나

The Reconstruction of Two Cities: Pyongyang and Hamhŭng

Inha Jung/ Kim Young-cheol

The reconstruction of North Korea's cities coincided with a period of political transition in the Soviet Union, namely the death of Joseph Stalin in 1953 and Nikita Khrushchev's ascension to power in 1958. As is well known, Soviet urban planning was deeply intertwined with the tastes of political leaders. For instance, the Lenin era favoured a radical approach to architecture and urban planning in an attempt to break down bourgeois culture and embody the new socialist ideology in reality. Following the Bolshevik Revolution in 1917, the Russian Avant-garde was the dominant stream; it was followed by the Disurbanist group, radicals who sought to abolish the distinction between city and countryside. However, as Stalin gradually came to power, this trend underwent a complete reversal. Neoclassicism was adopted as the main architectural style, while a Baroque-style planning method served as an important guideline in the reconstruction of cities destroyed in the Great Patriotic War (1941–1945). Stalinist socialist realism was subsequently abandoned under Khrushchev. In its place, the new leader promoted standardisation and mass construction of housing; this more practical approach aimed to improve the quality of daily life.

The North Korean regime was sensitive to these changes. The post-war reconstruction of North Korean cities occurred during the de-Stalinisation period; this made it possible to exploit new approaches to urban planning. Moreover, as North Korea's reconstruction projects harnessed international aid from socialist countries, architects and planners from various countries – including Soviet Russia, Germany, Poland, and Hungary – as well as North Korean architects educated in the Soviet Union, participated in these projects. This means that, in addition to reflecting the diversity of socialist urban planning following the death of Stalin, the reconstruction of North Korean cities had an influence on new directions in post-war socialist urban planning in general. Bearing these two historical particularities in mind, this chapter focuses on the reconstruction of two North Korean cities, Pyongyang and Hamhŭng.

International Aid

Japan's unconditional surrender to the Allied Powers on 15 August 1945 marked the liberation of Korea from Japanese colonial rule. However, the joy of liberation did not last long. The Allied Powers soon divided the peninsula into North and South Korea along the 38th parallel, designating North Korea a Soviet occupation zone. The Soviet Union subsequently launched a programme of social reform in order to communise North Korea. On 14 October the Soviet military government introduced Kim Il-sung as a guerrilla hero; on 8 February 1946 it established the Provisional People's Committee of North Korea. While dismantling landowners' and capitalists' social and economic bases through land reform and the nationalisation of industries, the Soviet military government reinforced the one-party dictatorship of the Joseon Labour Party. In July 1948 North Korea held a general election in which only candidates from the Communist Party could run. On 9 September it declared the establishment of the Democratic People's Republic of Korea (DPRK), with Kim Il-sung as the country's first prime minister.

When both North and South Korea established autonomous governments in 1948, the Korean Peninsula was gripped by political tension. The Soviet Union wished to communise the entire peninsula. In 1949 the communist takeover of China and the withdrawal of US troops from South Korea spurred Soviet and North Korean leaders to develop plans to invade South Korea. At 4:00 a.m. on 25 June 1950, with the support of the Soviet Union, the North Korean army launched an invasion across the 38th parallel, sparking a three-year civil war that wrought tremendous damage across the Korean Peninsula. Both US-led allies and Chinese troops participated in the Korean War (1950–1953), turning it into an international conflict. The war ended with the signing of a ceasefire in 1953. Both sides had suffered significant casualties and extensive structural and infrastructural damage.

The Korean War meant complete devastation for cities in North Korea. The US military, which was in charge of aerial operations, dropped significant quantities of bombs on North Korean cities.[1] According to North Korean official reports, more than 8700 factory buildings, 600,000 homes, 5000 schools, 1000 hospitals and clinics, 203 theatres and cinemas, as well as thousands of cultural institutions were destroyed during the war. The damage to large cities was even worse. An ancient city with more than 1500 years of history, Pyongyang lost its unique cultural identity in the aerial bombing. The majority of its historical sites, including old citadels, famous gate buildings, and provincial offices, disappeared without trace. In Hamhŭng, Korea's largest industrial city, US bombing campaigns concentrated on industrial facilities and railways, destroying more than 90 percent of the city's infrastructure. The extent of the damage is evident in aerial photographs of these cities taken after the bombings.

With no clear victory, the Korean Peninsula remained divided. As soon as the war ended, North Korea began recovery efforts, with the North Korean regime taking the opportunity to transform destroyed cities into socialist ones. Post-war restoration was carried out in two phases: from 1954 to 1956 through the 'Three-Year Plan for the Postwar Reconstruction' (*Jeonhu bokgu 3gaenyeon gyehoek*), and from 1957 to 1961 through the 'First Five-Year Plan for the People's Economic Development' (*Inmin gyeongje baljeon gaenyeon gyehoek*). Devised in close cooperation with the Soviet Union and other socialist countries, this economic-development plan replicated the Soviet planned economy. More specifically, the three-year plan was developed to restore North Korea's economy, which was based on heavy industry, to its pre-war level. Although the country's electricity, coal, and chemical industries did not reach pre-war levels,[2] reconstruction projects initiated during this phase produced significant results.

Parallel with this economic recovery, the North Korean government introduced several policies to facilitate the reconstruction of cities. The Ministry of Urban Construction, which had been established as part of the government in February 1951, appointed the State Construction Commission in June 1953. In 1954 the government adopted the cabinet's decision to proceed with the restoration of all cities based on urban plans. Accordingly, general plans for the urban reconstruction of Chongjin, Hamhŭng, Wonsan, Sariwon, Kanggye, Nampo, Sinuiju, Songlim, Kimchaek, and Pyongyang were prepared and plans were developed for 150 towns and autonomous districts across the country.[3]

North Korea lacked both the finances and urban-planning expertise necessary for reconstruction. Fortunately, the international environment at this time was favourable towards it. Indeed, the period of post-war reconstruction in North Korea was the first and only time that the Soviet Union, China, Soviet-aligned countries in Eastern Europe, and Mongolia cooperated on a large-scale economic project of this nature. This was a historical high point for 'international socialist solidarity.'[4] These countries were able to provide aid to North Korea because they had quickly and successfully recovered from the devastation of the Second World War. Thus the reconstruction of North Korean cities during this period was achieved thanks to aid from other socialist countries rather than North Korea's own resources. Foreign aid revenue constituted a significant proportion of the national budget in the first few years following the Korean War. In the 1950s socialist countries provided 1.76 billion USD in financial aid to North Korea, 75 percent (1.278 billion USD) of which was provided free of charge and the remaining 25 percent (428 million USD) as loans subject to interest.[5] Soviet sources provide a breakdown of foreign assistance to the DPRK between 1953 and 1960. This was divided roughly into thirds, probably at Moscow's suggestion: approximately 33.3 percent of reconstruction aid came from the USSR, 29.4 percent from China, and 37.3 percent from other countries.[6] However, foreign aid gradually decreased to 34 percent in 1954, 21.7 percent in 1955, and 16.5 percent in 1956.[7]

In addition to providing the various materials needed to rebuild North Korean cities, these countries despatched experts and engineers to help with urban planning and construction. The Soviet Union provided the largest amount of aid, most of which was used to reconstruct North Korea's textile factories, fertiliser factories, and steel mills. The Soviet Union also sent experts and engineers to Pyongyang, where they advised North Korean architects and supervised reconstruction projects. However, unlike Beijing, Soviet planners did not directly intervene in the planning of North Korea's capital. Instead, they chose to supervise Korean architects who had completed their studies in the Soviet Union. Meanwhile, China, which had directly participated in the war, helped North Korea in a different way. While China faced its own economic crisis after the Korean War, up to 34 divisions of the Chinese People's Volunteer Army, who were stationed in North Korea, provided free labour until they were withdrawn in 1958.[8]

East Germany adopted a different approach to North Korea's reconstruction. In 1954, Kim Il-sung and the prime minister of East Germany, Otto Grotewohl, selected Hamhŭng as the site for East German aid. On July 6 the East German government organised and despatched a group of architects, city planners, and engineers known as the Deutsche Arbeitsgruppe (DAG) to Hamhŭng, where they focused on urban planning, residential construction, and reconstruction of factories. Although the formal aid plan promised assistance until 1964, East Germany suspended financial support and reconstruction initiatives in 1962 due to the split between China and the Soviet Union. Other socialist countries – including Poland, Czechoslovakia, Romania, Hungary, and Bulgaria – also provided financial aid and expertise to help North Korea.[9] In November 1954, for instance, Poland sent city-planning experts to Chongjin; under the leadership of Piotr Zaremba (1910–1993), Polish experts spent 16 months helping in the city's reconstruction.

Hungary also despatched a design team to take part in reconstruction of North Korean cities. According to the literature, a Hungarian team submitted a proposal for the design of Kim Il-sung Square in Pyongyang.[10]

The reconstruction of North Korean cities was thus an international effort involving all the socialist states. Foreign experts stationed in North Korea also held meetings at which they exchanged information about North Korea and modified their projects accordingly.

Kim Jeong-hui (1921–1975): The Architect Behind North Korea's Reconstruction

Before discussing the reconstruction of North Korean cities, let us take a look at the life of the most prolific North Korean architect and planner, Kim Jeong-hui. One of the first North Koreans selected to study abroad with the support of Kim Il-sung, Kim Jeong-hui specialised in urban planning at the Moscow Institute of Architecture from September 1947 to July 1953. After returning home, he was put in charge of early plans for Pyongyang. Although he was prominent enough in North Korea for his life to be made into a movie,[11] little was known about his early education and formative years until the recent discovery of documents in the Russian Federal Archives.[12]

The archival documents tell us that Kim Jeong-hui was born to a farming family in North Pyongan Province on 9 July 1921. His personal submission to the Moscow Institute of Architecture reveals that his family gave him an anti-Japanese imperialist education; however, his parents' jobs and beliefs are not described. In 1934 he entered Osan High School, founded by the nationalist activist Lee Seung-hoon (1864–1930) in 1907. Around this time, his elder brother joined the Chinese Revolution, significantly impacting Kim Jeong-hui's 'communist education and the formation of [his] worldview'. However, in his personal submission Kim Jeong-hui claimed not to have participated in the partisan movement. In 1939 Kim Jeong-hui moved to Japan to study architecture at Nihon University, graduating from there in 1944.[13]

Nihon University has the second oldest architecture department after Waseda University. Under Sano Toshikata (1880–1956), head of the architectural department from 1920, Nihon University attempted to establish a new model for architectural education in Japan. Sano was at the centre of this educational reform. While studying the structure of reinforced concrete at Tokyo University, Sano pioneered the theory of seismic structures – an invaluable contribution to earthquake-prone Japan. He also contributed greatly to the 1919 Japanese Building Act, which was developed in cooperation with the Koto Shimpei-led Urban Planning Research Association. Sano actively sought to improve the quality of Japanese housing. He became deeply involved in the planning of apartment buildings erected by the Dojunkai corporation after the 1923 Kanto earthquake. With Toshiro Kasahara and other professors at Nihon University, Sano sought to cultivate 'engineer-architects' with engineering knowledge, as opposed to 'designer architects' versed in western architecture and artistic trends. Consequently, Tanigawa and Kuznetsov note, 'many graduates of this school grew to be excellent engineers in the structural field. In addition, this university produced many students who have become talented managers of government offices.'[14] The fact that Kim Jeong-hui became more interested in urban planning than architectural design reflects the atmosphere of this school. However, in 1943, the final year of his studies, Kim Jeong-hui was arrested and tortured by the Special Higher Police – known as the 'Tokubetsu Koto Keisatsu' or 'Tokko' – on the charge of being a member of a Marxist research group. After his release, Kim Jeong-hui graduated from college in 1944 and returned to Korea, where he began teaching at a technical school. After Korea's liberation in 1945, and the subsequent occupation of North Korea by the Soviet army, Kim Jeong-hui revealed his communist leanings and established the North Korean Union of Architects (NKUA), of which he was elected vice-chairman. On 5 July 1946 he joined the Communist Party of North Korea. He then studied as a graduate at Kim Il-sung University until 1 August 1947, leaving for Moscow two months later. According to Tanigawa and Kuznetsov, two things made up for Kim Jeong-hui's lack of a working-class background in his achievement of career success: his arrest and torture by the Japanese Special Police, and his ability to network at the NKUA. This demonstrated his legitimacy to the North Korean authorities, as well as his ability to hold an important position in the field of architecture. Furthermore, Kim Eung-sang, the chairman of the NKUA, had studied architecture with Kim Jeong-hui at Nihon University. Although Kim Eung-sang was five years older than Kim Jeong-hui, they appear to have known each other before Korea's liberation.[15] Kim Eung-sang brought Kim Jeong-hui into the inner circle of the North Korean architectural community.

In January 1951 Kim Il-sung ordered Kim Jeong-hui to return to North Korea from Moscow. The North Korean dictator needed an expert to lead the planning of Pyongyang's reconstruction. In September 1951, after ten months of work, Kim Jeong-hui submitted a general plan for the reconstruction of North Korea's capital city. His experience of this time was the basis for his doctoral dissertation at Moscow Institute of Architecture, where his thesis advisor was N. Kh. Polyakov, a renowned Soviet urban planner. Kim Jeong-hui remained in the Soviet Union until July 1953.

In November 1953, after returning to Korea, Kim Jeong-hui published a Korean translation of his dissertation under the title *Dosi Genseol* (Urban Construction). In the book's introduction Kim Jeong-hui wrote, 'After carrying out the assignment to devise a plan for North Korea's urban reconstruction in 1951, I developed it in the form of a thesis for about a year and a half, and [have now rewritten it] in an easier way.' Comparison of *Dosi Genseol* and Kim Jeong-hui's plan for Pyongyang provides insight into the actual intentions of his urban planning. Thus *Dosi Genseol* is worth examining because it provides clues that are important in understanding the reconstruction of North Korea's cities in the post-war era. Although Kim Jeong-hui admitted that his book lacked a clear structure due to its attempt to cover too wide a range of issues, *Dosi Genseol* laid the theoretical basis for the reconstruction of North Korean cities.

Dosi Genseol comprises six chapters, including an introduction and a conclusion. After the introduction, the first and second chapter briefly describe the history of urban development in Korea and the Soviet Union, with particular focus on urbanisation between the Bolshevik Revolution in 1917 and the reconstruction that followed the Second World War.

The third chapter, the most important in the book, presents principles for urban design and reconstruction in North Korea. In this chapter Kim Jeong-hui proposes various kinds of urban regulation – including of block size, population density, minimal dwelling size, maximal building height, and distance between buildings – primarily based on the Soviet experience of reconstruction. In addition to these regulations, he devotes several pages to the Soviet concept of the *kvartal* or city block, which he translated using the term *jutaekguheok* for the North Korean context.

This concept was used to define the basic unit of urban space in his plan for the reconstruction of Pyongyang. The third chapter also presents eight basic requirements for urban planning, namely: 1) guarantee future potential and growth for cities in line with a general outlook on economic development; 2) create new conditions for expansion of existing industrial facilities and transport and for development of new facilities; 3) create the most convenient working and living conditions for urban inhabitants; 4) predict the location of social, cultural, and household amenities for planned reconstruction; 5) create a complete architectural and artistic composition for the entire city and for parts of the city such as blocks, streets, squares, and so on; 6) create a green system (e.g. cultural spaces, pedestrian paths, and small parks) inside and around the city to improve sanitary conditions; 7) organise a suburban agricultural settlement directly connected to the city; and 8) ensure realisation of fire-prevention measures.[16]

The fourth chapter deals with the principles of architectural composition in the urban context. Kim Jeong-hui modelled these principles on the 1935 general plan for reconstruction of Moscow. Under the latter, all urban-planning projects should 'create unified cityscapes that incorporate diverse elements, such as squares, arterial roads, riversides, and parks, by utilising outstanding classic models, new buildings, and new construction techniques. Connection of various elements such as the ups and downs of Moscow's hills, the Moscow River, the Yauza River, and the city's parks is to generate potential for the creation of a truly socialist city.'[17] This thought represents the architectural and urban aesthetic of the Stalin era. Significantly, Kim Jeong-hui sought to apply this Stalinist approach to urban design in the context of North Korea.

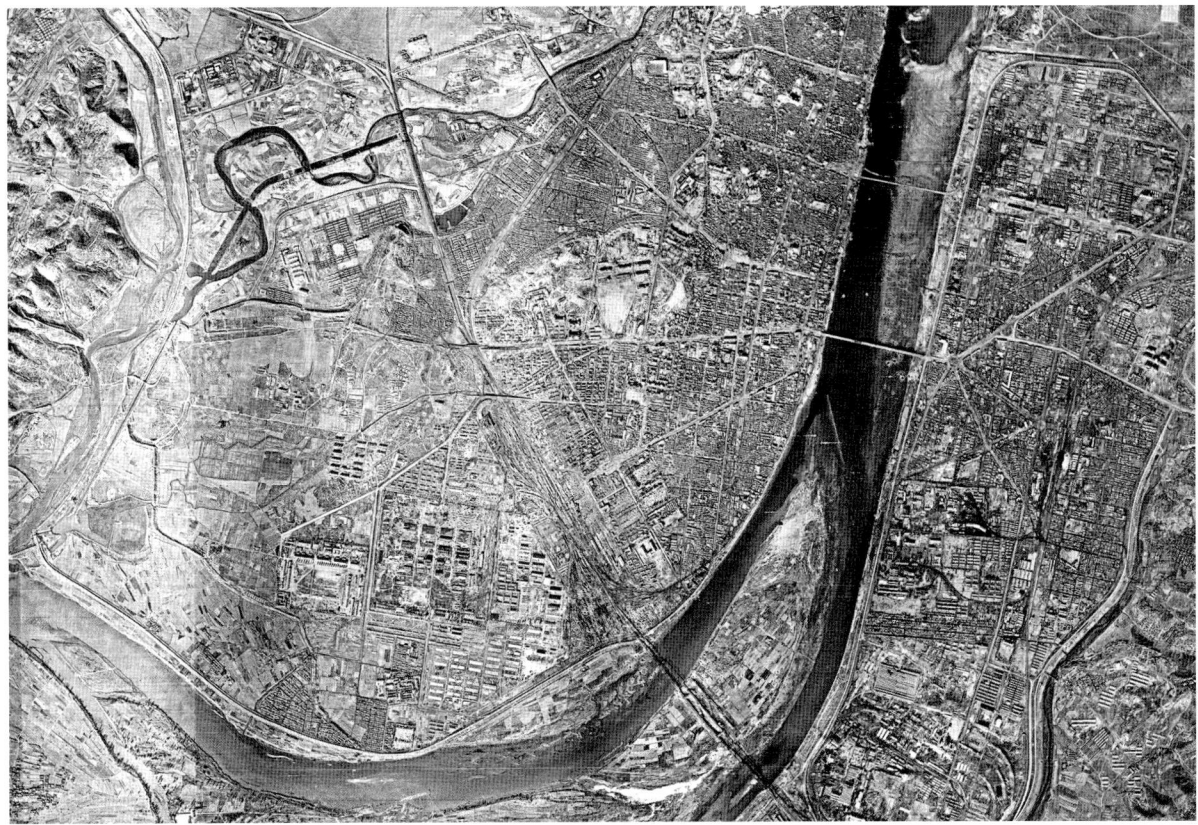

Aerial photo showing detruction of Pyongyang in the Korean War.
Source: National Geographic Information Institute

The Reconstruction of Pyongyang

The reconstruction plan for Pyongyang was revised several times, reflecting a variety of different approaches. Four plans show the reconstruction process for the city. The first was drawn up in 1938 and depicts Pyongyang's situation before North Korea came into being. The second was drawn up by Kim Jeong-hui in 1951 at the request of Kim Il-sung and illustrates Kim Jeong-hui's planning ideas. The third was developed in 1953 and was adopted as the basis for the city's reconstruction, particularly insofar as it framed the urban structure of downtown Pyongyang. The fourth plan, created in 1960, guided the expansion of Pyongyang's suburban area. Of these plans, we will focus on the planning process associated with the second and third plans.

On 21 January 1951, when the Korean War was in full swing, Kim Il-sung gathered North Korean city planners to develop a reconstruction plan for Pyongyang. At a meeting with them, he presented his own guidelines for their work: 'Pyongyang should not simply be restored to the original state of the Japanese colony; planners should create a contemporary city equipped with cultural and service facilities, eradicating the backwardness and abnormalities that were due to the Japanese imperialist regime.'[18] In May 1951 the city planners presented the first urban plan developed in

General reconstruction plan for Pyongyang, 1951.
Source: *Pyongyang geonseol jeonsa pyeonchan wiwonhoe, 1997*

accordance with Kim Il-sung's wishes: the General Reconstruction Plan for Pyongyang (hereinafter, the General Plan). The General Plan simply showed black-coloured city blocks and road networks. It primarily focused on correcting the city's urban structure, which had been deformed under Japanese colonialism. Comparison of the General Plan with the Pyongyang city plan drawn up in 1938 reveals that the North Korean planners were successful in this endeavour. The 1938 Pyongyang plan reflects characteristics typical of the colonial era: namely disconnection and heterogeneity. The spontaneous structure of the city's old town, located inside the inner fortifications, co-existed alongside the grid-like street network of the new Japanese town near the railway station. Although land readjustment projects were intended to expand the area on the east side of the Daedong River, these plans were never realised. Instead, military factories and airfields, necessitated by Japan's use of Pyongyang as a logistics hub for its invasion of Manchuria in the late 1930s, were scattered around the new town. Pyongyang was thus characterised by the coexistence of heterogeneous spaces.

In 1951 Kim Jeong-hui submitted his first plan for the reconstruction of Pyongyang. While markedly different from the 1938 plan, the General Plan still contained traces of Japanese colonialism because urban infrastructure, such as main roads and railway networks, cannot be fundamentally changed in a short period of time. Importantly, the General Plan unified the old Korean and new Japanese towns. It also established a more organised and efficient road network, with Stalin Street, a connecting path parallel to the Daedong River, as its centre. The General Plan reflects much of the know-how accumulated by the Soviet Union during its reconstruction period. The plan essentially sought to create a more consistent and connected urban centre. However, it paid little heed to protecting or reconstructing the historical heritage of the fortress city, Pyongyang, much of which had been destroyed during the Korean War.

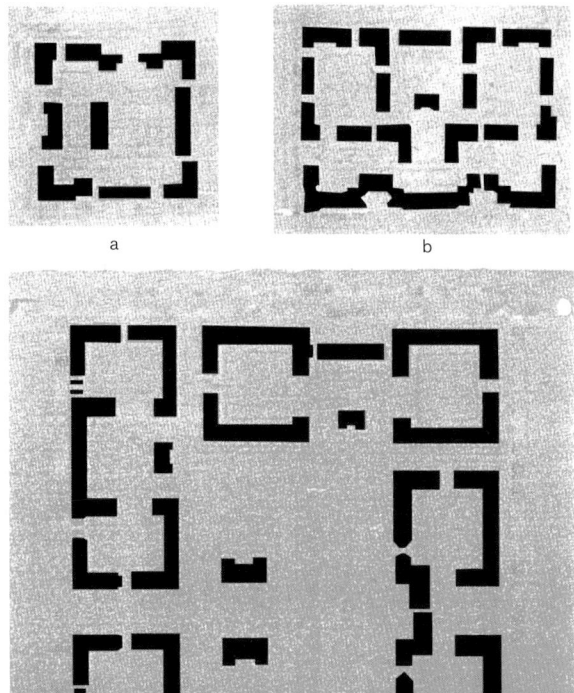

Three types of *kvartal*: a) peripheral (*jubyeon geonchuk bangsik*); b) mixed-type (*honhap geonchuk bangsik*); c) cluster (*group geonchuk bangsik*).
Source: Kim Jeong-hui, pp. 19, 243

Instead, Kim Jeong-hui's General Plan set out to create a harmonious cityscape with a natural environment. As Pyongyang is located on the main route from Manchuria to the Korean Peninsula, the city had long since been developed as a military stronghold harnessing the natural environment. It possesses unique geographical features, with the Daedong and Botong rivers flanking the two sides of the city wall and Moranbong Peak rising steeply to the north of the city, obstructing access. In addition, low hills, such as Namsan and Mansudae, are scattered throughout the city. 'Memorial buildings,' explained Kim Jeong-hui, 'will be situated in these places to emphasise the city's silhouette, or, if a site is inappropriate for building upon, it could be used as a green park for relaxation and walking.'[19] He similarly emphasised effective use of waterfronts, noting, 'we want to make the most of the waterfront by deploying the urban centre and other architectural assemblies around it.'[20]

In terms of transportation systems, the General Plan adopted a radial-ring road system, rejecting the grid-like street system proposed by modern architects. Citing the example of Manhattan, Kim Jeong-hui took the view that a grid street system and concentration of capitalist institutions in the city centre invariably result in high levels of congestion.[21]

Moscow's use of a radial-ring road system also served to reduce traffic in the city centre, while ensuring a beautiful urban landscape by creating grandeur on the radial arterial roads. This Baroque-style method had been applied to the construction of major cities in Russia prior to the Russian Revolution and was adopted in the reconstruction of Soviet cities such as Stalingrad, the ideal embodiment of the urban ideals of the Stalin era. Kim Jeong-hui had investigated this street system while studying in the Soviet Union. In the General Plan he used it to create an orderly arrangement of radial ring roads around the central square. In this respect the General Plan emphasised planning elements such as strong urban axes and boulevards, urban squares, and monuments.

The black-coloured urban blocks in the General Plan were designated as residential areas; these were the basic units of urban space in the reconstruction of North Korean cities. The idea of the urban block as the basic unit was rooted in the Soviet planning approach developed in the 1930s. Soviet planners proposed an urban block called a *kvartal* in the 1935 Moscow Plan, which reflected the dominant ideas of urban planning during the Stalinist period. The street blocks comprised buildings of a certain height on the perimeter, as well as various service facilities. Like the German concept of *Blockrandbebauung*, the *kvartal*'s perimeter comprises a series of four- to six-floor buildings, giving the city a consistent visual appearance. However, unlike its German counterpart, the *kvartal* is a self-contained unit possessing community facilities such as day-care centres, schools, and shops in the centre of the block. Soviet planners emphasised this difference, arguing that whereas the western neighbourhood unit was used in suburbs far from the city centre, the *kvartal* constituted the most economical approach to development of the urban area as a whole.

The *kvartal* approach was also completely different to the kind of collective housing promoted by the Russian Avant-garde, who designed independent buildings each equipped with the full range of socialist housing facilities. As illustrated by architect Moisey Ginzburg's Narkomfin building, the commune-house functioned as an autonomous community possessing a full range of service facilities. By comparison, Stalinist planners called for self-contained urban blocks connected to a green area and the radial-ring road system. In 1944 the basic principles for the Soviet city established the superblock as the basic city unit, with a single residential block (*kvartal*) becoming the centre of all social life. This later developed into the concept of the *mikrorayon* (microdistrict): each *mikrorayon* was a collection of such units.

In *Dosi Genseol* Kim Jeong-hui identifies three methods for designing a *kvartal*. First, the 'peripheral method' (*jubyeon geonchuk bangsik*), which places buildings at the edge of the block. While this is suitable for small blocks of less than four hectares, it makes it relatively difficult to organise the interior space of the block. Second, the more popular 'mixed-type method' (*honhap geonchuk bangsik*), which is suitable when the block size is large enough to include various service facilities in the centre of the block. Third, the 'cluster method' (*group geonchuk bangsik*), a newer approach whereby a block consists of several courtyards and a group of buildings, requiring a large area.[22] Based on this classification, Kim Jeong-hui suggested that *kvartal*s be planned in appropriate sizes in accordance with the urban context, building height, and orientation. Thus, after partitioning urban space into *kvartal*s, Kim Jeong-hui focused on architectural assembly using design elements such as buildings, roads, housing, and landscaping. He believed that the blocks should be united and adjusted to form an overarching composition, in the manner of a single artwork. This reflects the persistence of Stalinist ideas in socialist urban planning.

Kim Il-sung was satisfied with the General Plan. After listening to opinions from all sides to determine the final version, he held an exhibition at the Moranbong Theatre in May 1952, during which several plans, including for the Daedong River walkway, the city centre, high-rise housing, and public buildings were presented.[23] However, the General Plan was never realised: it was too schematic and unrealistic. Kim Il-sung ordered the development of a more concrete and practical plan for the reconstruction of Pyongyang. In 1953 a new reconstruction plan was commissioned following the publication of 'Cabinet decision no. 125 on the reconstruction of Pyongyang'. This decision determined the basic direction for the future Pyongyang reconstruction plan, which was required 'to preserve the base of the historical city; to correctly deploy housing, industry and transportation; to effectively organise residential areas guaranteeing residents' health; to make the Daedong River an urban axis; to build Kim Il-sung Square along the eastern foot of Mount Namsan; to lay out factories and businesses in the downstream Daedong area; to balance sanitation, education, culture, and amenities; and, finally, to create green spaces in residential areas and around the city.'[24] The 'Pyongyang General Planning Brief Plan' (hereinafter, the Brief Plan) was subsequently developed in mid-1953.

Brief plan for Pyongyang, 1953.
Source: *Arkhitektura SSSR, January 1955*

Reflecting the basic stipulations laid down by the North Korean regime, the Brief Plan contained three major changes that distinguished it from the General Plan. The first, most noticeable, change pertained to the proposed road network. While the 1951 General Plan was a conceptual diagram emphasising the radial-ring road system, the Brief Plan specifically reflected Pyongyang's existing street system; this made it more realistic. The radial-ring road system proposed in the General Plan was almost entirely abandoned in the Brief Plan, being only partially retained for East Pyongyang.

A second difference pertained to downtown Pyongyang. The General Plan proposed two urban axes: first, Stalin Street, parallel to the River Daedong; second, another axis intersecting with Stalin Street at right angles, linking the central square to the River Daedong and Mount Haebang. The Brief Plan retained the first axis but offered a more specific design, including a 2.4-kilometre-wide and 45-metre-long boulevard starting at the Pyongyang Grand Theatre on the River Daedong. Large public buildings – including Pyongyang Grand Theatre, Daedong River Hotel, Joseon Museum of Art, Joseon Central History Museum, and Pyongyang First Department Store – were attached to this road, forming the backbone of Pyongyang's urban structure.[25] Construction of Stalin Street got under way immediately after approval of the Brief Plan in 1953. The North Korean government subdivided the street into a number of zones, which it assigned to major national agencies. The official government newspaper, *Rodong Sinmun*, published reports on the progress of construction. A look at photos in *Rodong Sinmun* reveals that Stalin Street had the appearance of a Soviet city. Apartment blocks were built on both sides of the street in the Soviet manner. However, following the death of Stalin in 1953 and the subsequent purge of members of the Soviet Faction from North Korea due to their critical stance toward Kim Il-sung in August 1956, the street's name was changed to Seungri Street.

The second axis, on the other hand, was altered by the Brief Plan of 1953. The location of the central square was moved from the foot of Mount Haebang to the foot of

Namsan Hill. The reason for this change is not entirely clear. Arguably, since the Brief Plan did not retain the earlier plan's proposed radial-road system, there was no need to retain its positioning of Kim Il-sung Square, which had been intended as the centre of the General Plan. Moreover, given Pyongyang's terrain and position, the new location created a better silhouette of the city under Namsan. The new site also satisfies the traditional principle of 'mountain at the back and river in front', which Kim Jeong-Hui had emphasised in *Dosi Genseol*. After discussing the issue from various perspectives, the new location of Kim Il-sung Square was approved; this has been the main factor shaping the urban structure of downtown Pyongyang.

The third difference between the General Plan and Brief Plan is that the latter placed greater emphasis on green space: the intention was that most of the city's major facilities should be surrounded by forest. Indeed, green space had been one of the key principles in socialist urban planning since the Moscow Plan of 1935. The 1951 General Plan contained no specific proposals regarding green space; its focus was more on the transportation system and residential blocks. In contrast, the Brief Plan of 1953 presented a series of green belts intended to link individual parks and green areas to continuous bands of green space, while preserving the existing landscape; the objective was the creation of a broad green belt radiating from the city centre to the city's environs. Pyongyang's green areas extend from Moranbong to Mangyongdae on the Daedong River and the Botong amusement park in the south, from Jangsan and Amisan to Daeseong Mountain in the northwest, and from Mount Munsu to Sadong Park in the east.[26] As a result, Pyongyang's green space increased from just 4 m^2 per capita in the 1920s to 15 m^2 in 1961 and 48 m^2 in the early 1970s.[27] For this reason, many of the Chinese scholars who visited Pyongyang in the 1980s praised the city's system of green spaces. Kim Jeong-hui is believed to have been actively involved in the creation of this plan, presenting it at the fourth general assembly of the Union of International Associations (UIA) at The Hague in 1955.

General urban plan for Pyongyang, 1958.
Source: unknown, 1958

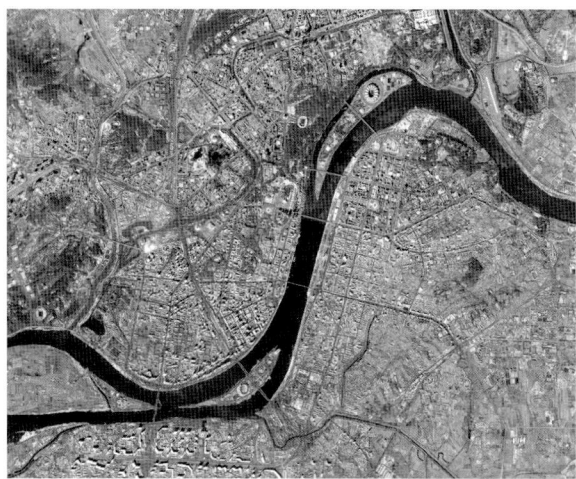

Downtown Pyongyang today.
Source: National Geographic Information Institute

Pyongyang's city centre was thus designed and completed in accordance with the Brief Plan of 1953. Thereafter, Pyongyang's urban planning focused on the city's outskirts. New planning initiatives published in 1958 were undoubtedly linked to urban expansion. Pyongyang had an urban population of 450,000 in 1949; this more than doubled to approximately one million in the early 1960s.[28] Consequently, the focus of urban planning shifted to responding to urban population growth. Developed in 1960, the Pyongyang City General Plan is noteworthy in that it features a circular road connecting the city's outskirts. Although the latter was also a feature of the Brief Plan, it was more clearly presented in the 1960 plan, which incorporated Seoseong Street, Gyeongheung Street, Hyeoksin Street, and Bifa Street. As Pyongyang continued to expand, such roads were needed to efficiently connect the surrounding suburbs. In fact, the plan featured a more detailed spatial partition for suburbs such as the districts of Sadong and Daeseong. It also reflects the introduction of the concept of district planning in Pyongyang's urban planning. Previously, Pyongyang had been separated into eastern and western sides by the Daedong River; travel between them was by bridges in the city centre. However, the expansion of urban functions made this road system increasingly cumbersome, resulting in the need for a ring-road system connecting the surrounding suburbs. However, recent maps of Pyongyang show that such attempts have only been partially realised.

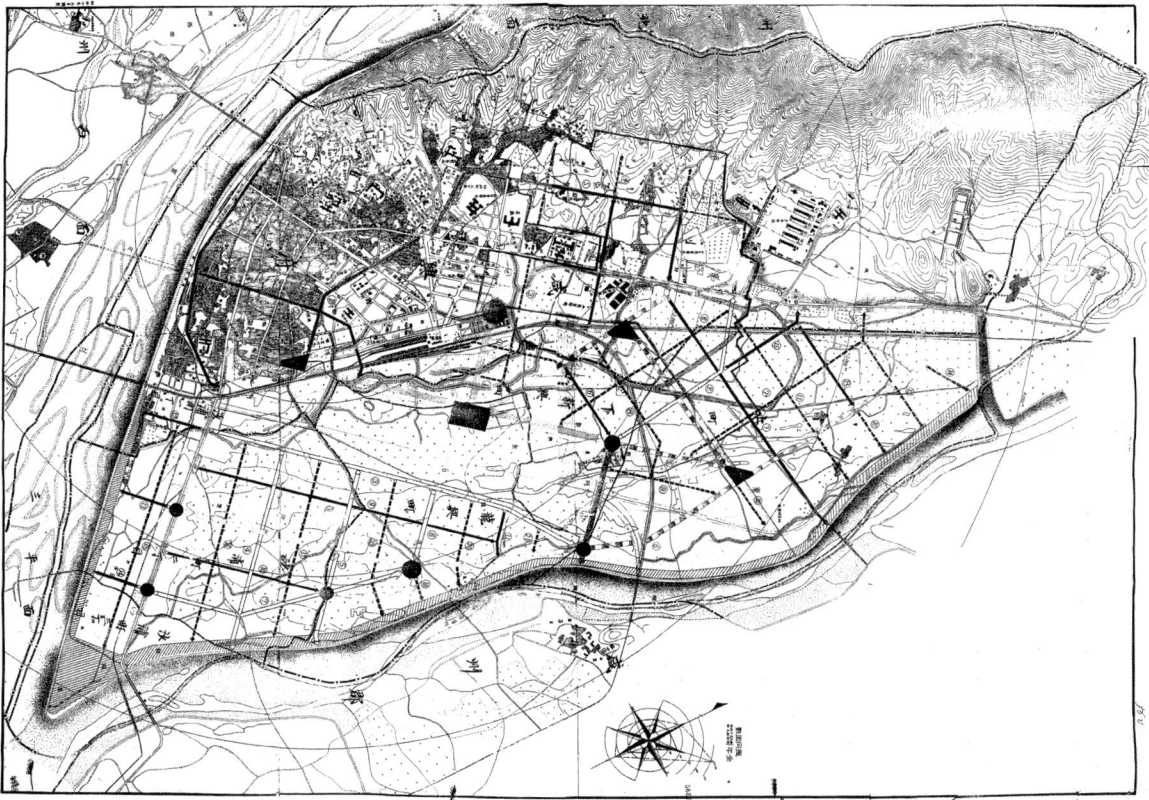

Plan for Hamhŭng drawn up by Japanese colonisers, 1938.
Source: National Archives of Korea

The Reconstruction of Hamhŭng

Hamhŭng is North Korea's second-largest city and the capital of South Hamgyeong Province. Possessing geographical conditions similar to those of Pyongyang, Hamhŭng is surrounded by the Hamgyeong and Nangnim mountains and is protected by two waterways, the River Seongcheon and the Horyeoncheon Stream. During the Joseon Dynasty, a strong defensive fortress was built here using the city's natural terrain, with villages scattered in surrounding areas. However, urbanisation in the colonial period completely altered the city's urban structure. Hamhŭng rapidly developed into a modern industrial city after a large nitrogen fertiliser plant was built at its seaport, Hŭngnam, in 1928. The subsequent emergence of large-scale factories in the 1930s saw Hamhŭng take on the role of a model industrial city in North Korea. The city's industrialisation was diverse, although primarily predicated on its abundant supply of natural resources. For instance, Hamhŭng is close to a rich supply of underground resources that are useful for the chemical industry, such as limestone, anthracite, and iron.[29] Moreover, the completion of the Bujeon River Hydroelectric Power Plant in 1929 supplied electric power to industrial facilities in this area. Industrialisation was further facilitated by the city's excellent accessibility, with public transportation boosted by several railway lines connected to surrounding regions.

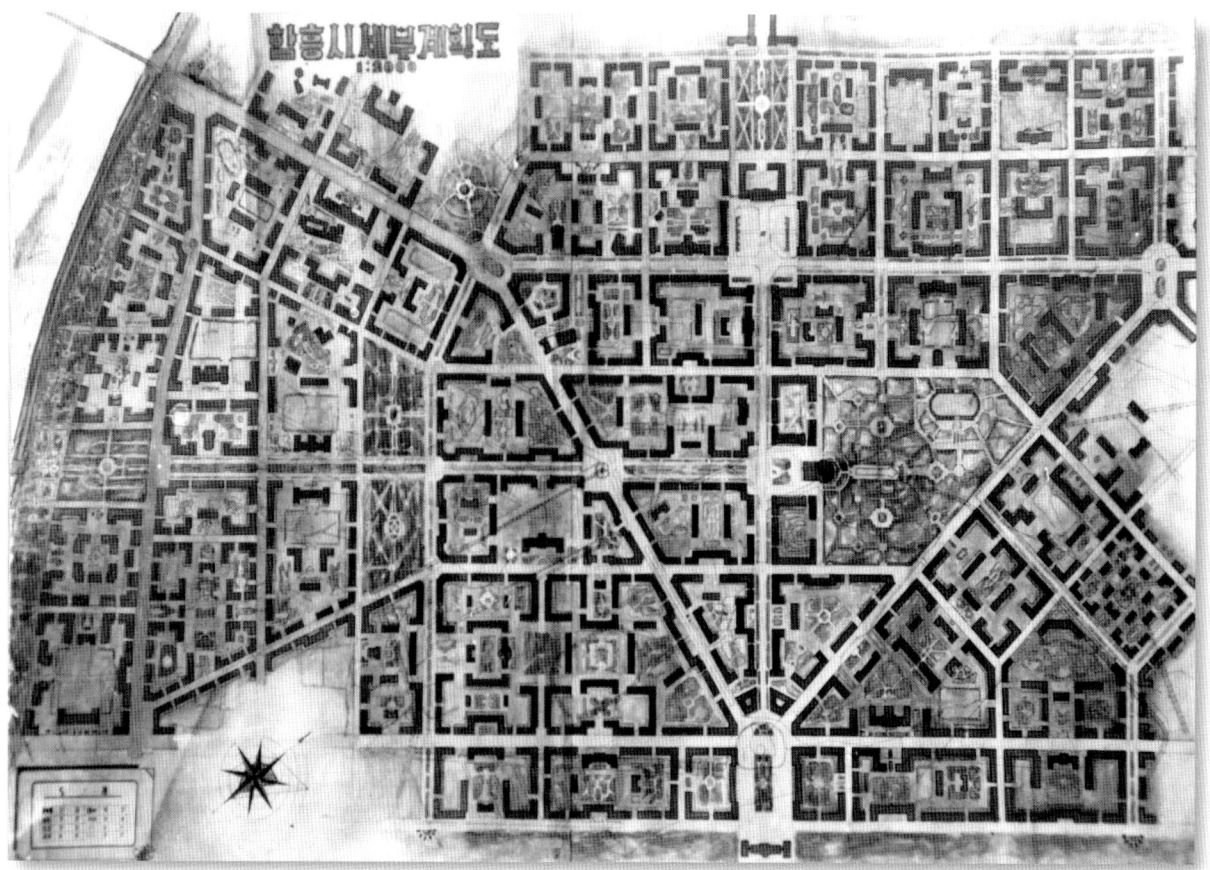

Reconstruction plan for Hamhŭng by Soviet planners.
Source: Bauhaus-Archiv Dessau, Konvolut-Püschel

The successive opening of the Gyeongwon Line in 1914, the Hamgyeong Line in 1928, and the Pyeongwon Line in 1936 made it easier to travel between Hamhŭng and Seoul, Pyongyang, and Wonsan. Consequently, numerous industries – including the textile, casting, glass, rubber, leather, and oil industries – flourished in Hamhŭng. The industrialisation of Hamhŭng led to a surge in its urban population, from 44,612 in 1934 to 122,760 in 1943. In response, the Japanese colonial government incorporated surrounding rural areas to expand the city's boundaries and initiated the urban planning of these newly urban areas. The National Archives of Korea hold urban-planning drawings executed for the Governor-General of Joseon (hereinafter, the 1938 Plan) in accordance with the Joseon City Planning Decree of 1934.[30] These documents show Hamhŭng's urban-planning process during the colonial period. The 1938 Plan covers the old town surrounding the city wall at that time, as well as newly expanded areas such as the Hoesang and Sapo districts, where land-readjustment initiatives were applied. A new railway station played a central role in the 1938 plan's design of the city's expanded urban space; the city's structure was determined by radial roads extending from the front of the station. However, colonial urban development was suspended when Japan launched the Pacific War (1941–1945).

After 80 to 90 percent of Hamhŭng was destroyed by US air raids during the Korean War, the city became the site of a large-scale reconstruction programme in the post-war period. The first reconstruction plan for Hamhŭng was drawn up by Soviet planners in 1953 and 1954.[31] The Soviet plan retained the radial roads extending from railway stations, while imitating the street systems of Soviet cities like St Petersburg and Stalingrad. The Soviet planners also highlighted a strong axis running from Hamhŭng Station Square to the provincial government building and added two radial roads to it. In addition to this axis, another extended from the city centre to the Seongcheon River. In this respect, the Soviet Plan reflects the seventh clause of the 16 principles of urban planning,[32] namely, 'In cities that lie on a river, the river and its embankments shall be one of the main arteries and architectural axes of the city.' The plan's centrality was also strengthened through the creation of a large park where the two axes meet in a T junction. The city's urban space was subdivided, with residential areas being divided into *kvartals*; the buildings on the perimeters of these blocks formed a consistent urban landscape. In this way, the Soviet Plan demonstrated a clear intention to create a harmonious urban structure integrating landscape, roads, and buildings.

The Soviet Plan was revised in April 1955, when the DAG (Deutsche Arbeitsgruppe), an East German reconstruction group, arrived in Hamhŭng.[33] The DAG was formed in 1954 following East German prime minister Otto Grotewohl's (1894–1964) promise to build a city for North Korea. The North Korean government designated Hamhŭng as the site for East German aid and pushed for joint reconstruction projects. Based on information gathered by two East German delegates, the East German government agreed to support a ten-year reconstruction effort in February 1955. The DAG – comprising approximately 170 architects, planners, engineers, and builders (bricklayers, carpenters, and electricians) – subsequently departed for Hamhŭng. Upon arriving in the North

DAG's Plan for Hamhŭng, Peter Döhler, 1955.
Source: Bauhaus-Archiv Dessau, Konvolut-Püschel

Korean city, the East German urban planners Konrad Püschel (1907–1997), Peter Döhler (1924–2008), and Georg Tegtmeyer began surveying the city. They were constrained by a tight schedule, having to determine the city's basic structure by 7 May and develop a site plan for the first microdistrict by 15 May.[34] In light of this, they decided to declare a design competition for the reconstruction plan before engaging in full-scale construction. They eventually adopted Döhler's plan – a proposal based on an entirely different logic to that developed by the Soviets.

The DAG disagreed with the Soviet Plan's decision to create a square in front of Hamhŭng Station to serve as a hub of urban life. The Soviet Plan had also placed administrative buildings in the north, near Mount Banryong, where administrative buildings had been situated during the Joseon dynasty. The East Germans disagreed with this arangement, advocating that the city's administrative buildings should be located on the central square instead. The DAG identified several other problems in the Soviet Plan. For instance, the creation of too many residential areas meant that the plan did not fully reflect the city's unique cultural heritage and natural environment, particularly insofar as it failed to sufficiently consider the link between the mountains and rivers and to revive traditional forms. The architectural design also appeared random, with little regard for location. The DAG proposed a new plan to address these problems.

Most notably, the DAG's plan extended the boundary of the district of Hamhŭng to Hamju on the left side of the River Seongcheon to Sapo in the south and Hoesang in the east. The DAG proposed establishing a strong urban axis to connect these districts to the city centre. As well as the urban axis, the DAG proposed creating two arterial roads –Wilhelm Pieck Street, extending through the upper side of the city, and the soon-to-be-renamed Stalin Street running parallel to the railway – to establish a more systematic urban structure. This idea was retained in subsequent plans. The scheme changed as new urban axes were established.

Largely designed by Peter Döhler, the new plan moved the positions of the three radial streets that had characterised Hamhŭng's urban structure during the colonial period. While eliminating the three radial streets emerging from Hamhŭng Station Square, the plan created a new axis extending from a monument building in the city centre to the River Seongcheon. Two radial roads were added to this new axis: one bound for the Manse Bridge, the central site for the city's traditional markets, and the other heading for a new bridge over the River Seongcheon. These roads emphasised the central axis of the urban composition, creating a trident spanning from the city's central park.

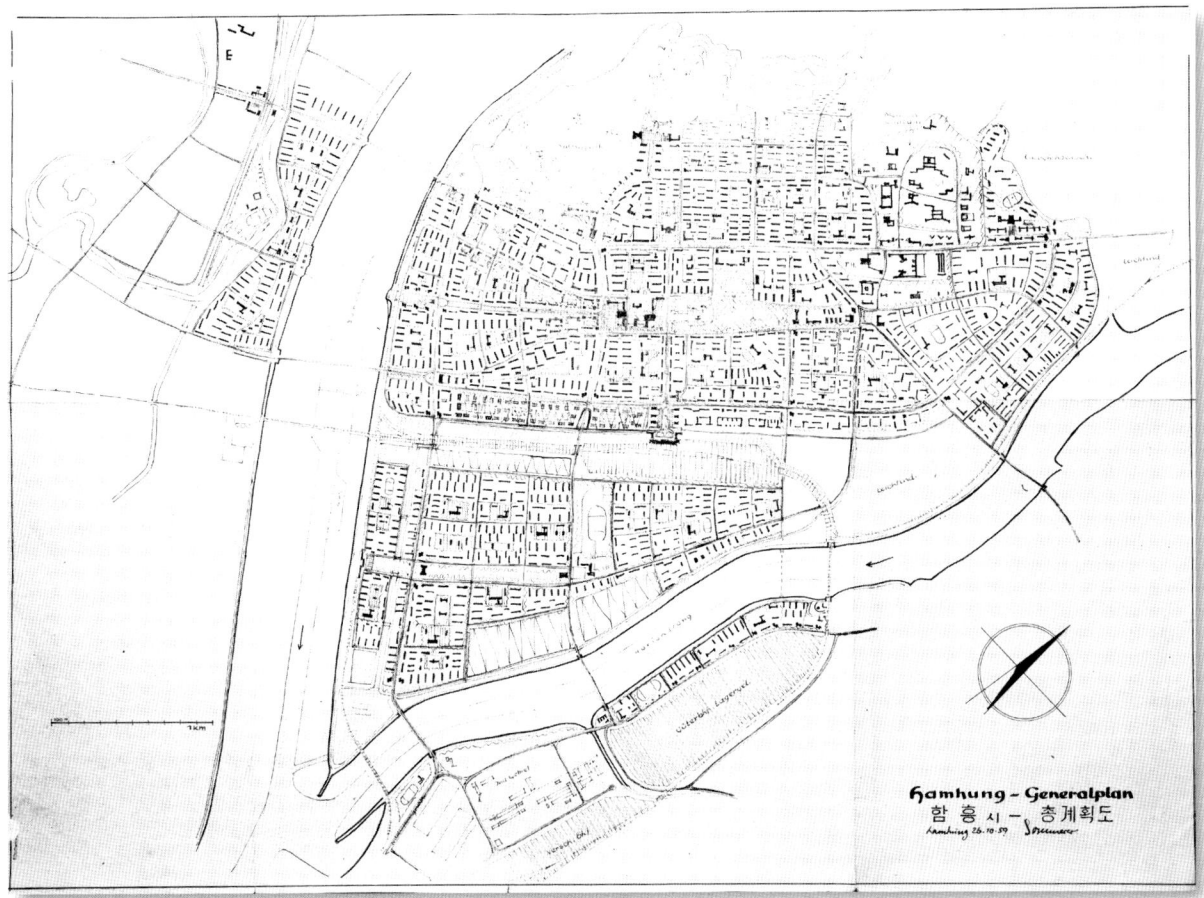

The DAG's Plan for Hamhŭng. Konrad Püschel, 1957.
Source: Bauhaus-Archiv Dessau, Konvolut-Püschel

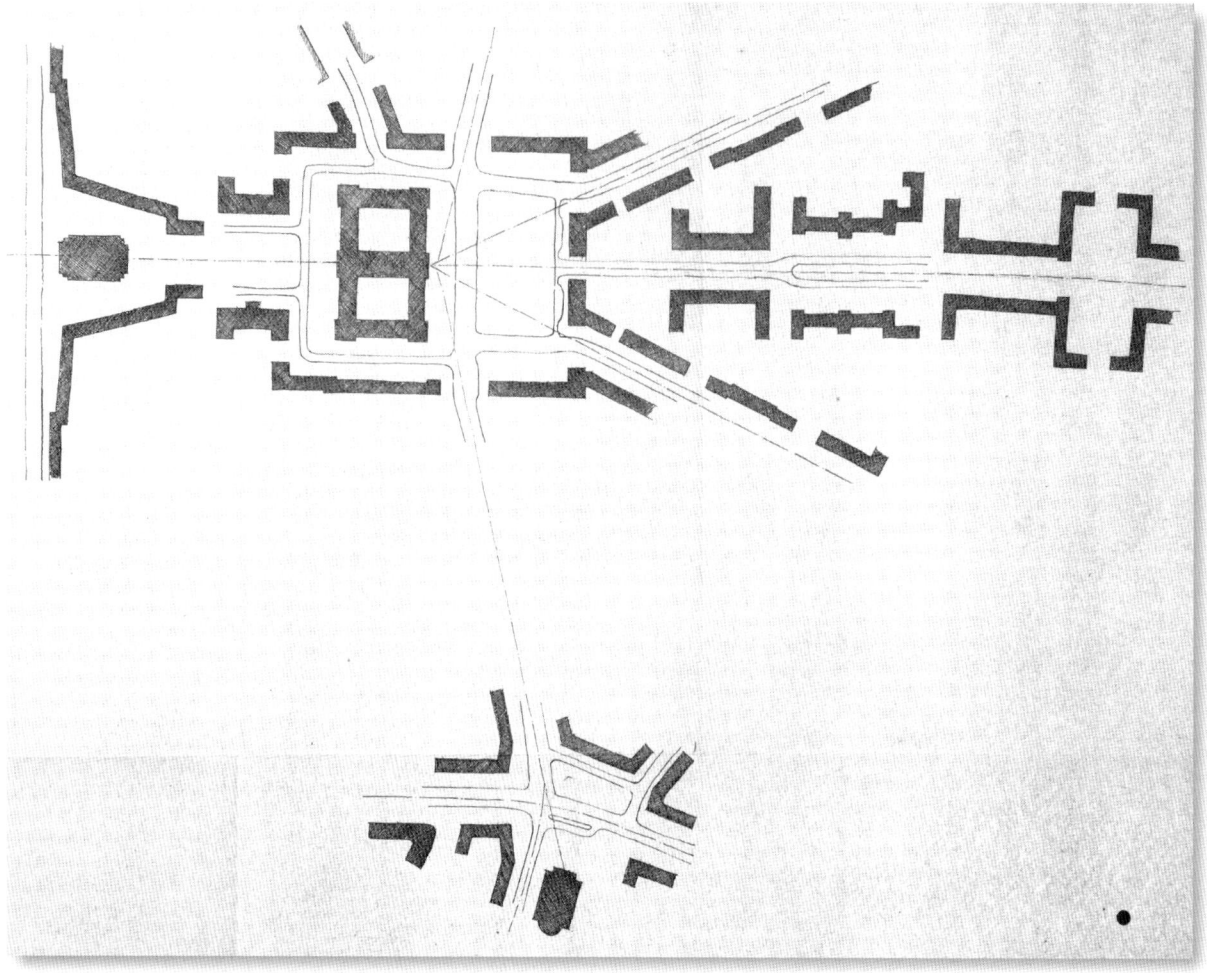

Hamhŭng's central square, Peter Döhler, May 1955.
Source: Bauhaus-Archiv Dessau, Konvolut-Püschel

The DAG looked for a means to highlight the city's identity as the capital of South Hamgyeong Province. Its solution was to locate administrative buildings such as the Provincial Office and City Hall in the city centre. Döhler often cited Beijing's Forbidden City as an example to justify his proposal.[35] This proposal was also supported by the 16 principles of urban planning, which dominated the East German approach to urban planning until 1955. In particular, the Hamhŭng plan reflected the ninth clause, which states that 'the city's visage – its individual artistic form – shall be defined by squares, main streets, and prominent buildings in the centre of the city.' Strongly influenced by Stalinist socialist realism, the central square in Döhler's plan was symmetrically designed around a monument building. Another historical square was created at the intersection of Kim Il-sung Street and Wilhelm Peak beneath Mount Banryong. This square is amorphous in shape, with the road leading to the central building curved to form a large semicircle.

The New Model of the Urban Centre

Following finalisation of the city's basic structure, the DAG turned its attention to reconstruction of residential areas and industrial facilities. Given the importance of such areas, the East German architects spent considerable time and effort on their reconstruction. 'By 1958,' Püschel noted in his diary, 'we built two residential complexes with amenities, several small housing estates on the city's outskirts, and schools, kindergartens, clubhouses, department stores and shops, administrative buildings, and bathhouses.'[36] The DAG also began developing a new plan for Hamhŭng, with Püschel as chief designer. Püschel took a leading role in the DAG from 1955 to 1959, maintaining a close relationship with Baustab Korea, an organisation in Berlin. His approach differed from that of Döhler, largely due to his educational background.

Püschel joined the Bauhaus design school in 1926 and was tutored there by famous artists such as Paul Klee, Wassily Kandinsky, and Laszlo Moholy-Nagy. He spent his second semester, which began in April 1927, studying wood sculpture under Marcel Breuer. In 1928 he undertook a building apprenticeship at the school and in March 1929 began studying architecture under Hannes Meyer.[37] His relationship with Meyer continued after his graduation in 1930. In 1931 he travelled to the Soviet Union as a member of the Bauhaus Brigade. Formed by Meyer and comprising seven former Bauhaus students, the Bauhaus Brigade participated in developing the plan for Greater Moscow, albeit without receiving the recognition it deserved. When Meyer disbanded the Bauhaus Brigade in 1932,[38] Püschel remained in the Soviet Union until 1937. Under the supervision of Hans Schmidt, he worked on the reconstruction of Orsk from 1934 to 1937; Schmidt's influence is evident in his later designs for North Korea. Thus the urban plan of Hamhŭng designed by Püschel bore many of the hallmarks of 1930s Soviet urban planning, adapted to the unique features of the cities and settlements on the Korean peninsula.[39]

Püschel's plan introduced two new planning concepts. First, he replaced the *kvartal* with the *mikrorayon*

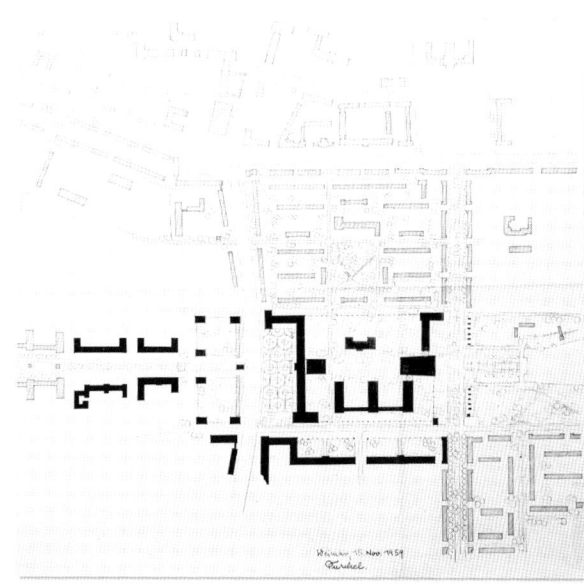

Hamhŭng's central square. Konrad Püschel, March 1959.
Source: *Bauhaus-Archiv Dessau, Konvolut-Püschel*

(microdistrict) as the basic unit of urban space. The concept of the *mikrorayon* as the primary element in a residential area emerged in the Soviet Union in the 1940s and 1950s. German architects participating in the planning of Soviet new towns used the notion of the *Wohnkomplex* in neighbourhood planning; this concept had its basis in the ideals of the socialist city. The characteristics of the *Wohnkomplex* include the positioning of residential, educational, public, recreational, and commercial facilities within walking distance in each district.[40] This idea inspired Soviet planners to create a new unit of urban space. The *mikrorayon* was larger than the *kvartal*. According to the Construction Rules and Regulations of the Soviet Union, a typical *mikrorayon* should cover an area of 10–60 hectares, although a *mikrorayon* could exceed 80 hectares and comprise multistorey apartment and public buildings. Additionally, the apartment buildings in a *mikrorayon* are more open to the outside; essential services must be located within a 500-metre radius of a residential dwelling. The adoption of this concept in Püschel's plan changed urban form in Hamhŭng.

In addition to the *mikrorayon*, Püschel's plan focused on the central square, employing a dynamic design based on Bauhaus principles. The central square was the most important element in Hamhŭng's urban plan, although its design was delayed due to disagreements among the East German architects. The task was complicated both by the need to define the square in a socialist manner and by growing criticism of Socialist Realism following the death of Stalin in 1953; this made it necessary for the DAG's architects to change their approach to designing the square. Drawn up by Püschel and Karl Sommerer in 1957, the DAG's plan for the city centre differed significantly from that proposed by Döhler.

Püschel, who took the leading role in designing Hamhŭng's central square, emphasised three focal points: function, location, and aesthetic principle. In terms of function, he designed the central square to play a symbolic role by placing provincial government buildings on its edges. These buildings' programmes and plasticity helped the square express the power of the ruling party, the workers, and the peasant government as embodied by provincial Party committees and the People's Committee. To symbolise this power, Püschel's design included a twelve-storey provincial government building. Another important function of the central square was as a gathering place for social life. Accordingly, the square was designed to hold 30,000–35,000 people for major events such as Worker's Day on 1 May and National Liberation Day on 15 August.

In respect to location, Püschel believed that the central square should be placed in such a way as to connect the railway station, the street, and spaces used for demonstrations. He also insisted that, 'the central square must not be part of the traffic network; through traffic should be avoided.' The plan of 1957 also connects the square to three radiating streets that extend to the River Seongcheon and a large park on the east side. Starting from the Seongcheon riverside, several urban spaces continuously converge on the central axis, reaching their culmination in the central square. To the east lie buildings, gardens, and green parks. Spatially, the main axis accentuates the buildings located on it; the monument is located at the axis' peak, and the axis culminates in the main building on the central square. In front of the park, the Hoesang district square (*Bezirksplatz*), urban park lake (*Stadtparksee*), and cultural centre / workers' palace (*Kulturhaus des Palasts der Arbeit*) face the main city hall building and the central square.

The greatest difference between Püschel and Sommerer's 1957 plan and Döhler's original proposal was one of aesthetics. While Döhler's plan emphasised spatial symmetry and was a highly authoritative expression of Stalinism, Püschel's design was based on a dynamic composition, with layouts reminiscent of the Bauhaus building in Dessau. Naturally, Püschel's design reflects the design principles of his Bauhaus education, with the legacy of the Stalin era retained in the composition of the boulevard stretching from the central square to the River Seongcheon. While both plans proposed streets lined with buildings of identical height, the 1957 plan suggested an entirely different layout for the central square. The elimination of the hierarchy and symmetry of historicist design was an important aspect of Bauhaus architecture. This objective is brilliantly illustrated in the Bauhaus building in Dessau, where the lack of symmetry in the building's structure creates a kind of aesthetic equilibrium in such a way that the building's form can only be understood by moving around it and viewing it from different angles.

In North Korea the idea of employing dynamic composition of buildings in urban spaces was first suggested by German urban planners, notably by Püschel. In an unpublished manuscript Püschel emphasised that the plan devised for Hamhŭng referenced Korean design traditions. He paid particular attention to the traditional long sequence of old palaces, in which 'the spaces gradually increase in size as they approach the main spot along a flowing sequence of axes and then fade away into gardens and parks.' In other words, a conceptual affinity between Bauhaus aesthetics and native Korean design led to the creation of a unique scheme. As noted, the direction of post-war urban design changed significantly after Stalin's death. Planners had more freedom to pursue different combinations of urban forms, including by grouping narrow buildings with long ones, high-rise buildings with lower ones, and angled buildings with round ones. The contrast between open and closed layouts resulted in a more abundant diversity of forms along the urban axis.

Completed in 1958, the new plan, which bore the mark of many of Püschel's ideas, was displayed at an exhibition during Kim Il-sung's visit to Hamhŭng that year. It was also sent to Baustab Korea in Berlin. In 1958 Alfred Förster, the head of the DAG, sent a letter to Kurt Liebknecht (1905–1994), the director of the Bauakademie in Berlin,[41] explaining the DAG's achievements in Hamhŭng. After providing an overview of the 1958 plan, the letter asked Liebknecht to give advice on the plan on the basis of his experience designing the central square in the reconstruction of Berlin. Förster's letter to Liebknecht illustrates the close communication between the German planners in Hamhŭng and Baustab Korea in Berlin. The planning of a city centre, writes Förster, revolves around three critical issues: natural conditions, trade, and socialist urban identity. The formation of the central square should be prioritised over other aspects, Förster explains, because it serves to express the city's soul; the design of Hamhŭng's central square was based on a series of ideas derived from natural situations, ethnic traditions, and the demands of the social order in socialist cities.[42] This approach, Förster continues, thus reflects those of East German urban planners, particularly Liebknecht, who had already developed several plans for the reconstruction of East German cities. East German urban planning emphasised natural conditions and national traditions,[43] as well as the need to embody social order in a socialist way. Summarising the principal ideas of the city plan to Liebknecht, Förster emphasises the location of the central square:

Surrounding nature, rivers, mountains, and plains clarify how its urban structure is located. Through the concentration of major squares, bridges, sports and cultural sites, industrial and residential areas, and various roads, its centre can be organically incorporated into the urban system, making it the vibrant heart of the provincial capital.[44]

However, following Püschel's return to East Germany in 1959, his successor, Karl Sommerer, revised the plan for the central square. Sommerer and Püschel had been colleagues at the Hochschule für Architektur und Bauwesen (Bauhaus University Weimar) before working in North Korea and had worked closely together in designing the central square in the reconstruction of Dresden. However, they had contrasting ideas regarding the significance of the central square and how socialist ideology should be expressed in urban planning and architecture. Sommerer's revision prompted Püschel, who remained in Germany, to draw up a new plan for the central square. Püschel's revised plan is a decisive cross-section of his disagreement with Sommerer regarding the formation of the central square; he criticised Sommerer's ideas as follows:

But how about the new plan that you showed me? It is full of cultural facilities, which occupy space that could be given to other important functions of life in the city. The silhouette of the centre, which should serve as a focal point, is surrounded by residential buildings. Worse, these are buildings containing small-scale apartments; so, if families grow larger in the future, as is likely, these apartments must also increase in size. Furthermore, because the composition of the central square itself consists mainly of cultural facilities, the square is visible as an ensemble only when it consists of low-rise development. The square's proportions are not clear, and the purity that was previously evident here has disappeared.[45]

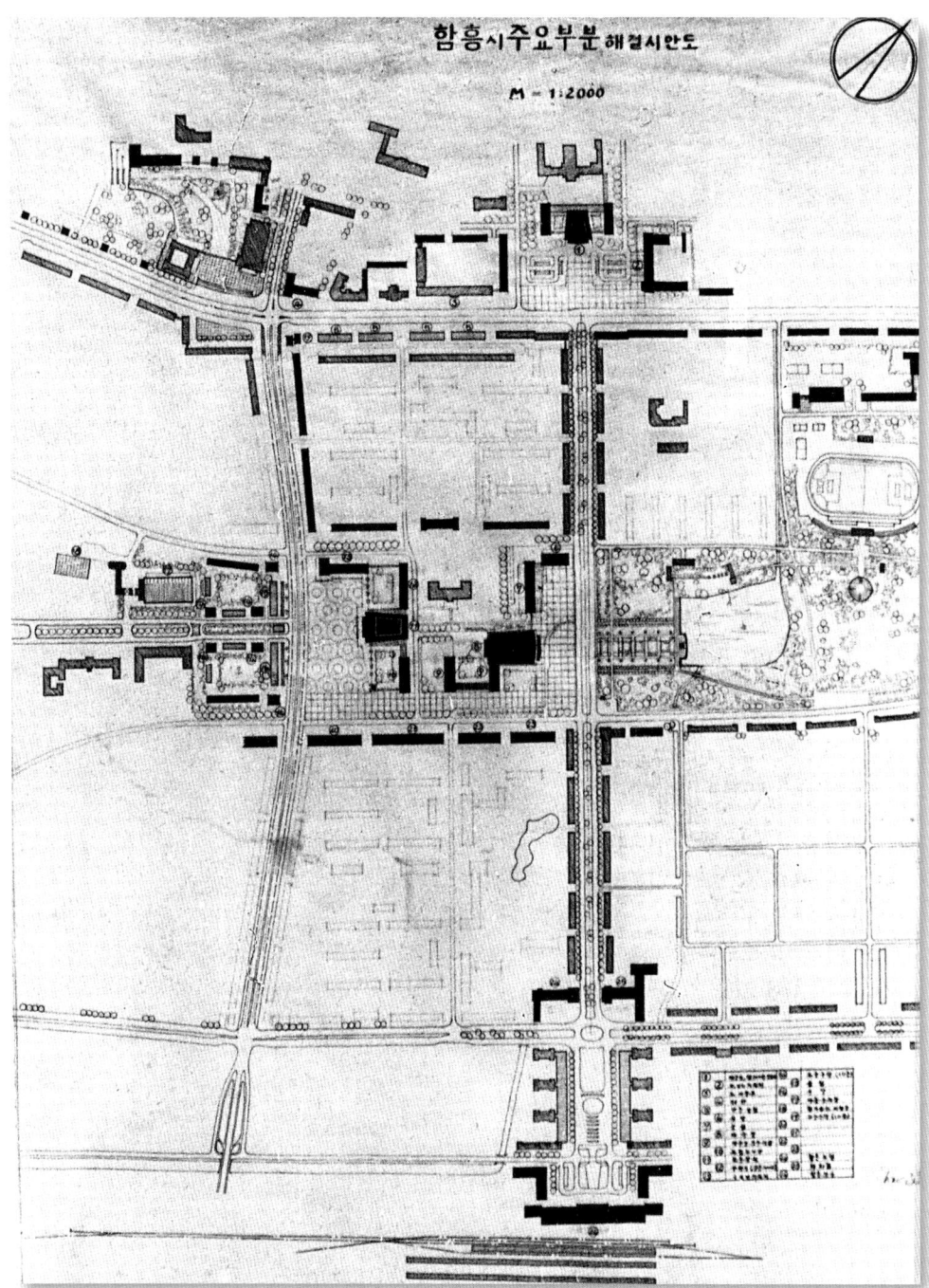

Hamhŭng's central square. Peter Döhler, May 1955.
Source: Bauhaus-Archiv Dessau, Konvolut-Püschel

32   Mass Housing and Urbanism in North Korea

In response to this criticism, Sommerer stated that, 'on the basis of past experience in the planning of Gera in Germany and given the resolution of the Central Committee, the cultural and commercial centre, not the administrative centre, should be the basis for the composition of the city centre.' This was not only recognised by the East German journal *Deutsche Architektur* but was also defined as the specific programme for the central square. Sommerer also had a more specific idea for an operational method governing how communist society should relate to architecture:

As for me, I am not, as you think, opposed to the construction of an administrative building to express the power of the state, and my comrades in Hamhŭng also agree that this administrative building is necessary. They also believe that the idea of showing power through architecture in the central square is incorrect. Rather, the power of a socialist society should be displayed, above all, through a highly developed culture and its facilities. …to add a word to your plan, rectangular blocks and skyscrapers are impossible. …because this is contrary to the composition of the central square and the entire surrounding area.[46]

Like Sommerer, Püschel recognised the importance of cultural facilities such as libraries, post offices, and the Palace of Labour. However, he believed that the power of communism could be effectively expressed through high-rise administrative buildings in the central square. Sommerer disagreed, resulting in the removal of administrative buildings from the 1959 plan. While Püschel insisted on the inclusion of high-rise administrative buildings as a symbol of state and government power, Sommerer advocated for the use of cultural facilities to express socialist ideology.

As Pyongyang's Kim Il-sung Square reveals, the North Korean government appears to have agreed with Sommerer. However, Sommerer's idea was never realised. He designed the Hamhŭng Grand Theatre, scheduled for completion in 1964 and intended as a focal point of the central square. As a result of the unexpected suspension and withdrawal of the DAG in 1962, German planners had to finalise the urban-design process between 1961 and 1962.[47] The completion of the square was an important achievement for North Korean architects. The view of Hamhŭng given by satellite photos today shows that the DAG's master plan has been realised almost in its entirety, except for the trident; a strange structure now occupies the central square. In 1984 the North Korean government constructed a monumental theatre in the classical style; this excludes all other options proposed by the DAG for the central square.

1. The US Air Force estimated that the destruction of North Korea was proportionately greater than that of Japan in the Second World War, when the US reduced 64 major cities to rubble and used atomic bombs to destroy two others. Compared to the 503,000 tonnes of bombs dropped across the entire Pacific during the Second World War, American planes dropped 635,000 tonnes of bombs, including 32,557 tonnes of napalm, on Korea (essentially on North Korea) during the Korean War. Cited in Rosemary Foot (Ithaca, 1990), pp. 207–208.
2. Lee, Kyo-duk, and Gong Seon-ja (Seoul, 2006), p. 358.
3. Li Hwa-seon(a) (Pyongyang, 1989), p. 343.
4. Armstrong, Charles K., 'The Destruction and Reconstruction of North Korea, 1950–1960', p. 4.
5. Lee, Kyo-duk, and Gong Seon-ja (Seoul, 2006), p. 358.
6. Armstrong, Charles K., 'Fraternal Socialism', p. 165.
7. Jeon, Seok-dam, (Pyongyang, 1960) p. 17.
8. Shen, Zhihua, and Xia, Yafeng, *China and the Post-War Reconstruction of North Korea*, p. 3.
9. Park, Jong-chol, and Jeoung, Eun-lee, 'Hangukjeonjaengihu Bukhanjaegeoneul', p. 59.
10. Kim, Jeong-hui, 'Pyongyangsi Kim Il-sung Gwangjanui Geonchukjeok', p. 27.
11. *The Story of an Architect*, a North Korean film focusing on Kim Jeong-hui's life, was released in 1987.
12. The collection comprises a total of 14 documents. The first is an excerpt from Volume 17 of the Minutes of the Moscow Institute of Architecture, July 6, 1953, titled 'Examination of Architect Kim Jeong-hui's PhD Dissertation Thesis, "The Principles of Urban Reconstruction of the Democratic People's Republic of Korea".' It provides an account of the Moscow Institute of Architecture's review of Kim Jeong-hui's doctoral dissertation, which he submitted in July 1953. This collection consists of the examination document, which is believed to have been written by the university, records (nine pages), personal reports (four pages), and an autobiography (one page) written by Kim Jeong-hui. All documents are in Russian. Tanigawa, Ryuichi and Kuznetsov, Dmitry, p. 1104.
13. Tanigawa, Ryuichi and Kuznetsov, Dmitry, 'North Korea's Urban planner Kim Jeong-hui-An elucidation and analysis of his career before the Korean Armistice (1953)', p. 1105.
14. Ibid., p. 1106.
15. Ibid., p. 1108.
16. Kim, Jeong-Hui (Pyongyang, 1953), pp. 122–123.
17. Ibid., p. 168.
18. Kim Il-sung (Pyongyang, 1980), p. 280.
19. Kim, Jeong-Hui (Pyongyang, 1953), p. 171.
20. Ibid., p. 172.
21. Ibid., p. 176.
22. Ibid., p. 194.
23. *Pyongyang geonseol jeonsa pyeonchan wiwonhoe* (Pyongyang, 1997) p. 144.
24. Li Hwa-seon (a) (Pyongyang:, 1989), p. 104.
25. Kim, Jeong-hui, *Pyongyangsi Kim Il-sung Gwangjanui Geonchukjeok*, p. 26.
26. Cho, Sung-hun, *Bukhanui Dosibaldal Yeongu*, p. 215.
27. Ibid., p. 215.
28. Ibid., p. 208.
29. Kim Myun, 'Dokil guklipmunseobogwanso', p. 95.
30. The 1937 Joseon City Planning Decree was the first modern urban-planning legislation in North Korea. Prior to the enactment of this decree, the Governor-General of Korea had issued Road Rules in 1911 and City Building Rules in 1913. The latter is a type of nationwide set of architectural rules believed to have been enacted under the influence of the Japanese Building Code. The Joseon Urban Planning Decree primarily comprises general rules, the designation of zones and districts, building restrictions, and land readjustment. The enactment of the Joseon Urban Planning Decree provided the first legal basis for land-use regulation and land-readjustment projects.
31. Shin, Dong-sam, *Die Planung des Wiederaufbaus der Städte Hamhŭng*, p. 97.
32. Proposed in 1950, the 16 principles of urban planning became the guiding principles for urban planning in East Germany over the next five years. These principles were shaped by the ideals of the 'socialist city' in accordance with the Soviet system of urban planning. For greater detail, see: Herbert Nicolaus and Alexander Obeth (Berlin, 1997).
33. Shin, Dong-sam, *Die Planung des Wiederaufbaus der Städte Hamhŭng*, p. 97.
34. Sin Dong-sam (Seoul, 2019). p. 82.
35. A statement by Gerhard Stiehler: Shin, Dong-sam, *Die Planung des Wiederaufbaus der Städte Hamhŭng*, p. 98.
36. Püschel, Konrad (Dessau, 1997), p. 117.
37. Ibid.
38. Tomita, Hideo and Ishii, Masato, 'The Influence of Hannes Meyer and the Bauhaus Brigade on 1930s Soviet Architecture', p. 49.
39. Hideo Tomita, Tomita, Hideo, *Wohnkomplexe in the 1930s USSR and 1950s North Korea*, p. 2288.
40. Ibid., p. 2289.
41. Letter from Förster to Kurt Liebknecht, July 7, 1958: Bauhaus Archiv Dessau. Püschel-Korea, I_010161_D, Hamhŭng, 7.7.58. p. 1.
42. Idid., p. 2.
43. Liebknecht's thinking on nature and tradition is commonly summarised as 'Ku-Li-na-tra' – an abbreviation of Kurt-Liebknechts-Nationale-Tradition. Simone Hain (Stuttgart, 1998), p. 193. The DAG (Deutsche Arbeitsgruppe Hamhŭng) attempted to investigate Korean cultural heritage sites and monuments to identify traditional themes, listing various types of Korean traditional house, spatial structure, and lifestyle.
44. Hain, Simone (Stuttgart, 1998), pp. 2–3.
45. Letter from Sommerer to Püschel, 18 November 1959 : Bauhaus Archiv Dessau, I_010202_D).
46. Letter from Sommerer to Püschel, 21 March 1960: Bauhaus Archiv Dessau, I_010254_D).
47. Jahresabschlussbericht Deutsche Arbeitsgruppe 1958 Perspektivplan Baustab Korea: Bundesarchiv-Berlin _1326/228.

War-time destruction led to an enormous housing shortage in North Korea. The simplest earthen buildings helped alleviate this deficit (1956).
Source: Hannelore and Matthias Schuberth Family Archive, Wismar (Germany)

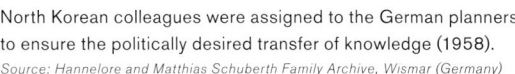

North Korean colleagues were assigned to the German planners
to ensure the politically desired transfer of knowledge (1958).
Source: Hannelore and Matthias Schuberth Family Archive, Wismar (Germany)

Konrad Püschel, trained at the Dessau Bauhaus in the late 1920s,
headed the 150-strong *Deutsche Arbeitsgruppe* (DAG) in Hamhŭng.
From 1955 to 1959 he was responsible for the rebuilding of the city of Hŭngnam.
Source: Stiftung Bauhaus Dessau (Konvolut Püschel – I 18498 F)

Houses for the German reconstruction workers were built
in 1956 using local materials. The families were housed in simple
barracks. Communal rooms, such as the dining hall and
laundry (left), expressed an ideal image of socialist society.
Source: Hannelore and Matthias Schuberth Family Archive, Wismar (Germany);
Stiftung Bauhaus Dessau (Konvolut Püschel – SBD I 18545 F 69293)

1. The Reconstruction of Two Cities: Pyongyang and Hamhŭng

The East German government also supplied a factory making concrete slabs. The Rostock architects could thus point to their first practical experience in concrete-slab construction technology after their return home. The success of the Rostock Südstadt estate also owed a lot to experience gained in Hamhŭng.
Source: Hannelore and Matthias Schuberth Family Archive, Wismar (Germany)

New housing construction in North Korea aimed to merge tradition
and modernity. The many chimneys on the roofs were necessary in order
to install traditional *Ondol* underfloor heating in the new buildings (1958).
Source: Hannelore and Matthias Schuberth Family Archive, Wismar (Germany)

From 1955 to 1962 the East German government ran a large-scale programme to reconstruct the North Korean cities of Hamhŭng and Hŭngnam, which had been severely damaged by US air raids during the Korean War. The photo above shows one of these construction sites in Hamhŭng in 1958.
Source: Hannelore and Matthias Schuberth Family Archive, Wismar (Germany)

Multi-storey residential buildings were erected in the city centre of Hamhŭng from 1958. The aim was not just to rebuild destroyed housing, but rather to construct an ideal socialist city.
Source: Hannelore and Matthias Schuberth Family Archive, Wismar (Germany)

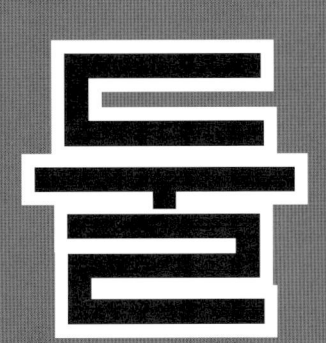

Piotr Zaremba and the Urban Planning of Chongjin

Inha Jung/ Kim Jong-yeon

After signing the armistice to end the Korean War on 27 July 1953, the North Korean government immediately turned to the task of reconstructing the country's war-torn cities. Lacking both the necessary financial resources and the know-how, North Korea was dependent on other socialist countries, including the Soviet Union, China, East Germany, and Poland. The latter sent an urban planning team to help in the reconstruction of Chongjin in 1954. As a result of the country's unique historical background, the Polish approach to urban planning was markedly different from the dominant socialist method at the time. As a result of the Polish government's relatively loose stance toward ideological control and foreign policy, the country had a more flexible approach to urban planning and establishing exchange programmes with socialist countries. Moreover, the country's rich post-war experience of reconstruction enabled it to accumulate and develop various different urban-planning theories and practices – as is clear from the Polish plan for the reconstruction of Chongjin.

The reconstruction of North Korean cities has been the subject of numerous studies. However, the reconstruction of Chongjin in the 1950s has been overlooked in this literature, particularly with respect to its urban planning. This oversight is primarily due to the relative difficulty, compared to other cities, of obtaining historical documents pertaining to the planning of Chongjin. However, this obstacle has been removed by the recent discovery of various documents and drawings produced by the Polish reconstruction team in the Szczecin State Archives (Spuscéizna Piotr Zaremby, Archiwum Panástowe Szczeciniie). Specifically, the collection comprises manuscripts, photos, and research materials collected and authored by Piotr Zaremba (1910–1993) during his stay in Chongjin. The archives also contain a wide range of works by the Polish urban planning team, including analytical drawings of Chongjin's natural environment and climatic conditions, draft design projects, proposals for the central square, and the reconstruction master plan.

Index Number	Date	Title (Main Content)
JEDN 76	1954–1958	Rękopisy Piotra Zaremby (manuscript by Piotra Zaremba titled 'Townscape Planning of Chinese and Korean Cities')
JEDN 77	1955	Rękopisy opracowań Piotra Zaremby (research manuscripts by Piotr Zaremba)
JEDN 152	1954–1957	Maszynopisy Piotra Zaremby (typescript titled 'Sketch programme for collective work: Korea, its cities and architecture'; author: Zaremba)
JEDN 154	1958	Maszynopisy Piotra Zaremby (typescript on 'Planning problems in China and Korea, based on works in these countries'; author: Zaremba)
JEDN 285	1956	Metody pracy urbanistycznej w Korei (*Miasto*, 1956, no. 2)
JEDN 286	1956	Metody pracy urbanistycznej w Korei (methodology of urban work in Korea)
JEDN 288	1956	W sprawie pracy ze studentami koreańskimi (on working with Korean students)
JEDN 289	1956	Podstawowe problemy rozwoju urbanistyki Koreańskiej (*Geonchuk gwa geonseol*, May 1956, no. 2)
JEDN 290	1957	Polski projekt koreańskiego miasta (*Miasto*, 1957, no. 1)
JEDN 291	1957	Metoda realistycznego planowania miast – Korei (*Geonseolja*, May 1957)
JEDN 292	1957	Metoda realistycznego planowania miast – Korei (*Geonseolja*, June 1957)
JEDN 632	1957	Kierunki rozwoju urbanistyki i planowania regionalnego w Polsce (directions for urban development and regional planning in Poland, 'Translation of City Construction') (城市建设译丛)
JEDN 905	1954–1960	Koreański rysunek planowania miasta – Czondzin (Korean city-planning drawing: Czondzin)
JEDN 907	1957	Materiały z prywatnej podróży Piotra Zaremby do Korei (letters and newspaper clippings from Zaremba's private trip to Korea)
JEDN 1049	1954–1957	Korespondencja prywatna piotra zaremby (private correspondence of Piotr Zaremba)
JEDN 1056	1955–1956	Korespondencja Piotra Zaremby zwiazana (Piotr Zaremba's correspondence, various)

The present chapter utilises these archival sources to investigate the Polish plan to reconstruct Chongjin – a 16-month project headed by Zaremba. Examining Zaremba's manuscripts and drawings, we highlight what makes his approach to urban planning distinctive, revealing pronounced differences from the approaches observed in Pyongyang and Hamhŭng. Despite taking place at the same time, these cities' reconstruction projects reflect different approaches to and understandings of urban planning. By tracing how Zaremba's approach was transferred to and embodied in post-war North Korea, we elucidate the diversity of socialist city planning before the mid-1950s and how such planning was transformed with Khrushchev's rise to power.

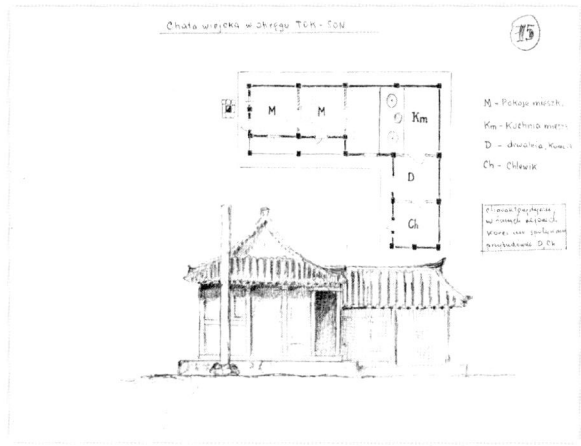

Sketches by Piotr Zaremba showing a North Korean house and landscape.
Source: Archiwum Państwowe w Szczecinie, Notatnik Chiny Korea 1954_0068, 0073.

Table 1. Archival material pertaining to the Chongjin project held by the State Archives in Szczecin, Poland.

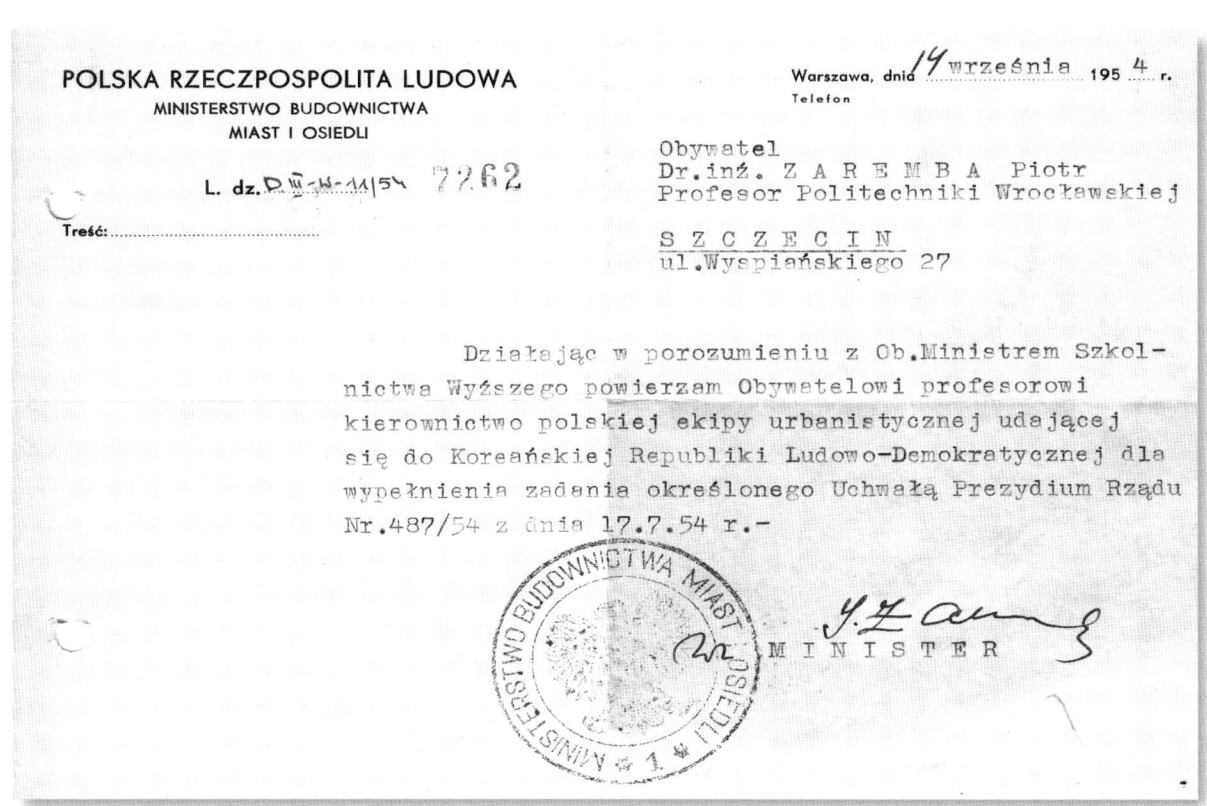

A letter of appointment from the Polish government.
Source: Archiwum Państwowe w Szczecinie, Spuścizna Piotra Zaremby, JEDN 907

Piotr Zaremba and the Polish Urban-planning Team

During the Korean War (1950–1953) Poland supported North Korea on the international stage, engaging in propaganda campaigns and spearheading initiatives to raise money for the country. Polish assistance did not end with the armistice. In answer to the North Korean government's request for humanitarian aid, the Polish government passed a resolution pledging economic support in 1953. Following this resolution, Poland founded an orthopaedic hospital in Hamhŭng, participated in the modernisation of the Anju coal mine, and despatched a number of professional personnel – including doctors, nurses, miners, and urban planners – to North Korea.[1] It also provided educational aid by accepting 230 North Korean students. The North Korean government was requesting two types of aid: aid for its starving population and help with reconstructing cities destroyed by war. In respect to the former, North Korea requested various relief goods, including clothes, daily necessities, food (particularly fat, meat, and fish), cotton fabric, and tools (e.g., hammers, sickles, and saws). In terms of reconstruction aid, the regime requested financial investment and transport machinery (e.g., vehicles and trains), which Poland promised to supply to North Korea through loans.[2]

The urban planning of Chongjin was a significant part of Poland's aid to North Korea. On 17 July 1954, the Polish Ministry of Cities, Real Estate, and Construction appointed Piotr Zaremba, a professor at Warsaw University of Technology, as the head of the Chongjin urban-planning team. The team had eleven members: the chief designer (Zaremba), five urban planners (Zasław Malicki, Bronisław Sekuła, Kazimierz Pencakowski, Zbigniew Karakiewicz, and Andrzej Jędraszko), and five industrial planners (Jerzy Gularski, Eugeniusz Pascal, Zygmunt Buczeń, Janusz Stankiewicz, and Jacek Nowakowski).[3] Their task was to develop a master plan, a phased development plan, and a plan for Chongjin's city centre. While such tasks fell under the typical scope of urban planning, the distance between Poland and Chongjin – some 13,000 km – constituted a significant hurdle, as did the different climate, people, and customs. The Polish team was also unaware of North Korea's construction capabilities, investment needs, financial resources, and unique urban forms.[4] These were the circumstances in which the Polish team opened an office on 15 November 1954 and began analysing the city's urban structure and dwelling culture. Sixteen months later, on 23 February 1956, the North Korean regime approved the Polish planning team's master plan.[5] Piotr Zaremba, the leader of the Chongjin project, is not well-known to the western planning community. A Chinese paper introduced his early career as follows:

> *Born to a noble family in Poland. Majored in civil engineering at Lviv College of Natural Science and Engineering in 1930–1934. Earned a doctorate at Warsaw University of Science and Technology in 1952. During World War II he worked as an air defence officer in Poland's civil-defence department, making use of his specialisation. In 1945, after the war's end, Zaremba was appointed the first mayor of the important Polish port city of Szczecin. During his five-year term he successfully implemented post-war reconstruction projects, earning a reputation as a prominent urban planner in Europe.*[6]

Zaremba's work in Szczecin proved a milestone in his career, fostering his ability to handle complex political and economic issues in a city. Szczecin was at the centre of debates regarding the establishment of the new Polish-German border after the Second World War. From the

Zaremba's team in Cheongjin with North Korean planners.
Source: Archiwum Państwowe w Szczecinie

late Middle Ages to 1945, Szczecin had had a predominantly German population and was known as 'Stettin' in German. On 5 July 1945 Stettin was ceded to Poland and renamed 'Szczecin'. The German population was subsequently expelled from the city and replaced with Polish refugees, mainly from eastern parts of the country. As the city's first mayor, Zaremba dedicated himself to uniting the existing population with the new settlers.

The successful restoration of Szczecin provided him with many opportunities to work in foreign countries. Between 1953 and 1959 Zaremba was invited to North Korea, China, and Vietnam to consult on various urban-planning projects. During his visit to China he gave lectures at Tsinghua University and cooperated with dozens of Chinese urban planners to develop a regional plan for Hangzhou.[7] After 1960 the Szczecin Institute of Technology became Zaremba's base for his academic activities. He also served as the chair of the Department of Construction, Housing, and Architecture, and established the Institute of Architecture and Spatial Planning. Additionally, from 1966 to 1994, in cooperation with UNESCO, Zaremba was responsible for coordinating advanced training in urban and regional planning for students from 47 countries (primarily Latin America, Asia, and Africa), ultimately educating some 500 planners.[8] His experience in East Asia made it easier for him to coordinate such international-exchange programmes.

Zaremba's Approach to Urban Planning

Before examining the Polish team's plan for the reconstruction of Chongjin, it is necessary to briefly analyse the main aspects of Zaremba's approach to urban planning. However, since Zaremba published in the region of 250 works (including books, scientific and popular articles, monographs, and dissertations) and participated in numerous urban projects, extracting his main ideas from these works is a challenging task. Accordingly, we shall focus on parts of his thinking that are relevant to North Korea.

It should be noted that Zaremba was highly critical of socialist urban-planning methods. His planning of Chongjin accordingly exhibits several differences from that of Pyongyang and Hamhŭng. As noted, Zaremba worked on several plans for North Korean and Chinese cities, frequently criticising the state-led uniform approach. Where urban planning in capitalist countries relies on a compromise between individual private property rights and public policies, all planning processes in socialist countries are implemented and supervised by the state. Despite the high efficiency of the rapid industrialisation and reconstruction in the Stalin era, this ultra-centralised planning produced urban spaces lacking diversity and vigour. As a result, socialist countries – including Poland – tried to move away from the Soviet model following Stalin's death. During the Cold War two ideological blocs confronted each other in urban planning. Rooted in entirely different political, economic, and social systems, the two approaches created contrasting urban landscapes. The capitalist approach to urban planning followed the principles of CIAM, as laid out in the Athens Charter. This approach prioritises the functional city. Cities were classified in terms of four functions – housing, leisure, work, and transportation – assigned to specific urban zones. The strategy tends to undermine a city's historical attributes and organic relationship with its natural environment; this is the principal criticism raised against many new towns created in accordance with the principles set out by CIAM.

By contrast, in reconstructing their war-torn cities, socialist countries took the principles of Soviet urban planning as important guidelines. Mainly defined during the rule of Stalin, the 16 principles of Soviet urban planning were formally recognised in 1948. Implemented through a top-down, state-led approach, these principles were uniformly applied to urban projects in socialist states, including East Germany, as a kind of dogma. In particular, the Soviet approach favoured deploying historical buildings or monuments as the city's main points, strategically placing them to form an ensemble. Soviet planners also emphasised the function of the city square as a site for political propaganda parades (principle 9). Meanwhile, residential blocks were partitioned in such a way as to incorporate necessary cultural, utilities, and social services, making them an important unit in urban space (principle 10). These principles are best illustrated in the 1946 plan for Stalingrad.[9]

When he took charge of the reconstruction of Szczecin, Zaremba was critical of both ideas; he accordingly developed his own approach. In particular, he was critical of the top-down character of Soviet planning. In a speech at the People's Great Hall of Hangzhou on 28 October 1957 he declared,

The leading governing bodies of cities and provinces do not have a deep understanding of the local economy and lifestyle. And if municipalities are subordinate to the institutions of the state, do not act as an independent agent, they are not aware of the potential of local, provincial, and urban areas. For this reason, the relationship between national, regional, and urban planning should be maintained horizontally, not in a top-down way.[10]

Additional negative outcomes of the top-down approach noted by Zaremba were imbalances in the industrial-production and residential sectors. 'Focusing only on heavy industry and neglecting light industry' in socialist countries, he wrote, led to 'emphasis of production and neglect of ordinary life.' Zaremba's critique of the state-led, top-down method derived from his experience working as an

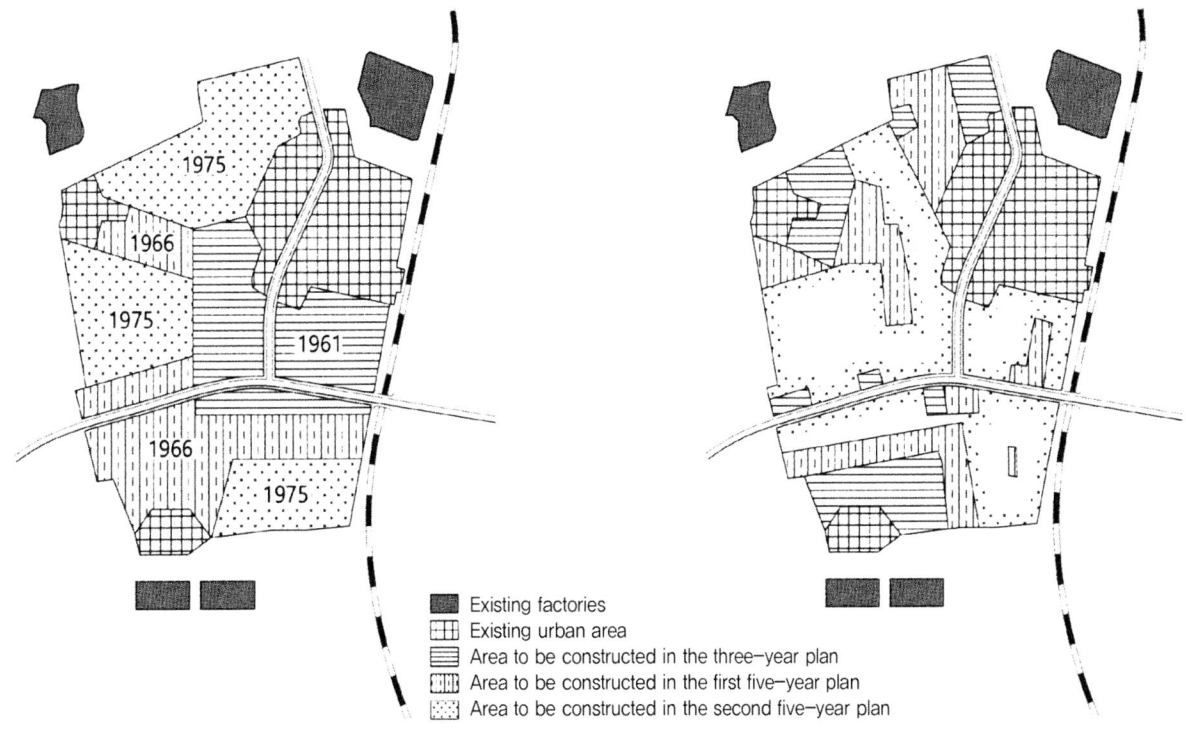

Comparison of two reconstruction plans: a) a phased development plan; b) a random plan without 'phased development'.
Source: redrawn from Geonchukgwa geonseol, February 1956, 29

urban planner during the reconstruction of Szczecin. The central government held a grudge against him due to his involvement in organising municipal self-government in Szczecin in 1945. Based on the system in Poznań, this system of self-government was retained until 13 April 1950, when the Soviet system of city administration was established. As Zaremba later recalled,

[In] defending the local government in Szczecin, I did not allow nationalisation of municipal enterprises, management of residential buildings, farms, and municipal forests. I objected to the liquidation of the municipal-planning studio, the repository of maps and plans, the municipal archive, the municipal measurement office, the municipal water administration, and the Oder quays. In this I had the full support of the City Council and social organisations.[11]

Zaremba put forward a 'phased implementation plan' as an alternative urban planning method.[12] According to Zaremba, after being refined over eight years of trial and error, the method had been in use in Poland since 1953. However, since Poland had completed its reconstruction, it was no longer useful for the Polish context.[13] Zaremba proposed applying the method to North Korean cities, where reconstruction had only just begun. North Korea had two further advantages: no pressure from the Polish central government and no need to apply Polish planning standards. Zaremba thus applied his 'phased implementation plan' to urban-planning initiatives in Chongjin. The 'phased implementation plan' has three parts: first, the development of design proposals; second, the development of a phased implementation plan; third, the development of a final master plan.

The first stage involves developing an outline design rather than providing specific details. The outline design is a plan at 1/25,000 scale identifying and proposing the major direction for a city's development for the next three decades. The location and size of each district, major industrial complexes, transportation networks, and green areas are largely determined at this stage. The urban-planning team presents several outline designs and selects one based on the regional environment. For Chongjin, Zaremba suggested two variants reflecting different visions of the city's future. His idea, based on his experience in Poland, was that this stage should involve close collaboration between urban planners and experts in sewage, transportation, and railways; the result would be a cooperative model of urban planning whereby the urban plan would be shaped by expertise of diverse kinds. 'At that time,' wrote Zaremba, 'there was no agreement between railway companies and urban planners over the railway line, so the master plan had to be constantly adjusted, and controversy arose over the already approved, finalised plans.'[14] To avoid such mistakes, Zaremba argued that the railway plan should be determined during the outline-design stage.[15] In following this approach, the reconstruction of Chongjin demonstrated the outstanding efficiency of the cooperative model. 'We learned from Chongjin,' wrote Zaremba, 'that the new way of implementing a project by developing a cooperative model is very effective, and that there is a need to change existing planning methods as soon as possible.'

The second stage involves dividing the development period into several stages and suggesting a direction for each stage – that is, developing an effective phased implementation plan. Zaremba illustrated the importance of the phased implementation plan using two examples. The first involved creation of a new urban area for temporary housing near the existing but destroyed urban centre. Subsequently, adjacent areas were gradually developed in accordance with each five-year plan and the phased implementation plan. Zaremba's second example involved the development of a new urban area without the use of a phased implementation plan. In this case new residential areas for workers were created around reconstructed factories without any consideration of growth of the urban area. This caused a serious problem that hindered restoration of the urban centre. Implementation of a reconstruction project without designating specific zones and identifying the appropriate timing for each development stage may jeopardise residents' living standards.[16] Thus a phased implementation plan is required to prevent the chaotic development of urban spaces and to facilitate participation in the project by residents.

Planners can use a sequential development plan to reach the final objective: a realistic and practical master plan with close links to the national planning process. In the final stage of the reconstruction of Chongjin, Zaremba and his Polish planning team developed a master plan titled 'Urban Development Prospect Plan'. This 1/10,000 scale master plan comprised designs for different zones, including street networks, residential areas, the city centre, industrial areas, port facilities, and green spaces.[17]

Zaremba's Approach to Planning Chongjin

After arriving in Chongjin in November 1954, Zaremba and his planning team began analysing the city's urban structure, which dated to the colonial period. Chongjin began as a small fishing village under the jurisdiction of the administrative district Boryeong-gun. It is situated in a bay. The Gomalsan Peninsula protrudes to the east; the deep seabed allows ships to anchor relatively close to the shoreline. Two low mountains, Mount Ssangyong-san and Mount Naktasan, are located above the Gomal-san Peninsula, while the Suseongcheon Stream and the Suseong Plain extend along the western part of the bay. Given such favourable mooring conditions, Chongjin became an important port for the supply and transport of Japanese troops during the Russo-Japanese War (1904–1905). In the wake of Japan's victory, Chongjin began to grow as Japanese merchants flocked to the fishing village, where they engaged in commerce from a fishing port on the eastern side of the Gomalsan Peninsula. Following Chongjin's designation as a treaty port in 1908, a new town was formed near the existing fishing village. As the population grew, the Japanese Government-General of Joseon designated Chongjin 'the city of Chongjin' in 1913.[18] Shortly afterwards, the Hamgyeong Railway Line Construction Plan was developed to transport military supplies and cargo to the Chinese mainland. Following the completion of the first railway line in 1917 and the opening of the Chongjin-Horyeong and Wonsan-Yeongheung lines in 1919, the entire Hamgyeong Line was completed in 1928.[19] The Hamgyeong Line remained relatively unchanged after the Korean War, with Zaremba harnessing it effectively for the Polish reconstruction of Chongjin.[20]

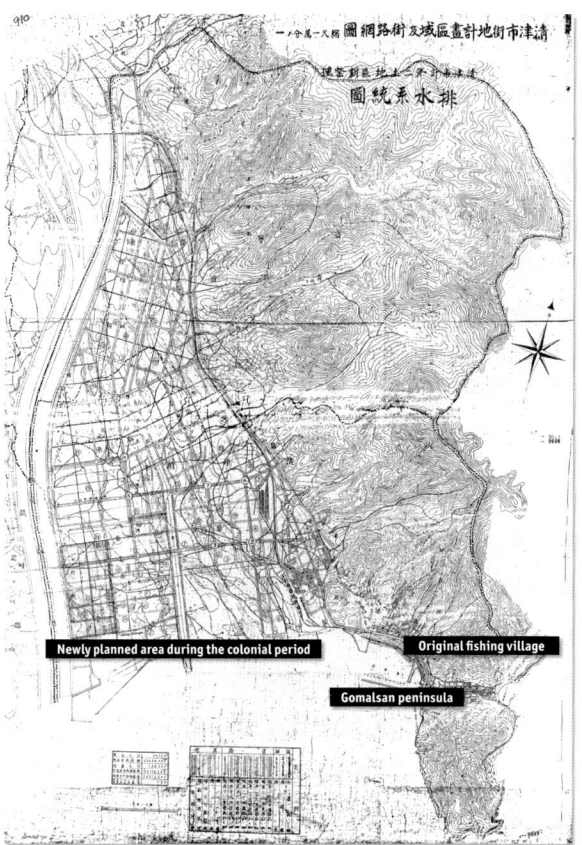

Plan for Chongjin, 1938.
Source: National Archives of Korea, CJA0016083

View of Chongjin after the Korean War.
Source: Archiwum Państwowe w Szczecinie

View of Chongjin after the Korean War.
Source: Archiwum Państwowe w Szczecinie

The opening of the Hamgyeong Line spurred the industrialisation of Chongjin. Notably, abundant sardine catches off the city's coast led to the construction of a processing plant for the production of hydrogenated oil, which is extracted from sardines. Industrial development resulted in an increase in the urban population from just 3915 in 1910 to 234,388 by 1942. This demographic surge forced the Japanese colonial authorities to expand the city's boundaries, incorporating surrounding areas. In 1936, after establishing a new pier on the coast near the Suseong Stream, the Government-General of Joseon adopted a new decision on urban planning. However, this policy – which provided for the construction of various industrial facilities, including steel mills – raised concerns regarding urban sprawl. Accordingly, in 1938, the colonial government greatly expanded Chongjin's urban boundary, designating a 'Land Readjustment Area' along the road connecting Chongjin and Nanam. The subsequent expansion of the Land Readjustment Area in 1941 served to fully incorporate Nanam into Chongjin city.

Chongjin was devastated during the Korean War. Photos taken by Zaremba's team document the extent of this destruction. Based on local surveys, the Polish team decided to reuse the city's existing infrastructure, including the road network and port facilities built by the Japanese colonial government. However, Zaremba identified several flaws in the Japanese colonial urban-planning strategy, which he considered a strange hybrid of American schematism and characteristics taken from European cities. Without giving any consideration to landform, the Japanese planners had employed rectangular grid plans and radial street systems that are very similar to the geometricising tendencies of late-nineteenth-century European urban planning.[21]

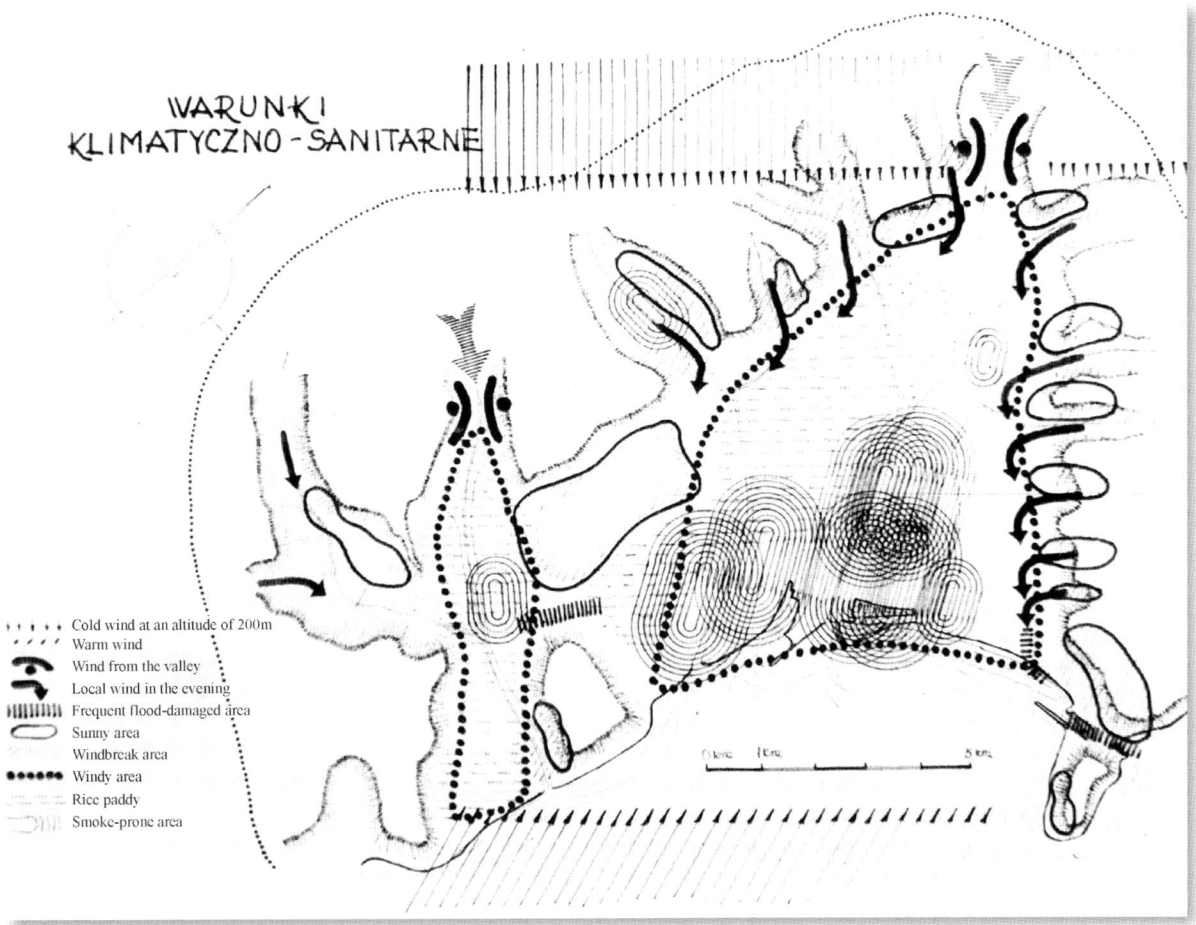

Climatic conditions in Chongjin.
Source: Miasto, no. 1, 1957

Zaremba and his team also investigated the city's geology and climate so as to use Chongjin's natural environment as a scientific basis for a more appropriate and finely tuned urban plan. They divided Chongjin into four districts – namely Minju, Songpyeong, Gangdeok, and Nanam – based on geographic and environmental attributes, with each district possessing a unique climate deriving from the mountains, valleys, and sea surrounding the city, as well as the flow of both natural and artificial waterways. In other words, the Polish team defined districts according to their natural environment and determined the appropriate urban structure and architectural form for each district.[22] Their conclusions can be summarised as follows. First, the district of Minju is located downstream of the Suseong Stream Delta, with cold air flows coming from the valley of the eastern ridge. Second, the district of Songpyeong is located west of the Suseong Stream; its low altitude and humid and windy conditions make it suitable for use as agricultural land. Third, the district of Gangdeok, located on a ridge, is subject to winds from the north but enjoys a relatively mild and consistent climate. Finally, while Nanam has a relatively mild climate, it is subject to winds from both the north and the south.

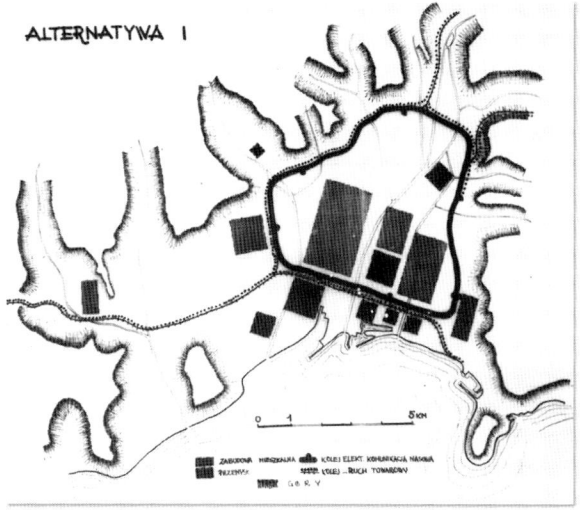 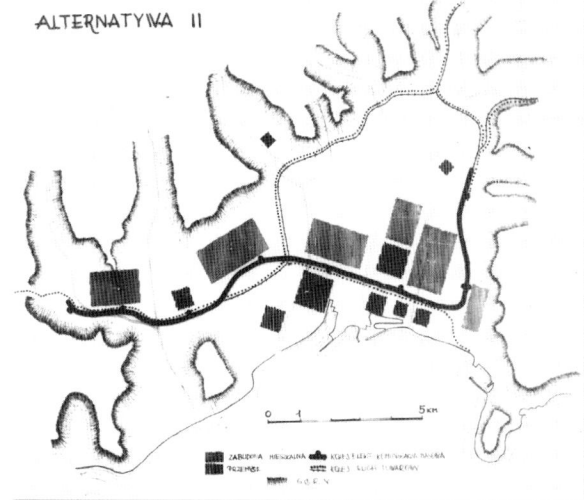

Two variants of the outline design for Chongjin.
Source: Miasto, no. 1, 1957

The Urban Planning of Chongjin

After completing their survey of Chongjin's environment, the Polish team proposed two outline designs at a scale of 1:25,000. The first proposal utilised a concentrated pattern, with the urban area concentrated around the districts of Songpyeong and Minju along the Suseong Stream Delta. The railway network was to ring these two areas, serving as the main means of transportation. Accordingly, this proposal reflects the centralised and radial urban form popular among socialist urban planners in the 1950s. Zaremba, however, identified four flaws in this design.[23] First, the relatively unfavourable geological and climatic conditions of the Suseong Stream Delta would make it difficult to construct diverse buildings in the area. In addition to possessing numerous irrigation channels, the land had been used for agriculture and was characterised by layers of excessively soft soil and sand 2–3 metres below the ground; this would hinder construction. Second, placing residential areas in the northern part of the delta risked residents being too far away from the industrial area in which they worked, resulting in long commutes between factories and residential areas and compounding traffic congestion in the city centre. Third, the plan necessitated the construction of numerous bridges to connect the Songpyeong and Minju districts. Fourth, the considerable distance between the city centre and Nanam would check the latter's growth, while the district of Gangdeok, which possesses favourable climatic conditions, would remain undeveloped. These issues presented a significant hurdle to developing Chongjin as a unified city.

Outline design for Chongjin.
Source: Archiwum Państwowe w Szczecinie

By contrast, the second proposal provided for a linear city stretching along the coastline and completely incorporated Nanam into the city of Chongjin. The district of Gangdeok – which is protected from the wind and enjoys sunny conditions – was to be developed as a residential area, rather than the northern part of Songpyeong, which has unfavourable soil conditions and a high risk of flooding from the Suseong Stream. The proposal also suggested repairing and using the city's existing railway lines as the main means of transportation, reducing the cost of construction. To this end, the plan proposed an 18-kilometre railway line extending from Minju to Namha, with eight railway stations. The Polish planners intended that this line should serve as the mainstay of the city's transportation system in conjunction with trolley-bus lines. Industrial areas and railways would be closely connected and situated adjacent to the coastline, while residential areas would be developed linearly along the railway. After comparing the benefits and drawbacks of the two proposals, Zaremba and his team chose the second outline design as the basis from which to develop their master plan.[24]

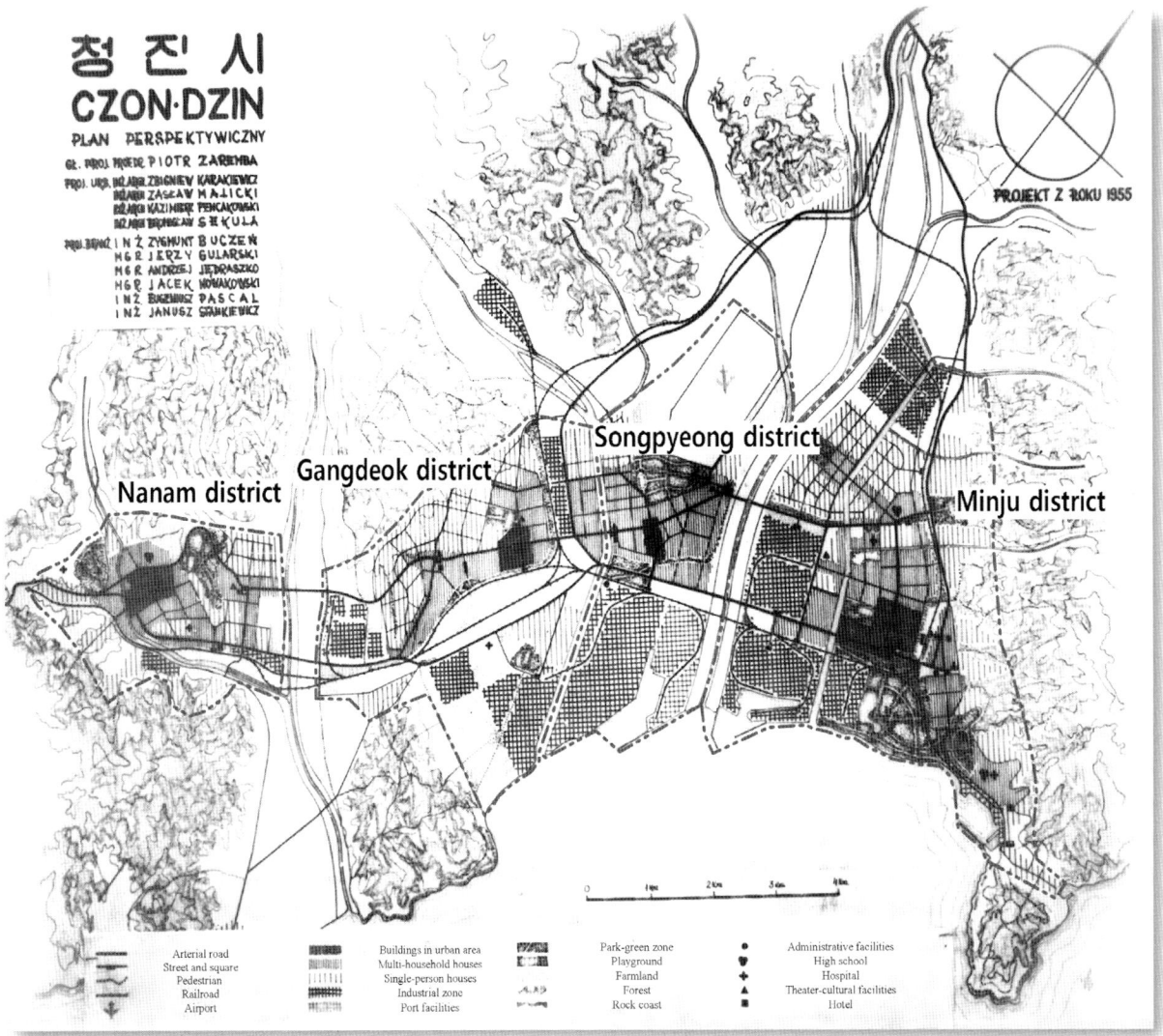

Master plan for Chongjin.
Source: Miasto, no. 1, 1957

The Polish team presented their master plan in early 1956. Reflecting all the work they had carried out over the previous 16 months, the plan encompassed provisions for the city's traffic network, land use, and locations of public buildings. Essentially, it involved developing a high-density city connected by an arterial road. In view of Chongjin's climate and geographical conditions, the city's industrial zones are located close to the coastline, while residential zones are located at higher altitudes. Residential development is subdivided into three categories: single houses; two- to three-storey, multi-household housing complexes; and four- or five-storey apartment buildings with no lift. However, given Zaremba's desire to have phased development, the master plan did not present detailed block plans. Realisation of the plan was accordingly left to North Korean architects.

The master plan divided the city into four districts – Minju, Songpyeong, Gangdeok, and Nanam – with each district possessing its own centre. The four districts were characterised as follows. First, Minju, located on the coastline, constitutes the city's central area and possesses a good street network. The central square – around which administrative buildings and public facilities are concentrated – forms the city's central axis. This district was designed to accommodate approximately 140,000 people. Second, shaped by its natural environment, the district of Songyeong possesses large factories and port facilities in the south and airports in the north, while its centre contains public buildings and multi-family housing. The plan envisaged a future population of 70,000 people for this district. Third, the district of Gangdeok was designated a residential area, with a lively environment guaranteed by its pleasant climate. Since Gangdeok is situated on a sloped ridge, the plan avoided high-rise buildings and opted for single-storey houses instead. This district was projected to have a population of 80,000. Fourth, like Gangdeok, Nanam possesses a favourable environment and was thus designated a residential area. However, as the terrain here is low and flat, the plan proposed two- to three-storey multi-household housing. This district was projected to have a population of 60,000. Thus Zaremba and his team distributed the city's population by district, taking geographical features, functions, and building height into consideration. For example, whereas single-storey houses are more appropriate for Gangdeok since this district is located on a slope and has a smaller population, multi-rise buildings are more appropriate for Minju, which accordingly has a larger population than either Gangdeok or the highly industrialised district of Songpyeong.

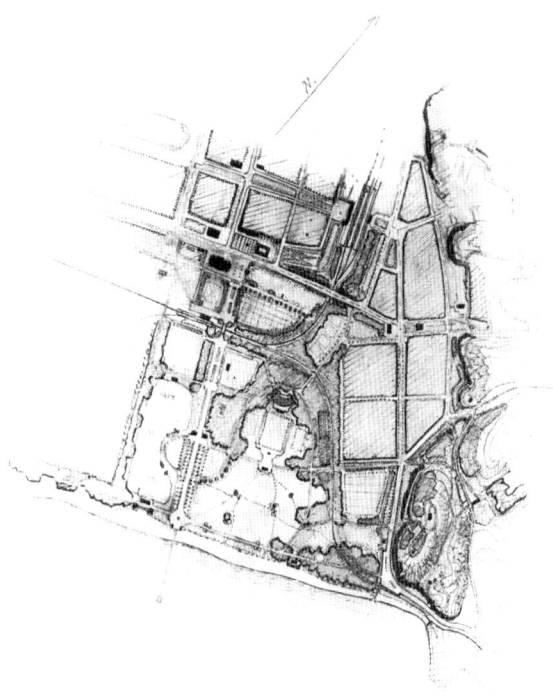

Plan of central district, Chongjin.
Source: Miasto, no.1, 1957

The City Centre

The creation of a central square connected to an urban axis had been a key objective in socialist urban planning since Stalin's reign. As nationalisation of land made securing the necessary land relatively easy, large central squares were placed in core areas to boost socialist ideology. As we see from the urban planning of Pyongyang and Hamhŭng, central squares were believed to represent the city's spirit and identity. Zaremba was equally aware of this significance. However, compared to the central squares of Pyongyang and Hamhŭng, the central square in Chongjin is markedly different in size, location, and function, illustrating how far Zaremba deviated from socialist urban planning.

In Zaremba's view, Chongjin's existing city centre was biased toward the district of Minju in the east, making it difficult to develop as a concentrated urban form. However, he also accepted the principle that the reconstruction of city should respect the old city centre in order to preserve its historical heritage. In consideration of these conditions, he planned to create a new city centre around Minju. The proposed city centre accordingly suffered from having a one-sided location. Zaremba employed various methods to compensate for this. Finding that the previous city centre lacked connectivity with other areas, he sought to link it with the new centre by means of arterial roads. His master plan accordingly proposed placing the central square on the side of the No. 1 arterial road, which connects the district of Nanam with the eastern border of Minju. As Zaremba explained in an article in the North Korean magazine *Geonseolja* (Builder),

> In the new plan the city must respect the traditional location of the historical centre. The new centre must be connected to the existing one and be naturally formed as a continuous part of it. Thus we decided to create a new centre near the existing centre. Since there are not yet any industrial buildings on this part of the coast, we can build a cultural park on the beach in the future.[25]

The master plan proposed that the Communist Party building and the three-to-four-storey multi-household housing complexes for party officials should be erected to the north of the square. To the south of the square, a drainage channel was intended to prevent flooding and direct overflow into the Suseong Stream. A park was to be situated across from the drainage channel and alongside the railway, with a school at its centre. South of the square's axis and the school site lay the coast, where Zaremba planned to create a grand park as a space for culture and relaxation.[26] The central square itself was relatively small, with dimensions of 120 × 80 metres, and was situated at the

Detail planed of main square, Chongjin.
Source: Miasto, no. 1, 1957

corner of the urban area. Moreover, since the axis ran from the square to the large park on the coast, it did not create a spectacular scene, making it difficult to see it as a key element integrating the entire urban structure. Service facilities such as bookshops, markets, and hotels were laid out around the park and the axis. In this way, Zaremba did not follow the existing socialist planning approach. His master plan clearly reflects a move towards de-Stalinisation.

2. Piotr Zaremba and the Urban Planning of Chongjin

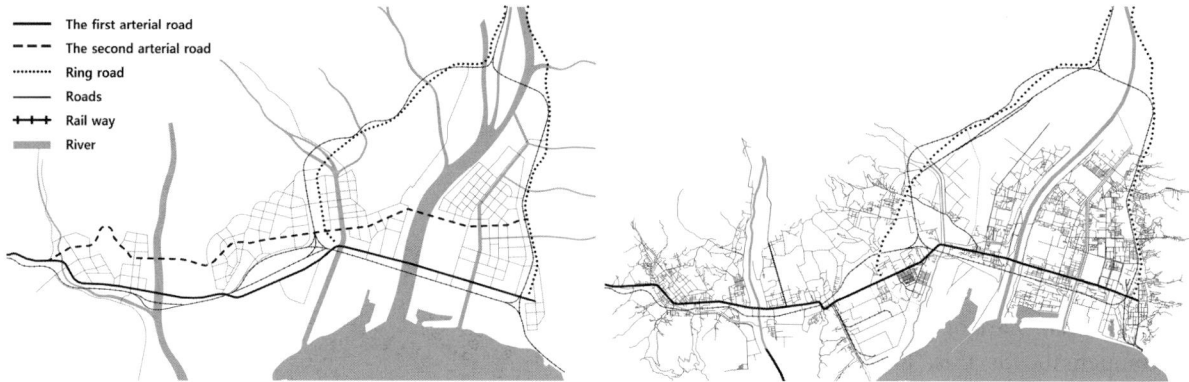

Chongjin's road system: a) the road system in Zaremba's masterplan of 1956; b) the current street system.
Source: *Miasto*, no. 1, 1957

The Urban Structure of Contemporary Chongjin

Chongjin grew to become the third largest city in North Korea, with a population of about 670,000 – that is, over 120,000 more than Zaremba and his team anticipated. The Polish master plan for Chongjin opted for a phased-development method instead of the top-down method typically employed in socialist countries. By contrast with the concentrated urban form prevalent in socialist countries in the 1950s, in consideration of the city's topography and natural environment, the Polish planners designed the new Chongjin as a linear city. The North Korean government accepted their proposal and approved its implementation; however, aerial photos of the reconstructed city show that the Polish plan was only partially fulfilled. A comparison of Zaremba's master plan with an aerial map of contemporary Chongjin reveals how the plan was in fact implemented.[27]

Following the withdrawal of the Polish planning team, North Koreans were responsible for turning the master plan into reality. Rather than using the aid offered by other socialist countries as an opportunity to learn advanced urban-planning theory and practice, North Korean planners submitted to external pressures. For instance, the Polish team had suggested constructing four- to five-storey apartment buildings without elevators in lower-lying areas, artificially raising them off the ground to avoid the risk of flooding. However, the North Korean implementation ignored this suggestion as too expensive; the consequence is that this residential development is confronted with regular damage caused by flooding. Similarly, while the Polish plan suggested placing the industrial facilities in the district of Nanam on the coastline, the aerial map of Chongjin reveals a mixture of factories and housing in the district's centre. Many North Korean defectors who lived in this district have complained of intolerable noise and pollution. Such instances prompt us to ask how flexible Zaremba's phased-development plan actually was.

Both the street and railway networks in contemporary Chongjin differ from the Polish master plan. While Zaremba's master plan retained and utilised the railway network built during the Japanese colonial era, it separated the lines according to function, into cargo and passenger lines. However, this separation was never implemented. The railway network in Chongjin today is identical to that built in the colonial period. This railway line runs from the eastern end of the district of Minju to the end of Nanam, before turning south to Gyeongseong County. However, the circular line which the master plan proposed should encircle the Suseong Plain and the district of Songpyeong and connect Gangdeok Station to Chongjin Station was realised during reconstruction of the city.

Like the railway lines, Chongjin's current street network differs from that proposed by the Polish team's master plan. The street network in Zaremba's master plan largely comprises two arterial roads and one outer ring road. The master plan used the existing road network passing through the central square of the district of Minju and south along the railway line as the first arterial road. The second arterial road was supposed to cut through the district centres of Songpyeong, Gangdeok, and Nanam, leading to the outer ring road of Minju district. The planners thought this road necessary to connect the districts. In the master plan the ring road ran from the eastern outskirts of Minju down the northern ridge of Songpyeong to meet the first main road near Songpyeong Station.

In contemporary Chongjin the first arterial road, originally constructed in the colonial era, is wider than that proposed by the Polish team. It has been renamed 'Asia Highway 6' (AH6). The second arterial road, however, was not realised as shown in the Polish team's master plan. Since two of the four district centres proposed by the master plan were never built, this road proved unnecessary. While the Polish team had envisaged that the ring road would run parallel to the railway line and lead to Songpyeong Station, it was actually constructed on the west side of Namgangdeok Station.

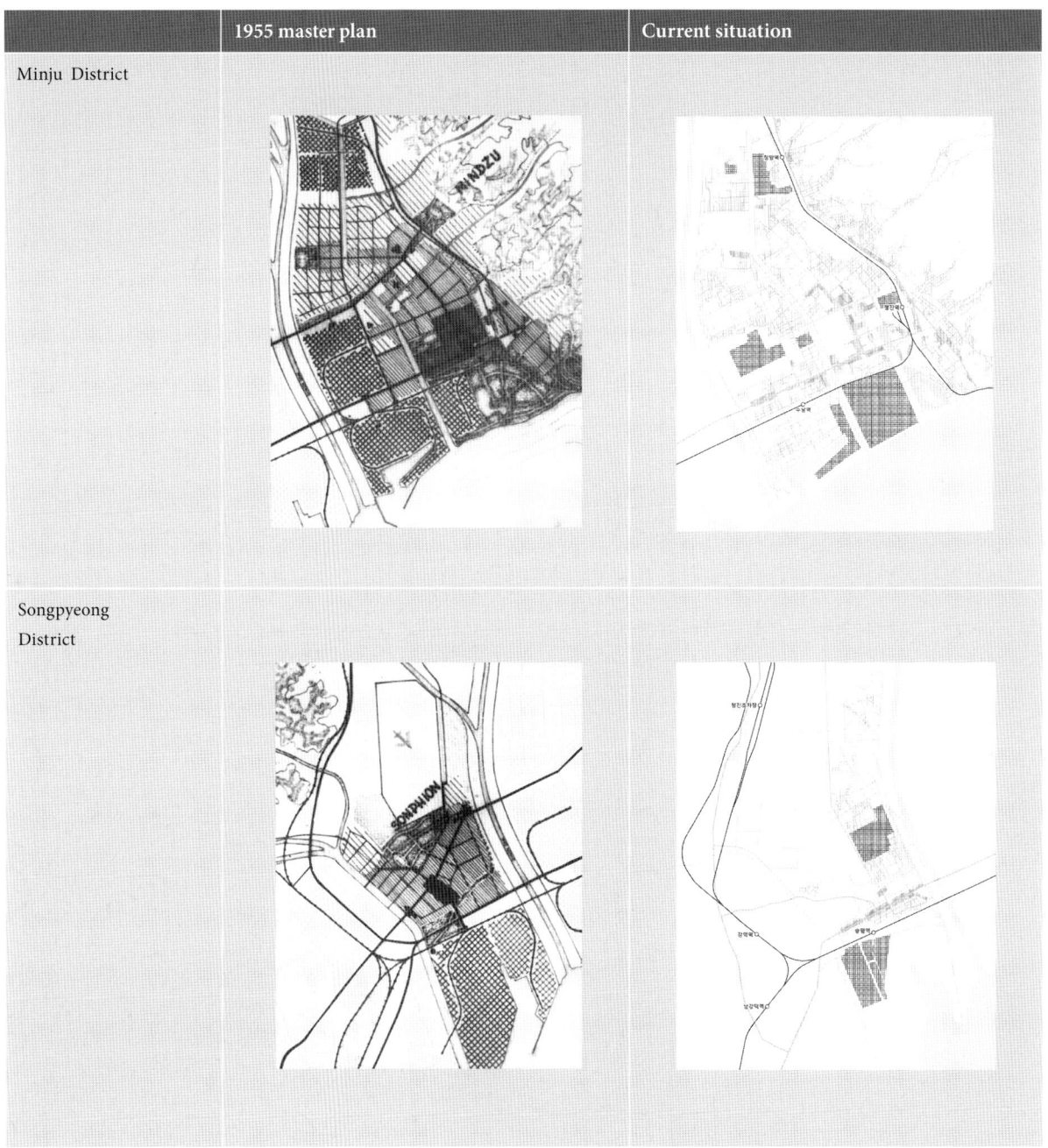

Table 2. Comparison of masterplan and current situation.

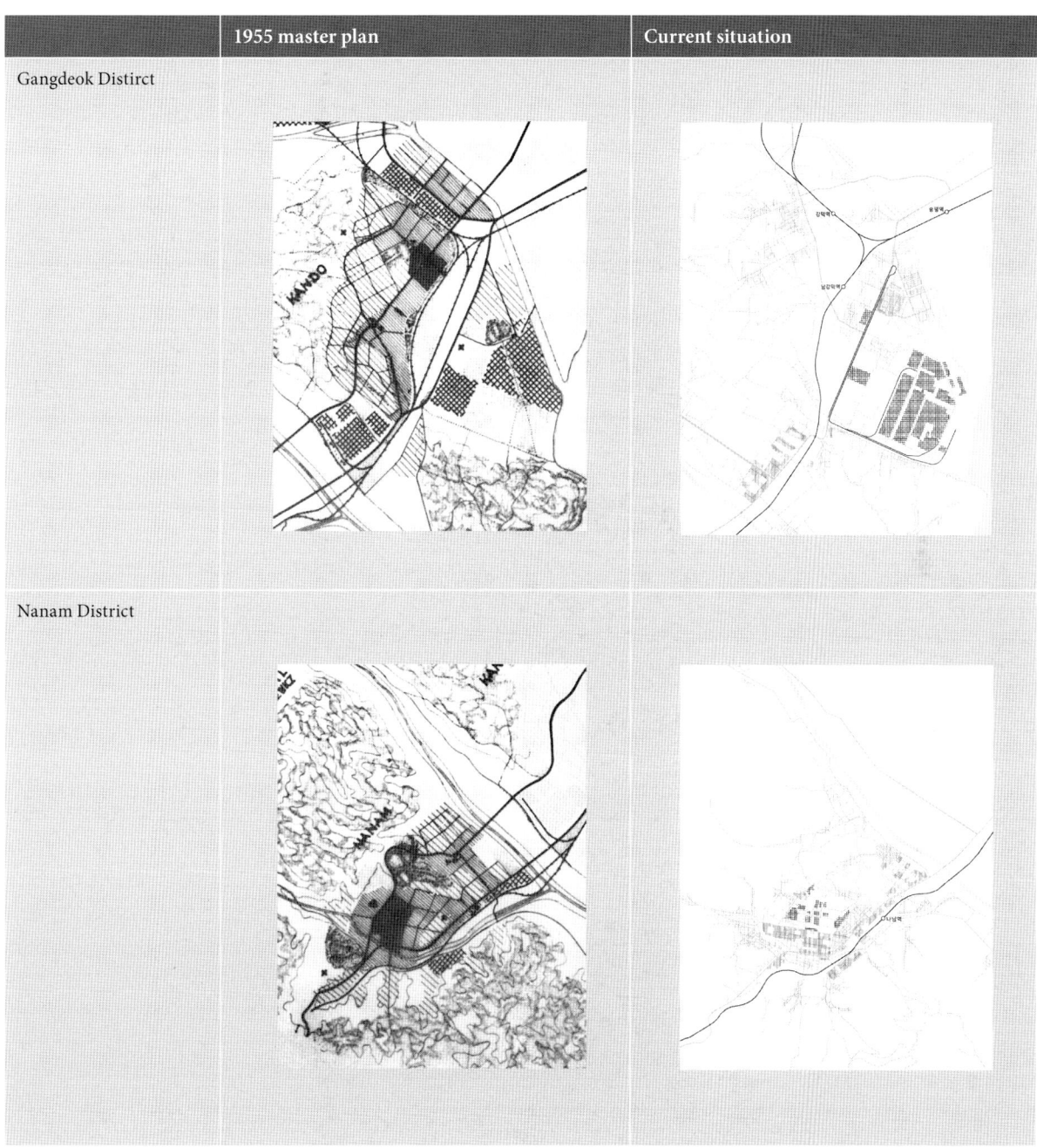

2. Piotr Zaremba and the Urban Planning of Chongjin

Of the four districts, the Polish master plan was realised relatively well in Minju, contemporary Chongjin's largest district and where the city centre is located. There are three railway stations in Minju: Chongjin Station, Chongam Station, and Sunam Station. Chongjin Station appears to utilise the building erected in the colonial era. In the city centre, the central square and administrative buildings were constructed in accordance with Zaremba's master plan, as was the proposed drainage system to the south of the square. Although the park was constructed as planned, the school at its centre was not; instead, high-rise buildings were erected on the parkland to the east. Meanwhile, the large park, the most important element in Minju, was built on a much smaller scale and named 'Chongjin Youth Park'. Low-rise buildings were concentrated in the area adjacent to the railway, while industrial facilities were developed on sites adjacent to the urban axis. Significantly more low-rise dwellings were constructed in Minju than planned; additionally, they were located in the valley of the Gomalsan Peninsula, an area which the Polish team had assigned to industrial facilities. Moreover, only 30 percent of the four-to-five-storey walk-up apartment complexes were realised; detached single houses predominate instead. Built on industrial sites south of Sunam Station, these complexes are in different locations from those proposed by the Polish master plan.

The other three districts were not reconstructed in accordance with Zaremba's master plan. First, although the district of Songpyeong was the intended site for an airport, port facilities, industrial facilities, and areas of small-scale residential development, these functions were never realised. The site intended for an airport remains as rice paddies to this day; irrigation channels were never constructed as planned. Only a small number of houses were constructed in the vicinity of the Suseong Stream and the AH6. As envisaged by the master plan, the centre of Songpyeong was to have had its own square, as well as administrative and cultural facilities opposite Songpyeong Station. However, instead of this urban centre, a small park was created without irrigation channels. For Gangdeok, in view of its excellent climate, the master plan proposed the construction of large-scale housing complexes. However, this intention was only realised around South Gangdeok Station; the other areas remained unchanged. By contrast with the Polish plan, four-to-five-storey apartment complexes were constructed along the AH6 near the river. Additionally, unlike in the design proposed by the Polish team, a haphazard street network was built on the hillside. Third, the street network of Nanam underwent considerable modification. Additionally, without the planned parks and road network, many of the plains remain virgin territory; instead, residential areas were constructed along the AH6 and single-storey detached houses on the sides of the valleys. While parks, walk-up apartment complexes, and administrative buildings have been constructed in its centre, most of this district is occupied by industrial facilities.

Conclusion

The master plan developed by Zaremba and his Polish planning team differed from the Stalinist approach that dominated socialist urban planning at the time. These differences are clear when we compare the Polish master plan with those developed for Pyongyang and Hamhŭng. The plan for Chongjin should accordingly be recognised as an important example of the diversity of post-Stalinist planning.

Rejecting the top-down approach, Zaremba pursued an urban-planning strategy that guaranteed participation by residents. This explains his choice of a master plan for Chongjin based on the phased-development method. Instead of pursuing speedy completion of urban development, Zaremba's phased-development plan was intended to develop the city progressively over an extended period of time. This was a provisional springboard rather than a final and complete outcome.

The Polish master plan for Chongjin differs from those for Pyongyang and Hamhŭng, especially given that the latter sought to express the superiority of the socialist system and the power of the North Korean government. Pyongyang and Hamhŭng were planned as centralised cities with a central square symbolising political power and a radial road network representing a Stalinist-type spatial hierarchy. By contrast, the plan for Chongjin took the city's natural conditions and lifestyles into account in its proposal for a linear city with a public central square and a high degree of connectivity ensured by an extensive road network. This plan had no room for buildings lining the city's boulevard to create impressive urban landscapes.

1. Levi, Nicolas, *Zarys Historii Stosunków Między Polską*, p. 737.
2. Kim, Jong-suck, 'Polish Aid for North Korea during the Korean War', p. 169.
3. Zaremba, Piotr, 'Polski Projekt Koreańskiego', pp. 4–11.
4. Zaremba, Piotr, 'Metody Pracy Urbanistycznej w Korei', p. 22.
5. Ibid.
6. Hou, L., Sheng, Y., Stanek, L., Gzowska, A., Bujas, P., 'Zhongbo jiaoliu beijing xia', p. 85.
7. For further details regarding Zaremba's interventions in Chinese cities, see: Zhou, Buyi, *Jianzhu Xuebao*, no.1, 1956.
8. Hou, L., Sheng, Y., Stanek, L., Gzowska, A., Bujas, P., 'Zhongbo jiaoliu beijing xia', p. 85.
9. Ptichnikova, Galina and Antyufeev, Alexey, p, 5.
10. Hou, L., Sheng, Y., Stanek, L., Gzowska, A., Bujas, P., 'Zhongbo jiaoliu beijing xia', pp. 83–85.
11. Krasiu. Prezydent Piotr Zaremba Odpiera Atak. W: Sedina. pl Portal miłośników dawnego Szczecina (published in *Architektura i Urbanistika*) [on-line] 6 January, 2007.
12. Piotr Zaremba's Polish article in *Miasto*, 1956, no. 2, uses the term 'plan etapowej realizacji', the English translation of which is 'phased-implementation plan'. In an article in *Architecture and Construction* 1956, no. 2, published in North Korea, this term was translated as 'stepped plan' (*Gyedan Gyehoek*).
13. Zaremba, Piotr, 'Metody Pracy Urbanistycznej', p. 31.
14. Ibid., p. 23.
15. Zaremba, Piotr, 'Siljejeokin dosigyehoekui munje 1', p. 60.
16. Zaremba, Piotr, 'Joseon dosi geonseolui baljeonwonchike', p. 39.
17. Zaremba, Piotr, 'Metody Pracy Urbanistycznej w Korei', pp. 22–27.
18. Shim, J., Lee, H., Min, W., 'Iljegangjeomgi Chongjinui', pp. 138–141.
19. Song, Kue-jin, 'Hangyeongseon buseolgwa Gilhoeseon', pp. 328–330.
20. Zaremba, Piotr, 'Joseon dosi geonseolui baljeonwonchike', p. 39.
21. Zaremba, Piotr, 'Metody Pracy Urbanistycznej w Korei', p. 23.
22. Zaremba, Piotr, 'Polski Projekt Koreańskiego Miasta Czon-dżin', p. 4.
23. Zaremba, Piotr, 'Siljejeokin dosigyehoekui munje2', p. 78.
24. Zaremba, Piotr, 'Metody Pracy Urbanistycznej w Korei', p. 31.
25. Zaremba, Piotr, 'Siljejeokin dosigyehoekui munje 2', p. 80.
26. Ibid, pp. 78–84.
27. For comparison, this chapter utilises Google Maps (www.google.co.kr/maps/) and North Korea Information Portal Maps (nkinfo.unikorea.go.kr/NKMap/).

The Creation of Kim Il-sung Square in Pyongyang

Inha Jung

One of the most distinctive features of socialist planning was the creation of a central square at the centre of a city. If collective housing reflected the socialist way of life, the square projected socialist ideology into urban spaces. In addition to serving as the site of workers' rallies and demonstrations, the central square was designed to guide people's thoughts and facilitate their embrace of the socialist system; its grandeur was intended to make a country's citizens believe in the superiority of socialism and their regime. Socialist regimes accordingly paid close attention to the design of their central squares, as we can see from the formation of Red Square in Moscow and Tiananmen Square in Beijing. The post-war reconstruction of North Korean cities also established a central square at the city centre as an organic link between major public buildings and green spaces. Of these, Kim Il-sung Square in Pyongyang is the most politically symbolic. Indeed, whenever the North Korean regime exhibits new weapons during military parades, Kim Il-sung Square becomes the focus of global attention. Established in 1951, the square was gradually developed into a true socialist space over the next 30 years. This development ended in 1982, with the completion of the Grand People's Study House at the front of the square and the huge Juche Ideology Tower across the Daedong River.

This chapter traces the formation of Kim Il-sung Square in Pyongyang, identifying the design principles applied in this process. The history of this square's creation in the country's capital is especially revealing since it displays in microcosm the tensions between communist ideals and Stalinist retro trends that affected North Korea's post-war urban planning in general. The square's history further reveals an ongoing search for North Korea's national identity. The radical urban experiments of the Soviet Avant-garde never took place in North Korea. Instead, North Korean planners pursued national identity through manipulations of urban scale and axiality, placing traditional-style monuments at key points. By these means they sought, as Kim Il-sung put it, to create a North Korean version of 'national in form and socialist in content'.[1] North Korean architects and designers aspired to create a socialist city, as well as one which would showcase the legitimacy of their own national identity. These dual aspects of post-war urban design served as engines driving change in North Korea's urban landscape. Our investigation of the creation of Pyongyang's Kim Il-Sung Square will make clear both the roles of the participants in North Korea's urban planning and their design principles, helping us understand a decision-making process that has not been sufficiently examined until now.

Pyongyang's Urban Centre Before the Korean War

In the wake of the Russian Revolution (1917–1923), the city centre – where the bourgeoisie had long accumulated assets – became the most controversial subject in socialist urban planning. Amid fierce debates, the proponents of a thorough break from the past argued for ruthless destruction of monuments in city centres. In Moscow, Kazan Cathedral and the Iberian Chapel were demolished to create Red Square. Even St Basil's Cathedral, one of the most important monuments in the Soviet capital, was slated for demolition.[2] Similarly, Beijing's Tiananmen Square was created after the demolition of a T-shaped road in front of the Tiananmen Gate and surrounding buildings. Government buildings, museums, and the Mao Zedong Memorial Hall were then constructed on the new square.[3] However, this tide of destruction did not last long. A resolution issued by the Central Committee of the Soviet Communist Party in 1931 called for existing cities to be transformed into foci of culture, technology, and advanced economy.[4] Traditional urban centres now began to play a key role in residents' leisure and cultural life. This change in perception is conspicuous in the General Plan for the Reconstruction of Moscow of 1935; the Communist Party's Central Committee declared that 'an urban-planning strategy must begin by preserving the basis of the historical city.'[5]

After the ceasefire of 1953, however, North Korean planners encountered a different situation. Pyongyang's city centre had more than 1500 years of history behind it but had been neglected during the colonial period and then devastated by US airstrikes during the Korean War. 'The city has been so thoroughly destroyed', said a report submitted to the International Union of Architects, 'that rehabilitation would be almost tantamount to building a new town.'[6] Accordingly, North Korean planners faced two challenges: on the one hand, they needed to restore the old city centre in order to compete with the historical legitimacy claimed by the South Korean military regime; on the other, they were required to establish a new urban space to embody the North Korean regime's socialist ideals.

Before modernisation, Pyongyang's rich history had been reflected in its urban form. During the Joseon dynasty, Pyongyang had been a heavily fortified military stronghold, a commercial hub for trade with China, and a city known for its pleasures. As one of eight provincial capitals, it had approximately 18,000 inhabitants living within its innermost city wall;[7] of these, 63 percent were engaged in commercial activities and 13 percent in farming.[8] Four rings of city walls located between the Daedong and Botong rivers marked the city limits; the principal urban axis was the main road leading from the Daedongmun Gate to Daedongguan House. The Daedongmun Gate served as the city's main point of entry from the River Daedong, while Daedongguan House was where local government officials held ritual ceremonies and entertained foreign envoys, a symbol of the king's authority. Chinese emissaries from Beijing frequently visited this house en route to their final destination, Seoul.

A new era in Korean history began with the Joseon government's signing of the Treaty of Ganghwado in 1876. When freedom of religion was protected in 1882, an influx of Protestant missionaries followed – including William J. Hall, an American Methodist who opened a mission station in Pyongyang in 1892. As home to several of the most devout Christian establishments on the Korean Peninsula, Pyongyang acquired a reputation of being 'the Eastern Jerusalem.'[9] Two mission stations were located outside Pyongyang's inner-city wall. American Methodist missionaries established a clinic and chapel on Namsan Hill; this compound soon expanded to include a 500-m² church, as well as various mission houses, schools, and clinics. American Presbyterian missionaries arrived in 1893, establishing their compound around the Botongmun Gate and building an L-shaped church with a vernacular roof on Jangdaehyeon Hill, the highest site in the city. They were followed by Catholic missionaries led by Louis LeMerre of the Foreign Missions Society of Paris, who erected Saint Michael's Church on Jangdaehyeon Hill in 1900. Photographs from the colonial period show church spires soaring above the hills as if taking command of Pyongyang's urban landscape.

The centre of Pyongyang in the colonial period.
Source: National Geographic Information Institute

IIn 1906 new Japanese residents flocked to Pyongyang. Although Japanese settlement in Pyongyang had been legalised in 1899, prospective Japanese settlers had initially hesitated due to the prevalence of anti-Japanese sentiment. Japan's victory in the Russo-Japanese War in 1905 gave Japan control of the Korean Peninsula; nevertheless, Japanese immigration was only triggered by the completion of the Gyeongui Railway line in 1906.[10] This led to Pyongyang's urban area expanding from the inner wall to the outer city wall and to an increase in the number of Japanese colonists to 8670 – that is, 19 percent of Pyongyang's total population – by 1915.[11] Japanese settlers built a new town around the railway station, accelerating the dismantlement of the old walled city. As the old city centre gave way to newly constructed military barracks and administrative buildings, colonial Pyongyang gradually became more heterogeneous and fragmented.

After liberation from Japanese colonial rule, Korea was divided in two by the United States and the Soviet Union; Pyongyang became the provisional capital of North Korea. Although the municipal People's Committee requisitioned all Japanese public buildings in the city, Pyongyang still lacked an extensive open space suitable for large-scale public events. Kim Il-sung's first address to a large assembly on 14 October 1945 had to be given at Pyongyang's public stadium.[12] In an effort to provide more space, the interim government replaced the wide crossroads in front of Pyongyang's city hall with a public square. The roads themselves, however, were still too narrow to accommodate a mass rally; accordingly, a number of small roadside buildings were demolished to create a temporary square. In 1948 the founding of the Democratic People's Republic of Korea was declared in this makeshift space, which served as Pyongyang's central square until the creation of Kim Il-sung Square. Although the North Korean regime immediately set about constructing a formal central square in Pyongyang, the project took a considerable amount of time to complete. Kim Il-sung Square was redesigned no less than four times between 1951 and 1982, with different building principles applied each time.

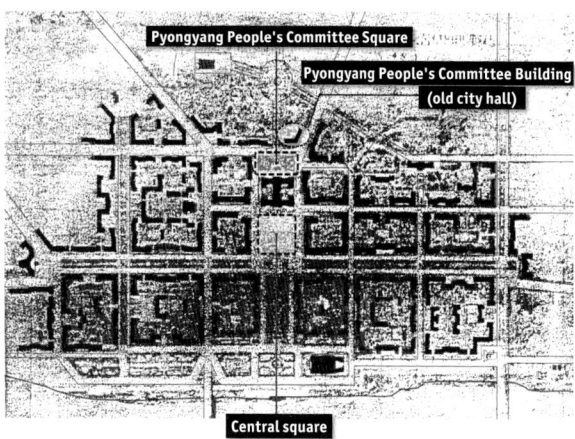

The central square in the General Reconstruction Plan for Pyongyang.
Source: Kim, Jeong-Hui, 1953, p. 347

Kim Jeong-hui's 1951 Plan for Pyongyang's City Centre

Key documents show that the creation of a new central square in Pyongyang was intertwined with the overall reconstruction project for the city.[13] The planning process was initiated on 21 January 1951, when Kim Il-sung met with a group of architects and instructed them to develop a reconstruction plan for Pyongyang. Kim Jeong-hui (1921–1975), one of the first North Koreans to be sent to study abroad, was put in charge of urban planning. In respect to the city centre, Kim Il-sung offered these guidelines: 'it would be good to place it in proximity to the municipal People's Committee building or at the foot of Namsan Hill. The ideal location will balance the city's needs with the convenience of its workers.' With regard to Stalin Street, which was to pass through the city centre, Kim Il-sung told the planning team, 'without remodelling the currently disorderly through road, we must create a new street parallel to the Daedong River, going from Moranbong to Pyongyang station.' Finally, 'regarding the location of a [new] central square, I think it would be best to place it in front of the municipal People's Committee building.'[14] The site indicated by Kim Il-Sung was that of the temporary square in front of the former city hall, now occupied by the Pyongyang People's Committee.

Based on these guidelines, Kim Jeong-hui submitted the General Reconstruction Plan for Pyongyang (hereinafter 'the General Plan') on 10 May 1951. The General Plan envisioned an entirely new kind of urban space – a conceptual leap that was made possible by starting with a blank slate. In addition to a strong axis, broad boulevards, large public squares, and imposing monuments, the General Plan provided for an arterial road system that divided the city into urban blocks. Kim Jeong-hui's *Dosi Geonseol* (Urban Construction), published in 1953, elucidates his approach to Pyongyang's reconstruction. 'The new principles that all socialist cities should follow,' he wrote, 'have already been demonstrated in urban planning implemented by the Soviet Union. All I have done is to apply those achievements to the urban reconstruction of North Korea.'¹⁵

In addition to the General Plan, Kim Jeong-hui prepared a special plan for the city centre. As he explained in *Dosi Geonseol*, 'the architectural assemblage in the city centre must be conceived at the same time as the General Plan, so that the composition of the city centre can respond to the city's future development.'¹⁶ The plan's most noticeable feature in the city centre was an urban axis linking the Daedong River to the municipal People's Committee building (the former city hall). In *Dosi Geonseol* Kim Jeong-hui identifies three reasons for the selection of this site: first, 'it must be located in an area where the traffic flow will be convenient for citizens'; second, 'the natural environment must also be considered. This area is linked to the waterfront, and it has mountains for a backdrop, as well as a scale which is appropriate for a central square'; third, 'we must conserve the historical centre as much as we can, but if a new centre is needed for reasons of size, the new one must not be located too far from the historical centre.'¹⁷ Accordingly, the General Plan placed the city centre just three blocks from the traditional axis leading from the Daedongmun Gate to Daedongguan House.

Kim Jeong-Hui's sketches and plans reflect the strong influence of Stalinist-era urban design in several respects. The urban space does not consist of independent objects but remains a unified whole.¹⁸ At this time Soviet planners, like the Avant-garde, rejected the concept of the city as a collection of self-contained buildings; instead, they returned to traditional urban forms as the basis for a homogeneous spatial order. Kim Jong-hui's ideas may be clearly identified through his frequent use of the terms 'assemblage' and 'composition'; the key principle of his methodology was 'to create an urban ensemble from a unified architectural assemblage'¹⁹ This tenet subsequently became the essential motif of postwar urban design as practised by North Korean architects. According to Kim Jeong-hui, it provided a means to secure a city's spatial and architectural unification.

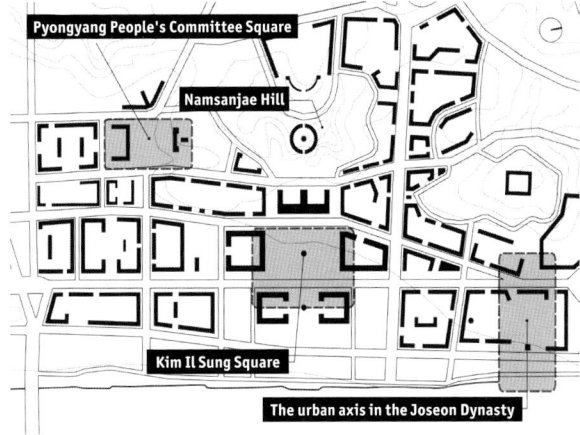

Comparison of the locations of Pyongyang People's Committee Square, Kim Il Sung Square, and the urban axis during the Joseon dynasty.

Kim Jeong-Hui's concept for Pyongyang's city centre looked to diverse precedents. In addition to being familiar with the city centres of Leningrad (St Petersburg), Moscow, Paris, Beijing, as well as the old city centre of Seoul during the Joseon dynasty, he paid attention to newly reconstructed cities such as Stalingrad (now Volgograd) and Istra.²⁰ In doing so, he identified two types of relationships between the river flowing through old cities and the urban axis. In the first the urban axis lies parallel to the river; such is the case in Paris, where the narrowness of the Seine dictates the arrangement. In the second type of relationship the axis is perpendicular to the river, as is the case in Leningrad and Stalingrad. In his evaluation of Pyongyang Kim Jeong-hui concluded that the latter arrangement – particularly that of Stalingrad – would be more suitable.

After the almost total destruction of Stalingrad at the hands of the Germans in 1943, its reconstruction was an urgent and top-priority project for the Soviet government. Among the issues debated, one of the most controversial was how – or whether – to restore the city's heritage.²¹ Eventually, the Communist Party instructed that the city 'be developed as an ensemble in which administrative buildings and monuments would be organically integrated.'²²

Following this guideline, a team led by the architect Vasily Simbirtsev put forward a plan for a new city centre parallel to the Volga River, thereby creating a new axis perpendicular to the river. At the back of the square stands a majestic memorial hall commemorating the victory at Stalingrad. In front of the square is a 110-metre-wide boulevard linking it to the river.[23] Similarly, in Kim Jeong-hui's plan for Pyongyang the city centre has a new urban axis perpendicular to the Daedong River. The plan even provided for the possibility of extending the axis across the river by creating another square on the opposite side. Although Pyongyang's city centre has since undergone a number of changes, Kim Jeong-hui's original layout has largely been retained.

A closer look at Kim Jeong-hui's plan for the city centre reveals that there are in fact two squares around the main building. This arrangement indicates the difficulties faced by Kim Jeong-hui at the time. As noted above, Kim Il-sung had suggested that the central square face the People's Committee building; Kim Jeong-hui chose to implement this suggestion in an original manner.

He initially considered orienting the central square toward the river, like the central square in Stalingrad. However, this raised the worrying question of whether he was following Kim Il-sung's instructions closely enough. He therefore designed two squares: one in front of the People's Committee building to honour the suggestion made by North Korea's foudner, and a second, larger square open to the river so as to fulfil his own vision. Between the two squares, he left sufficient space for a public building whose function would be determined later. This was a daring compromise with the supreme leader's instructions, and his success in gaining approval was, at the time, an extremely rare occurrence in this embattled communist country.

In *Dosi Geonseol* Kim Jeong-hui went into great detail regarding the size and form of the central square and surrounding buildings. First, he believed that a 'regular form is better and is particularly favourable for squares.'[24] The square was thus given a geometrical shape from the outset.

With regard to the forms of the buildings around the square, Kim Jeong-hui identified three styles: open, semi-open, and closed. Of these, he preferred the open style because 'the closed inner courtyards of a palace surrounded by city walls or the cloisters of the Joseon dynasty are not suitable for today's democratic temper.'[25] He believed that a public square needed to be easily accessible. Second, in terms of size, Kim Jeong-hui insisted that the square need not be unnecessarily large.[26] In his experience the appropriate ratio of building height to the width of a square lay between 1:3 and 1:6. The General Plan shows Kim Il-sung Square as measuring approximately 120 metres by 130 metres and surrounded by 25-metre-high buildings; the square's dimensions accordingly fit this formula. In accordance with Soviet best practice, the design was capped by the installation of an obelisk at the centre of the square.

Kim Jeong-Hui also noted that 'a direct link between the central square and leisure park and cultural facilities was to be recommended.'[27] Given his bird's-eye perspective, he did not presume to specify what sort of buildings would occupy the square, although he did assume that the square itself would be surrounded by administrative buildings and cultural facilities. These buildings were envisaged as having a traditional Korean roof style. Kim Il-sung grasped his intent immediately, explaining that his architect was seeking to revive native Korean identity through the use of this roof form. Together with public buildings, Kim Jeong-hui provided for the construction of nearby housing blocks, the layout of which followed the Soviet style preferred during the Stalinist era. According to *Dosi Geonseol*, buildings can be placed in an urban block in accordance with three methods, resulting in perimeter, mixed, or cluster types of development.[28] In the city centre of Pyongyang, the apartment buildings stand at the perimeter of each block, making for a consistent street view.

The City Centre in the 1953 Brief Plan for Pyongyang

TThe North Korean regime prioritised and accelerated reconstruction projects following the end of the Korean War on 27 July 1953. In the process Kim Jeong-Hui's initial plan – the General Plan drawn up in 1951 – underwent several changes. The resulting 'Brief Total Plan for Pyongyang' (*Pyongyangsi chonggyehoek yakdo*; hereinafter 'the Brief Plan') put forward an entirely new plan for downtown Pyongyang. The date of the Brief Plan's creation is unclear. Citing two references, Park Dong-min, a Korean architectural historian, estimates that the Brief Plan was drawn up after the middle of 1952. First, in his memoir, *Tracing the History of the Construction of the Juche* (1998), Kim Eung-sang writes, 'I saw the plan in autumn 1952 in Moscow.'[29] Second, in his speech on 21 April 1952 Kim Il-sung declared, 'the reconstruction of the post-war city should be prepared in advance,' leading Park Dong-min to conclude that the 1951 version differed from the plan of 1952. 'This testimony,' notes Park Dong-min, 'was supported by a North Korean documentary film made in 1982 and named "Beyond the Ashes", which dealt with the reconstruction of Pyongyang. A new plan appeared at a construction exhibition held in 1952.'[30]

However, despite these claims, the Brief Plan was most likely developed after the middle of 1953. Four points support this argument. First, in *Joseon Geonchuksa* (A History of Joseon Architecture), Li Hwa-seon, a North Korean architectural historian, writes, 'The plan for the reconstruction of Pyongyang was drawn up in 1951, exhibited at the Moranbong Underground Theatre in May 1952, and displayed at the World Architects' Conference in Warsaw in the autumn of 1952, which impressed architects from all over the world.'[31] This makes it likely that when Kim Eung-sang recalled meeting North Korean colleagues in Moscow in the autumn of 1952 – colleagues 'who had been despatched to the Warsaw Conference by our party' – he was referring to Kim Jeong-hui's group. Accordingly, the plan they reviewed together in 1952 was the General Plan, which Kim Jeong-hui submitted in May 1951. Following a year during which it was reviewed, the General Plan was adopted as the official reconstruction plan until at least autumn 1952.

Second, guidelines for the reconstruction of Pyongyang were presented in Cabinet Decision no. 125, 'On the Reconstruction of Pyongyang City', which was published on 30 July 1953. These guidelines are faithfully reflected in the Brief Plan. It is difficult to imagine a reversal in the order between political decisions and urban planning in North Korea. This means that the Brief Plan was likely drawn up after the decision taken by the cabinet.

Third, Kim Jong-hui's doctoral dissertation submitted to the Moscow University of Architecture in July 1953 addressed key aspects of and examples from North Korea's reconstruction plan. His dissertation was subsequently translated into Korean and published in November 1953. If Park Dong-Min's assertion is correct, and the Brief Plan was put together by 1952, then it would be reasonable to expect Kim Jong-hui's dissertation to expound on the plan in significant detail; however, it does not.

Fourth, as soon as the newly drawn-up urban plan was approved, construction began on government complexes nos. 1 and 2 around Kim Il-sung Square. Their erection indicates when the Brief Plan was drawn up. The first government complex, designed as a four-storey building by the architect Li Hyeong, was built between March 1954 and August 1955, while the second was completed by the architect Han Deok-gun in December 1955. Other major public buildings in downtown Pyongyang – including Pyongyang Railway Station, Moranbong Theatre, the International Inn, the former Korea Liberation War Victory Hall, and Daedongmun Cinema – were constructed around 1954 and 1955 in the Socialist Realist style. So, it is probable that the Brief Plan and its proposal for Kim Il-sung Square were only drawn up after the 1953 cabinet decision. Indeed, the plan made its first appearance in North Korea's architectural media in 1955, first in the January 1955 issue of the Soviet architectural magazine *Arkhitektura SSSR* and then in the December 1955 issue of *Geonchukgwa Geonseol* (Architecture and Construction).[32]

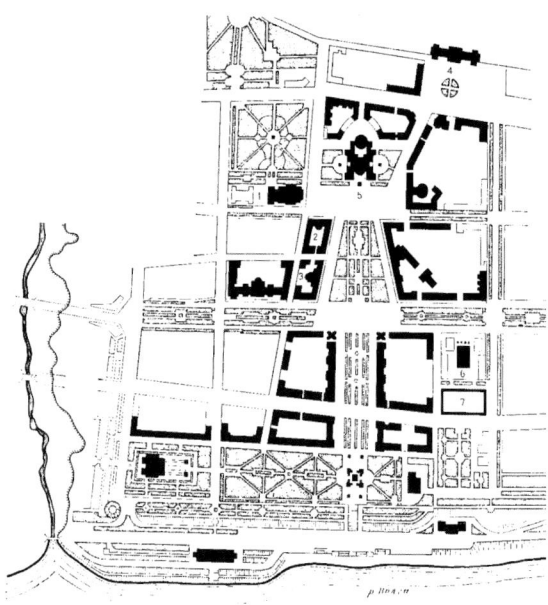

Stalingrad city centre.
Source: Ptichnikova, Galina, and Antyufeev, Aleksey, 2018, p. 3

Although the identity of the author of the Brief Plan is unknown, it seems highly probable that this was Kim Jeong-hui, given the plan's similarities to the General Plan and its practical application of ideas expounded by Kim Jeong-hui in *Dosi Geonseol*. Kim Jeong-hui returned to Pyongyang immediately after receiving his doctorate from the Moscow Institute of Architecture on 6 July 1953. Until his deportation to Anju, Kim Jeong-hui held several major posts in North Korea and was responsible for coordinating the reconstruction of North Korean cities. Evidence of his influence on reconstruction projects across the country is to be found in a number of different sources. For instance, German planners consulted Kim Jeong-hui when developing the plan for Hamhŭng; his name also appears in Piotr Zaramba's plan for Chongjin.[33]

The Brief Plan of 1953 is entirely consistent with ideas and concepts laid out in Kim Jeong-hui's *Dosi Geonseol*. It also bears marked similarities to the 1951 General Plan, notably in that it retains the dual axes of the earlier plan. Stalin Street, inspired by Gorky Street in Moscow and Stalinallee in East Berlin, ran parallel to the Daedong River and connected three important public spaces, namely Station Square, Grand Theatre Square, and Kim Il-sung Square. This design was intended to integrate the fragmented urban space resulting from the construction of the Japanese new town and indigenous neighbourhoods in the north. The second axis was perpendicular to the Daedong River, running through Kim Il-sung Square to Namsan Hill.

Of course, the two plans also have distinct differences. For instance, while the 1951 plan was drawn up in accordance with instructions from Kim Il-sung, the 1953 plan was based on the cabinet's decision of 1953. Additionally, whereas the 1951 plan possessed a somewhat schematic design, the 1953 plan adhered closely to the actual situation in the city; it contained far more detailed information on land use, transportation, and green areas than the 1951 plan. In this respect, the Brief Plan was much more specific in its treatment of the design of the city centre and central square.

Compared to the 1951 General Plan, the Brief Plan proposed three primary changes to the design of the central square. First, the Brief Plan positioned the central square at the foot of Namsan Hill, 480 metres to the north. It is unclear why the 1953 plan made this change. Arguably, the central square was moved because the Brief Plan abandoned the radial-ring road system proposed by the previous plan. Additionally, the Brief Plan's proposal for the city centre involved a central square oriented toward the river and positioned against a mountainous backdrop. Seen from the Daedong River, the new location offered significantly more potential for creating a unified, dramatic skyline. The alignment of this second urban axis is in perfect harmony with traditional geomantic concepts, called *baesanimsu* in Korean, which favoured locations with 'a river at the front and mountains at the back.'

Second, the Brief Plan also increased the size of the square to 130 by 190 metres, making it rectangular in form. This change was likely a response to internal criticism that the square proposed by the 1951 plan was too small to accommodate events on a national scale, as well as military parades. Critics pointed out that Pyongyang's square would inevitably suffer unfavourable comparisons with the 880-by-500-metre immensity of Beijing's Tiananmen Square and the 330-by-70-metre expanse of Moscow's Red Square.

Third, whereas the 1951 plan envisaged a centripetal space with an obelisk at its centre, the 1953 plan emphasised the axial link between the square and the river with two towers, enhancing the square's openness toward the river. Moreover, two *cours d'honneur* were to be created close to the waterfront promenade to highlight the monumentality of the square's buildings when seen from a distance. Again, whereas the perimeter layout of the buildings in the 1951 plan suggested a closed urban structure, the new plan sought to increase the square's openness, drawing the green swaterfront space into the city centre.

Based on the new location and size of the central square, the planners considered two proposals. Although both proposals placed the square in the same location and and

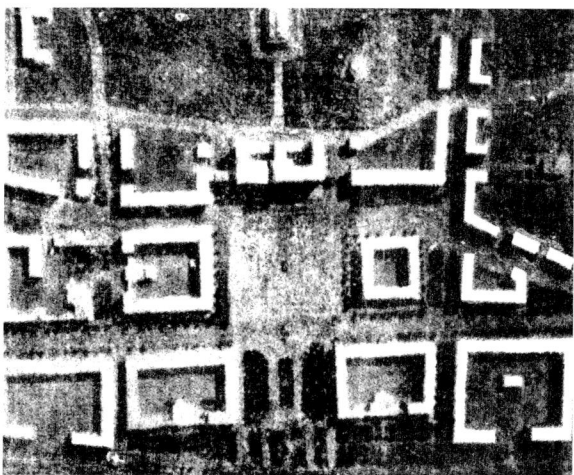

Variant 1 of Kim Il Sung Square in the Brief Plan for Pyongyang.
Source: Jeon Man-Gil, 1993

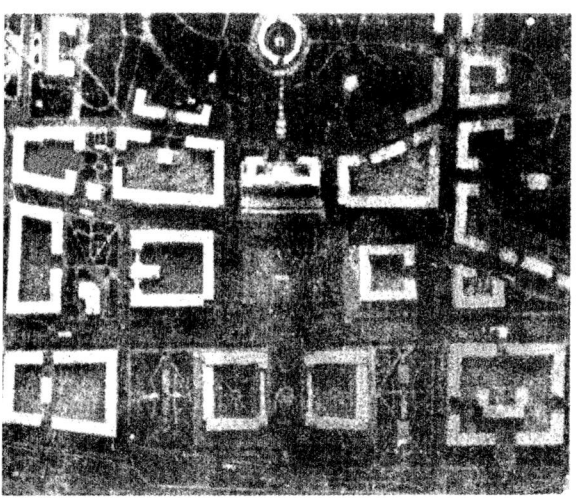

Variant 2 of Kim Il Sung Square in the Brief Plan for Pyongyang.
Source: Jeon Man-Gil, 1993

North Korean government building 1, elevation.
Source: *Geonchuk gwa Geonseol*, May 1956

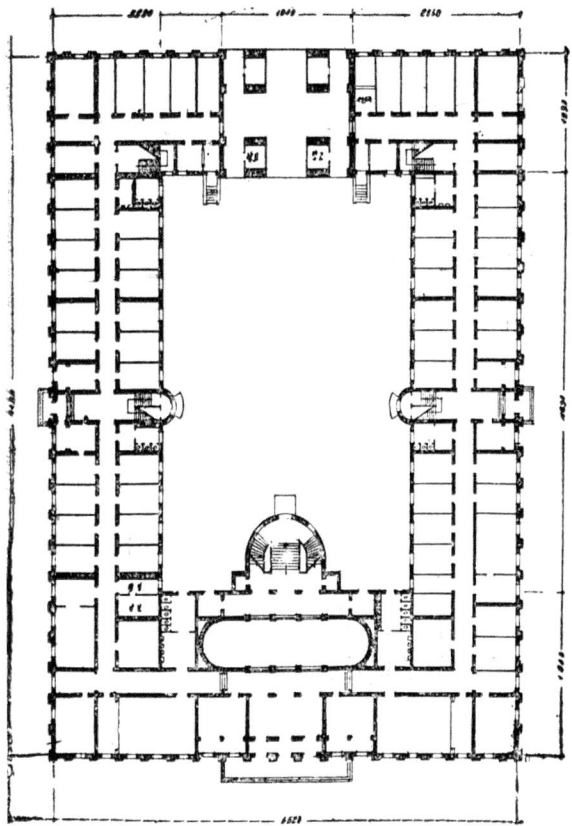

North Korean government building 1, plan.
Source: *Geonchuk gwa Geonseol*, May 1956

made it the same siye, the way in which they connected the square to the Daedong River differed. The first proposal suggested creating two *cours d'honneur* in front of Government Complex nos. 1 and 2 on Il-sung Square in order to connect the square and green spaces along the Daedong River. The second proposal suggested eliminating the *cours d'honneur* and connecting Kim Il-sung Square and the riverside more directly.

The 1956 Plan for Kim Il-sung Square

However, the 1953 plan was never implemented: Kim Il-sung Square today possesses an entirely different shape from that proposed in the Brief Plan. Kim Jeong-hui explained the reason in a 1956 article in *Geonchkgwa Geonseol* (Architecture and Construction), a North Korean architectural journal:

The design of Kim Il-Sung Square is not simple given that so many outstanding architects participated in addressing the complicated problems. They drew up a number of different solutions. Many proposals came from the urban-design institutes at the Ministry of Construction, the Pyongyang People's Committee, and the 583rd Military Construction Bureau. The Hungarian Architects Group, who were visiting Pyongyang for the aid porgramme, also suggested ideas.[34]

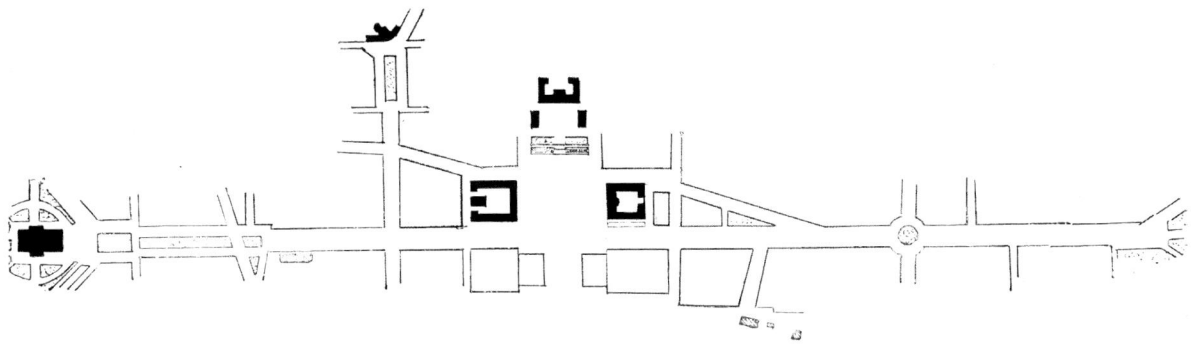

Architectural composition of Stalin Street, Pyongyang.
Source: Geonchuk gwa Geonseol, May 1956

This process put Kim Jeong-hui's initial proposal in competition with others; in the end, a different proposal was selected by officials.

Kim Jeong-hui's 1956 article in *Geonchkgwa Geonseol* presents the four projects that competed for selection. Of these, Variant 1 is likely Kim Jeong-hui's own, as it is very similar to the second version of his 1953 plan. Despite distinct differences, the projects all have government complexes 1 and 2 surrounding the proposed central square because these buildings had already been constructed by 1955. Among the four proposals, Variant 3 is the closest to the current layout of Kim Il-sung Square. According to Kim Jeong-hui, the final selection of this plan followed six principles:

1) The square must have a traffic-circulation layout suitable for organising military parades and demonstrations.
2) Buildings surrounding the square must have sufficient volume (height and width) and be of an architecturally refined and formal character.
3) Roads from the square to the river and adjacent buildings must have a more relaxed and friendly character (for both use and appearance), and the square must be directly connected to the green space of the walkways and gardens.
4) The square must not be restricted to a closed area;

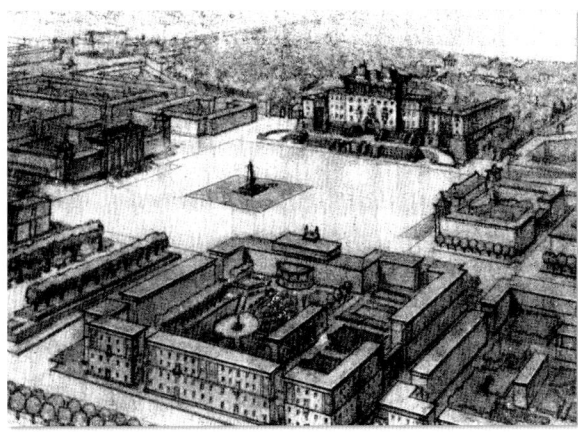

Kim Il Sung Square, as published in *Arkhitektura SSSR,* January 1955.

rather, it should include the surrounding larger space and nature.

5) The square and the river should not be linked through a street, but by means of a sufficiently large connecting space. The front of the main buildings in the square should be wide open toward the Daedong River so that these buildings can take command of the panoramic scene.
6) The main building, which will play a leading role in the square assembly, must fully and effectively utilise the natural variations in the terrain of Namsan Hill.[35]

3. The Creation of Kim Il-sung Square in Pyongyang

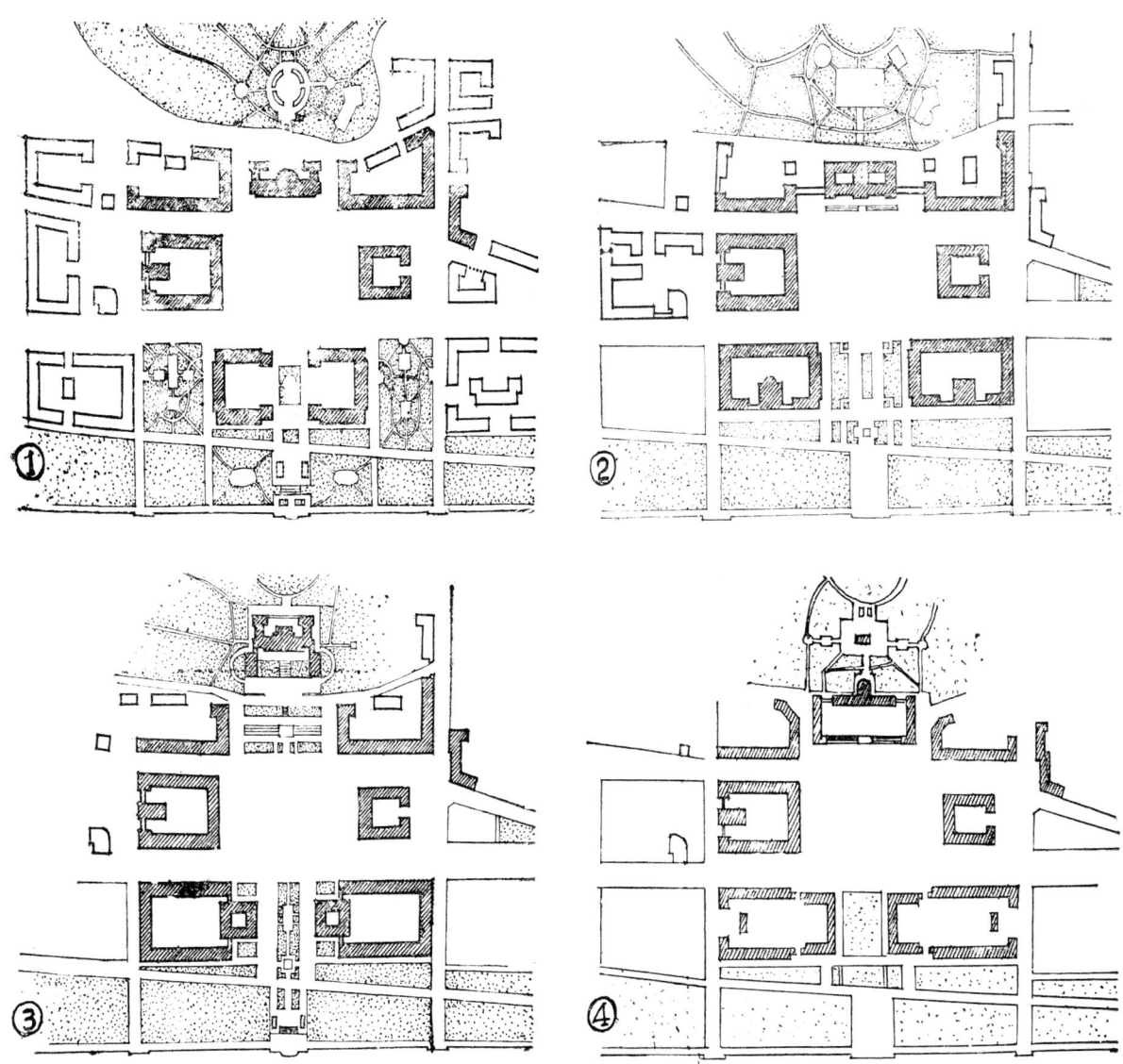

Four variants of the proposal for Kim Il Sung Square.
Source: Geonchuk gwa Geonseol, May 1956

Comparison of variants 1 and 3 reveals two major differences. The first involves the space connecting the square to the river. In this respect, Variant 3 does a good job of embodying principles 4 and 5 above. According to Kim Jeong-hui, the planners shared the idea that 'the square must have a passage wide enough to ensure a panoramic view of the square from the river.' To this end, 'this passage should not be as narrow as a single road, nor should its width be as large as the width of the square.'[36] In Variant 3 two low buildings protrude from the main body of two buildings housing cultural facilities in order to check the width of the passage running from the square to the river.

The second difference involves the central building on the square. In Variant 3 this has been shifted to Namsan Hill in accordance with principle 6. As Namsan Hill is just 20 metres high, positioning the main building on it signals its importance to the square. Moreover, shifting the main building to Namsan Hill allowed for the creation of an elevated platform on which leading figures of the North Korean Workers' Party can observe the parade. Ultimately, it was the failure of Kim Jeong-hui's proposal to meet the six principles – which reflect the intentions of North Korean politicians – that resulted in its rejection.

Variant 3, submitted by the Central Urban Design Institute under the Ministry of Construction, was selected as the official plan in 1956. However, construction of streets and buildings around the square had already begun. On 12 August 1954 Kim Il-sung attended a ribbon-cutting ceremony to celebrate the paving of the square and Stalin Street. It had taken just over two months for approximately 8000 students, soldiers, and public officials to complete the job.[37] In accordance with the layout proposed by the Brief Plan of 1953, the construction of two major buildings on the square – government complexes 1 and 2 – also commenced around this time.[38]

Variant 3 of the proposal for Kim Il Sung Square.
Source: *Geonchuk gwa Geonseol*, May 1956

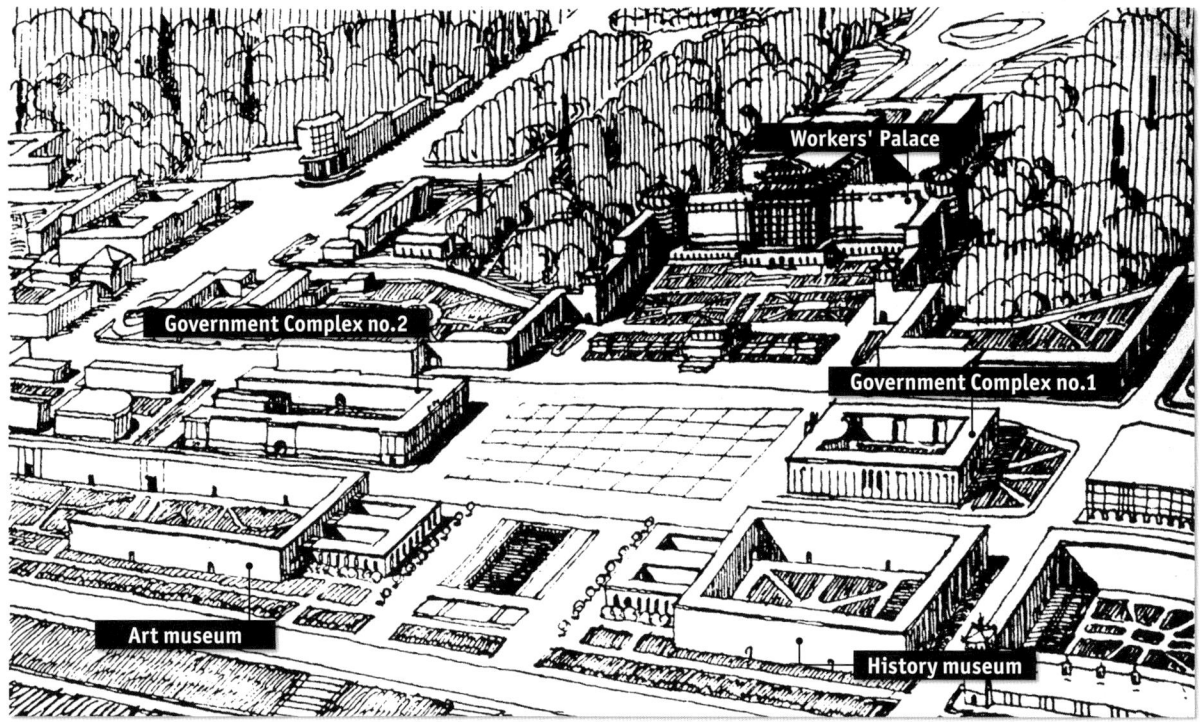

Illustration of Kim Il Sung Square and buildings published in *Rodong Simmun* newspaper, July 13, 1958.

The Construction of the Grand People's Study House and Juche Tower

As we can see from an aerial view of the square published in an issue of *Rodong Simmun*, dated 13 July 1958, as well as Li Hwa-seon's *History of Joseon Architecture*,[39] the Pyongyang Urban Design Committee presented a layout for buildings on the square. The layout has the Workers' Palace located in front of the square, a public building situated on the left side, and a workers' apartment complex on the right. Moving towards Daedong River, government complexes nos. 1 and 2 stand on the left and right sides of the square respectively. One block further, two museums stand on the left and right sides before the embankment of the Daedong River. The buildings surrounding the square exhibit no particular architectural style. However, the design and identity of the main building in front of the square became the subject of prolonged debate among the planners. This contest was only settled when Kim Il Sung decided upon a workers' palace, a multipurpose facility that would house many different types of activity. As he had said earlier, 'if a bustling district is to be created in the vicinity of a large square, it would be better to construct palaces, theatres, and cinemas for workers rather than government buildings.'[40]

For the workers' palace, architects designed a building with colossal wings so that sightlines would converge on the central block: the adoption of a classical method to emphasise monumentality (examples from earlier times are Trajan's Forum in ancient Rome and the Palace of Versailles in the Baroque period). At that time North Korean architects conducted considerable research on 'how to embody national characteristics in an urban formation.' They prioritised 'having traditional types of buildings placed at key locations in the city so that national characteristics are distributed throughout the city.'[41] This idea is reflected in a bird's-eye view of the reconstructed city in 1958.

View of Pyongyang in 1961.
Source: Pai, 2014

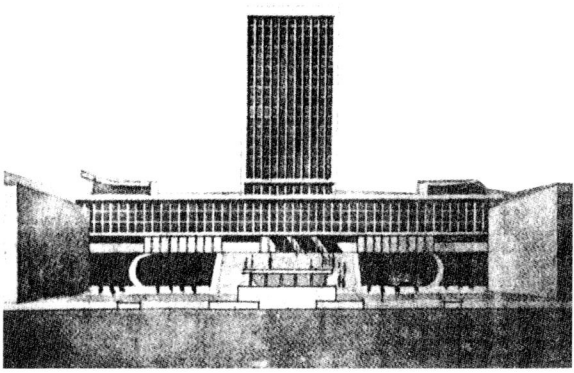

Competition entries for the workers' palace on Kim Il Sung Square.
Source: Jeon, Man-gil, 1993

An aerial photo taken in 1961, however, reveals that the central part of the square remained vacant. Only an elevated platform from which the nation's leaders could watch and be watched during mass celebrations had been built at the upper end of the square. This suggests that architects and planners were still debating the optimal type of building for this location. Various architectural designs were proposed for the workers' palace. For instance, the August 1962 issue of *Architecture and Construction* contains a particularly modern design. Nevertheless, this part of the square remained vacant until December 1973, when Kim Il-sung put an end to the debate. Wanting the square to become a busy urban centre, he decided that instead of a workers' palace, the central building would be a national library – namely, the Grand People's Study House – to complement the grand theatre, the people's cultural palace, the students' and children's palaces, and the gymnasium that already adorned the city centre.[42]

Work on this new project proceeded slowly until Kim Jong-il, Kim Il-sung's son, emerged as his prospective successor in 1975. Kim Jong-il urged the planners to speed up construction so as to complete the library before his father's seventieth birthday. An architectural competition for the library was held in 1979. Based on the winning entry, submitted by Professor Ham Ui-yeon (1941) of Pyongyang University of Construction and Building Materials Industries,[43] the Grand People's Study House was completed in 1982.[44] That same year saw the dedication of the 170-metre-tall Juche Tower, which faces Kim Il-sung Square from its location on the opposite bank of the Daedong River.[45] Both monuments were completed in time to commemorate the founder's seventieth birthday.

While the completion of the square meant that Kim Jeong-hui's vision had finally been realised, much of its original significance – associated with the revolutionary spirit – had changed over the 30 years. This was due to the ambition of Kim Jong-il, who was officially designated Kim Il-sung's successor at the Sixth Party Congress in October 1980. Adopting a different approach to urban planning from that of his father, Kim Jong-il used architecture and urban design to justify and strengthen his succession to power. Kim Il-sung had cultivated an identity as the charismatic leader who had galvanised anti-Japanese resistance during the 1920s and 1930s, founded an independent country, and guided post-war reconstruction. Lacking such magnetism, Kim Jong-il used the urban projects of the 1980s to identify himself with the fount of power as well as to routinise and artistically sublimate his father's achievements.[46] To this end, he directed and produced five revolutionary operas and erected monuments throughout the city. Designed on an overwhelming scale, the new monuments sought to convey grandeur, sublimity, and perpetuity to the utmost degree.[47] In effect, North Korea became a kind of theatre state, one which was mobilised for spectacles.[48]

Grand People's Study House in Pyongyang (Ham Ui-yeon, 1982).
Source: Meuser, Philipp, vol. 2, 2012, p. 36

Juche Tower in Pyongyang (2008).
Source: Meuser, Philipp, vol. 2, 2012, p. 116

3. The Creation of Kim Il-sung Square in Pyongyang

Two Models for the Design of an Urban Square

Kim Il-sung Square in Pyongyang and the central square in Hamhŭng provided two different models for North Korean urban planners in the 1960s. When cities such as Wonsan, Sinpo, Nampo, and Hyesan created new city centres, they followed the established models, simply adjusting their size. These two models shared three common elements: an urban axis, large-scale buildings as symbolic monuments, and an open space for military parades and mass rallies.[49] However, as the decade progressed, urban design in North Korea shifted from the symbolic approach taken in the Stalinist era to dynamic and asymmetric compositions. The seeds of this change were sown in Hamhŭng by architects from the Bauhaus. A close look at the plans developed for North Korean cities in the 1960s illustrates this change. The plan for the Haean Geori (Beach Street) area of Wonsan, a port city on the westernmost shore of the East Korean Sea, is a good example. Four successive urban schemes for this area's development, dating from 1956 to 1963, can be found in North Korea's architectural magazine, *Geonchuggwa Geonseol* (Architecture and Construction),[50] allowing us to trace the evolution of North Korean urban design during this period. In the first scheme, published in 1956, 'the urban planners placed a central square close to the coastline, retaining the existing street system. They also created three radial roads so that flows of traffic converge on the square.'[51] This arrangement was similar to Kim Jeong-hui's 1951 plan for the city centre of Pyongyang, which aligned buildings of identical height along the perimeter of the urban blocks. However, Kim Il-sung regarded this plan as flawed since it prevented adjustments to buildings' orientation to maximise exposure to the sun during the severe winters. He therefore instructed the planners to create a more diverse layout of buildings, thereby bringing more life to the city's streets.[52] The second scheme, proposed in 1959, saw significant changes. A 120-metre-wide beach park was envisaged along the coastline, shifting the central square to the north, where a workers' palace, museum, and art gallery were clustered.

This scheme's downside was that it permitted the central square to divide the beach park into two parts – an issue which Kim Il-sung noticed immediately. The third scheme, created in 1961, accordingly separated the central square from the beach park, allowing the latter to become a single green space. Nonetheless, a new controversy arose over the composition of buildings facing the square. While the third scheme employed a symmetrical composition to express grandeur and solemnity,[53] the fourth, developed in 1963, features an asymmetrical composition.[54] This was considered the best choice if elements such as the natural environment, street system, skyline, and building orientation were to be taken into account. Recent aerial photography confirms that this fourth plan was realised without significant modification.

The plan for a town centre at Sinpo, developed in 1965, exemplifies this trend. A port city on the coast of the East Korean Sea, Sinpo had significant potential for development as a base for the fishing industry. To cope with the area's growng population, the North Korean regime built a new town to the west of the existing city. Covering two hectares, the new town was located in an open area between a sandy beach and pine forest. The town centre formed a green axis perpendicular to the sea, with public facilities such as the municipal building, a meeting place for the fishing industry, a theatre, an aquarium, a department store, a hotel, and specialty shops flanking the axis. While planners placed the fishing industry building at the centre, they opened the view by narrowing the upper part of the building.[55] The design of this building, in particular, is strongly reminiscent of the Bauhaus style. While the types of building constructed in the town centre followed the precedents set by Kim Il-sung Square in Pyongyang, the approaches taken to their layouts and designs were very different. More specifically, while the left side of the axis comprised a harmonious composition of three four-storey buildings, two six-storey buildings, and a single-storey shop, the right side was connected to the end of several apartment buildings, the layout of which facilitated easy circulation around the axis.

A similar method guided the development of Munsu Street in East Pyongyang in the 1960s. Located at the north end of the right bank of the River Daedong, this area was used as a runway by the Japanese Army air corps during the colonial era. It remained undeveloped until the early 1960s, when the Pyongyang Urban Planning and Design Institute sought to revive it, obtaining approval for the final version of its proposal in 1964.[56] As in other cities, the most important task was to come up with a concept for a central square and a main street. A comparison between this plan and that for Kim Il-sung Square reveals just how much North Korea's urban-design practices had changed over the ten-year period. Here, unlike in Pyongyang itself, there was no need for an urban axis because this area was to be developed as a suburban centre. Instead, the principal road ran parallel to the river. A stadium was located at the end of this road, with the town square positioned alongside so as to function as an auxiliary space accommodating spectators of sporting events. A 180-metre-wide promenade included recreational facilities, offering pedestrians a variety of views. Thus, despite the fact that Munsu Street is situated some distance from the city centre, this is a case of dynamic and asymmetric urban composition in Pyongyang.

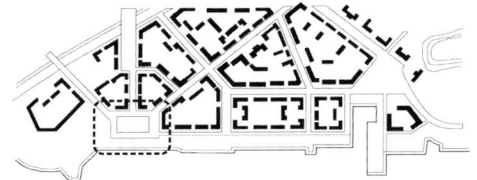

a.

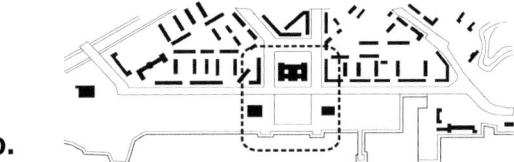

b.

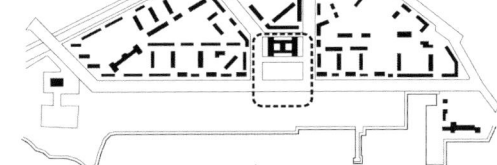

c.

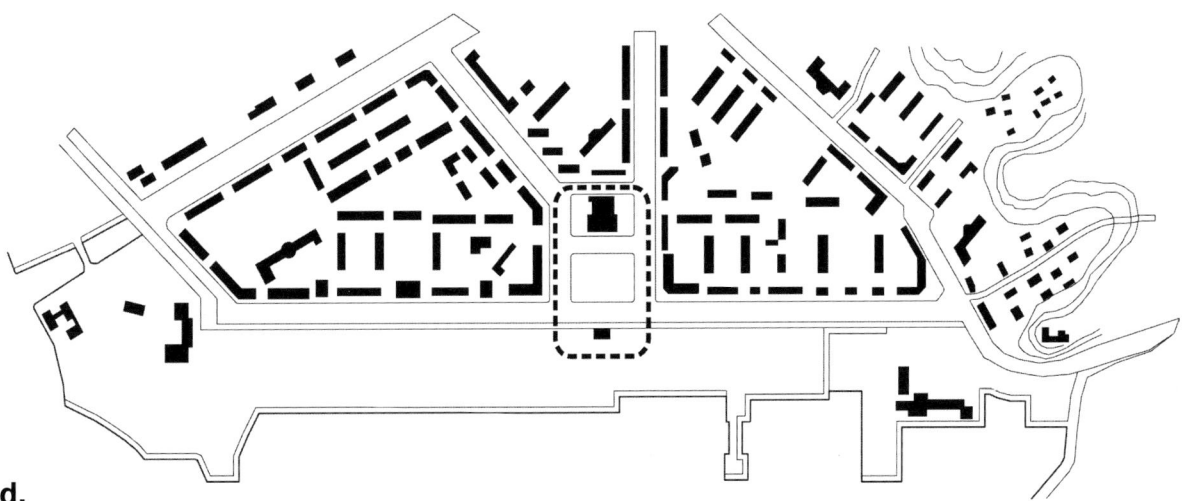

d.

The planning process for Sinpo town centre.
Source: Jeong Myeong-geun, February 1965

Conclusion

In North Korea's large cities public squares served as a starting point for urban design, while connecting major roads became a kind of spine holding together subsequent development. In the mid-1950s Stalinist central squares with radial roads and solid block perimeters dominated urban design. However, around 1957, this approach began to change as a result of the influence of East German planners helping with North Korea's reconstruction. In tune with the tenor of the Bauhaus-style layout, dynamic and asymmetric combinations of buildings became the preferred method of composition for public squares. The history of Kim Il-sung Square in the nation's capital illuminates the early stages of this development and provides insight regarding the decision-making framework shared by Party members, cabinet officials, planners, and politicians. The creation of squares in North Korea took a different path from urban projects in democratic countries; the main reason for this was that the autocratic leader's thoughts became official decrees laying down guidelines for subsequent urban planning.

Kim Il-sung was determined to make Pyongyang a showcase of Korean-style socialism. Planners interpreted his ideas as best they could, presenting alternative designs for scrutiny before the adoption of a final plan. Arguably, the role of urban planners devolved to that of technical practitioners. However, analysis of the creation of Kim Il-sung Square reveals the surprising role played by the lead planner, Kim Jeong-hui, in the planning process. Committing to an idea for the square that differed from the that of Kim Il-sung, he was able to secure acceptance for his plan and position the square with 'a river in front and a mountain at the back,' thereby creating a strong axis that defines the heart of Pyongyang to this day. Finally, it is worth noting that attention to urban form and landscape has been an enduring element of North Korea's approach to urban planning.

Li Jae-seon, a researcher at the Pyongyang Urban Planning and Design Institute in the 1960s, argued that a city's master plan must balance the essential ingredients of a unified skyline, clear directionality, and cityscape to achieve a desirable character. This perspective seems congruent with the direction emerging in the West at the time. Urban theorists such as Kevin Lynch, Colin Rowe, Aldo Rossi, and Christopher Alexander were critical of the visual monotony characteristic of the new towns that had sprung up based on modern planning methods; they suggested alternatives. However, while the image of the city was a crucial theme in their discourse, it is important to note that the North Korean concept of the cityscape, as expressed by Li Jae-seon, came from a completely different context. In the 1960s western theorists began looking at the city from the standpoint of users rather than planners. As Lynch explained, clear legibility can enhance users' grasp of the identity of a city. In North Korea the importance of urban form and landscape lies in their capacity to express socialist ideology. For North Korea's rulers and planners, the urban form largely functioned as a stage for theatrical display. In official North Korean photo albums, many pages depict scenes of Kim Il-sung in the act of instructing urban experts with regard to the architectural models they are inspecting. This trait became even more pronounced under Kim Jong-il.

1. Kim Il-sung (Pyongyang, 1982), pp. 39–40.
2. Bater, James H. (Beverly. Hills, 1980), p. 122.
3. Wu, Hung (Chicago, 2005), p. 402.
4. Zigurds L. Zile, 'Programs and Problems of City Planning in the Soviet Union', p. 31.
5. Kim, Jeong-hui (Pyongyang, 1953), p. 66.
6. IUA Inquiry, Moscow (1958), Bauhaus Dessau Archives, I 010299 D.
7. According to the *Yeojidoseo* (Book of National Geography), published from 1757 to 1765, Pyongyang had a population of approximately 18,255 during the Joseon dynasty; this number remained relatively stable until the end of the nineteenth century. Acoding to Pyongyang sian (Pyongyang City Statistics) (Seoul: Uijeongbu, 1906), the city had a population of approximately 5088 at the start of the twentieth century.
8. For statistics, see *Pyongyang yoram* (A Booklet of Pyongyang) (Pyongyang: Pyongyang-bu,1909) and *Minjeoktogyepyo* (Census Registration Statistics) (Seoul: Government General of Joseon, 1910).
9. Kim Jin-hyeong (Seoul, 2006), p. 165.
10. Kang, Myeong-suk, 'Hanilhabbangijeon ilbonindeul-ui Pyongyang chimtu', p. 172.
11. Kwon Tai-Joon, 'Iljesidae-uidosihwa', pp. 290–91.
12. Located in Gaeseon-dong Moranbong-guyeok, Pyongyang, this stadium was called 'Girimri Gongseol Stadium'. It was subsequently renamed 'Pyongyang Gongseol Stadium' after the liberation of Korea and 'Moranbong Stadium' after its 1969 renovation. Finally, the stadium was remodelled for the celebration of Kim Il-sung's seventieth birthday on 11 April 1982 and renamed 'Kim Il-sung Stadium'.
13. Numerous documents elucidating the design process were produced between 1951 and 1954: (1) Kim Il-sung's guidelines dated 21 January 1951; (2) Plan for Pyongyang, dated 20 May 1951, by Kim Jeong-hui; (3) Cabinet decision no. 125, 'On the Reconstruction of Pyongyang', dated 30 July 1953; (4) Cabinet decision no. 126, 'On the Implementation of Construction Planning to Guarantee the Reconstruction of Our Cities', dated 30 July 1953; (5) Kim Jeong-hui's *Dosigeonseol* (Urban Construction), published in 1953; (6) and the general reconstruction plan for Pyongyang, dated 1953.
14. Kim Il-sung (Pyongyang, 1980), p. 280.
15. Kim Jeong-hui (Pyongyang, 1953), p. 4.
16. Ibid., p. 201.
17. Ibid., pp. 202–3.
18. Rolf Jenni, 'Learning from Moscow: planning principles of the 1935 General Plan for Reconstruction and its political relevance', http://www.raumbureau.ch/files/Learning_from_Moscow.pdf, accessed 19 March 2015.
19. Kim Jeong-hui (Pyongyang, 1953), p. 104.
20. Ibid., p. 180.
21. Andrew Day (Ithaca, 2003), pp. 177–181.
22. Kim Jeong-hui (Pyongyang, 1953), p. 180.
23. Andreï Ikonnikov, (Paris, 1990), pp. 244–45.
24. Kim Jeong-hui (Pyongyang, 1953), p. 180.
25. Ibid., pp. 213–14.
26. Ibid., p. 213.
27. Ibid., p. 206.
28. For these styles, see the appendix of figures in Kim Jeong-hui's *Dosigeonseol*.
29. Kim, Eung-Sang (Pyongyang, 1998), pp. 64–65.
30. Park, Dong-Min, *Journal of an Architectural Historian*, p. 131.
31. Li, Hwa-seon(a) (Pyongyang, 1989), p. 104.
32. L. Abramov, *Arkhitektura SSSR*, pp. 31–37.
33. His writings can be found in *Spuścizna Piotra Zaremby (1910–1993),* Archiwum Państwowe w Szczecinie, JEDN 152, 1954–1957, *Maszynopisy Piotra Zaremby* (Typescripts by Piotr Zaremba).
34. Kim, Jeong-hui, 'Pyongyangsi Kim Il-sung Gwangjanui Geonchukjeok Guseonge daehayeo', p. 27.
35. Ibid., p. 28.
36. Ibid., p. 29.
37. *Pyongyang geonseoljeonsapyeonchan-wiwonhoe* (Pyongyang, 1997), p. 157.
38. Lee Wang-kee (Seoul, 2000), p. 190.
39. Li Hwa-seon(a) (Pyongyang, 1989), p. 344.
40. Kim Il-sung (Pyongyang, 1982), p. 89.
41. Li, 1967.
42. Jeon, Man-gil, 'Itjimothal Namsanjae', p. 9.
43. Ham Ui-yeon, one of North Korea's most prominent architects and academics, is credited with the design of major buildings such as Pyongyang Sports Centre, East Pyongyang Grand Theatre, Mangyongdae Children's Palace, and the Grand People's Study House.
44. Lee Wang-kee (Seoul, 2000), p. 228.
45. *Juche* is generally translated as 'self-reliance'. Sometimes referred to as Kimilsungism, *Juche* is the term coined by Kim Il-sung for the idea that the Korean people are the masters of their country's development.
46. Kwon, Heonik and Chung, Byung-Ho (Seoul, 2013), pp. 214–15.
47. Oh, Dae-yeong and Ha, Gyeong-ho (Pyongyang, 1989), p. 8
48. See : Clifford Geertz (Princeton, 1981); Kwon and Chung (Seoul, 2013).
49. Yim Dong-woo (Seoul, 2014).
50. The official magazine of the National Construction Committee and Joseon Architects' Union (Joseon geonchukgadongmaeng), this was published monthly from 1956. It dealt with construction methods, architectural planning and design, urban planning and design, housing planning in rural areas, and architectural history.
51. Jeong, Myeong-geun, 'Wonsansi Haeangeori Geonchuk Hyeongseong-e daehayeo', p. 46.
52. *Pyongyang geonseoljeonsa* (Pyongyang, 1997), p. 169.
53. Jeong, Myeong-geun, 'Wonsansi Haeangeori Geonchuk Hyeongseong-e daehayeo', p. 47.
54. Ibid.
55. Han, Jong-ok, 'Sinposi jungsimbuui geonchuk hyeongseong', p. 26.
56. Kim, Yeong-bok, 'Munsudong gwangjang mit juyogarogeonchuk gyehoek', p. 23.

넷

The Emergence of Mass Housing in Post-war North Korea

Inha Jung/ Shin Gun-soo

A mere decade after the armistice that ended the Korean War (1953), North Korea's cities began to recover, and the country's urban spaces filled up with large numbers of modern buildings. The reconstruction of the capital, Pyongyang, was particularly astonishing. North Korea had remained largely an agrarian state until the outbreak of the war, although it had become partially industrialised and urbanised during the colonial period, i.e. prior to the war. Technologically, the country was not yet sufficiently advanced to build multi-storey housing; its post-war reconstruction accordingly relied on financial aid and material support from the Soviet Union and the Eastern Bloc. This foreign support was the platform on which North Korea's urban housing was built in the post-war era. However, the imported housing models needed significant modification. This led to the emergence of new models reflecting North Korea's traditional way of life. The purpose of this study is to understand how North Korean architects and planners appropriated and adapted the 'socialist way of life' through standard housing in large cities and to identify major causes of this transformation in the nation's housing culture.[1]

The Development of Mass Housing in North Korea

Most urban housing in North Korea had been destroyed during the Korean War.[2] Its reconstruction in effect entailed new construction. North Korea's rate of urbanisation rose from 17.7% in 1953 to 40.6% in 1960.[3] During the war the North Korean regime prepared a reconstruction plan; a competition for standard housing designs was held in May 1952 to guide the future development of urban housing. The guidelines drawn up included improvements to the unit plan, the provision of multi-storey housing, speedy construction, use of local materials, a focus on economic feasibility, and mechanised assembly.[4] These guidelines were developed under the influence of Soviet reconstruction projects. During the five years from the ceasefire to the Chollima movement in 1958,[5] three housing models emerged in North Korea. A type of urban housing with staircase access called 'sektsiia' after an element in Soviet housing was the first model introduced in the post-war era.[6,7] After abandoning attempts to create an architecture that communalised everyday life in the 1930s, Soviet architects studied urban-housing design as practised in the West.[8] This

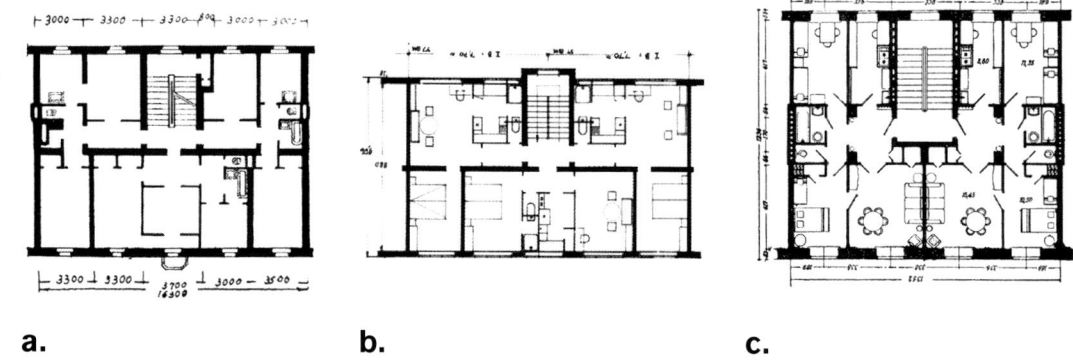

Comparison of *sektsiia* plans in North Korea, Germany, Soviet Union: (a) Pyongyang Worker's apartment (1954), (b) housing plan by Walter Gropius (1930), (c) Soviet *sektsiia* plan (1939).
Sources: *Pyongyang geonseoljeonsa 2; The Walter Gropius Archive, The Busch-Reisinger Museum, Harvard University, 1991; Arkhitektura SSSR, 2(1939).*

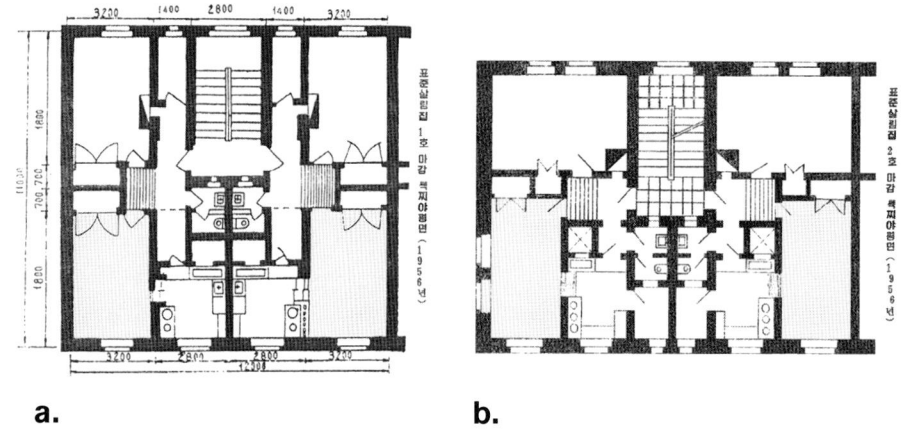

Housing models devised by DAG.
Source: *Bauhaus Dessau Archives, I_010013_D*

research led to the development of the type of housing based on the *sektsiia* (section). The workers' flats built in Pyongyang in 1954 with Soviet financial aid followed this type of housing design. Although it did not specifically refer to a housing type in the Soviet Union, North Korean architects labelled it as such, thus creating mixed versions, such as the single-corridor-access *sektsiia* type and the single, detached *sektsiia*.

However, the unit plan of the 1954 Pyongyang workers' flats did not make a good match with traditional North Korean housing and lifestyles. In particular, it did not suit the *ondol*, the traditional North Korean underfloor heating system that transfers heat by means of furnace flues built under a thick masonry floor. It was almost impossible to install the *ondol* in modern multistorey housing due to technical problems. Instead, workers' flats in Pyongyang used a Soviet-style heating system, with radiators on the upper floors; this was inconvenient for North Koreans. Architects accordingly first utilised the *ondol* on the upper floors in two standard plans created in 1956 for the Pyongcheon district by the Pyongyang Urban Design Institute (PUDI).[9] Compared with the typical Soviet *sektsiia* plan, the layout of these units was altered to accommodate the *ondol* by moving the kitchen to the position of the living room in a Soviet *sektsiia*. This difference presaged inevitable problems in the modernisation of North Korean housing.

As well as housing models imported from the Soviets, the involvement of East Germany from 1955 to 1962 had a strong formative effect on North Korea's standard housing model. In 1955 the Deutsche Arbeitsgruppe Hamhŭng (DAG) was sent on orders from the prime minister, Otto Grotewohl, to assist in the reconstruction of Hamhŭng, North Korea's second largest city. Bringing together advanced technologies for the production of construction machinery and materials, this group set out to create a model socialist city in Hamhŭng.[10] In undertaking these housing and urban projects, East Germany contributed the second-largest amount of funds to the development of North Korea's urban planning and housing planning.[11] East Germany's contribution was lauded at a meeting

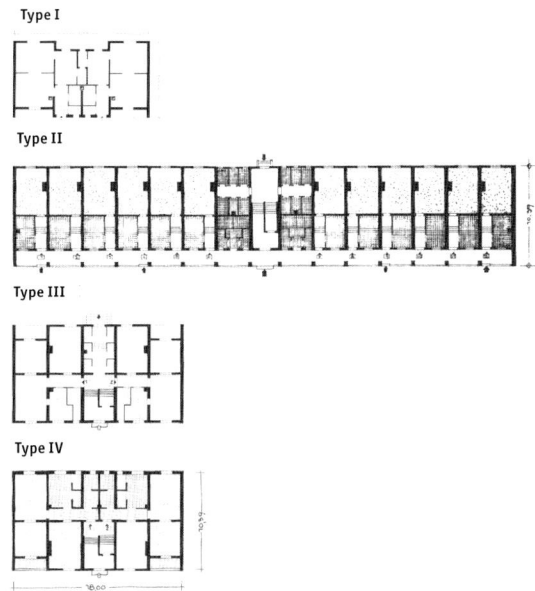

Unit and building plans for a single-corridor-access apartment PUDI 1958 (redrawn by the authors).
Source: Geonchukgwa Geonseol, Sep. 1958

of the International Union of Architects in the USSR in 1958 that highlighted Pyongyang and Hamhŭng as examples of successful reconstruction projects.[12]

The hallmark of the East German team's projects was the development of a single-corridor-access apartment house that later became the most popular standard design in North Korea. The German team developed six basic types of housing (with variants) in 1956; the methods used in combining these types and variants varied. By 1959 approximately 6000 housing units had been constructed under the guidance of DAG.[13] Most of the six types consist of one or two-storey structures with fewer than six residential units in each, although type II has 28 units with single-corridor access. In terms of the spatial organisation and distribution of rooms, the GWT 1956 type II used a repetitive bay system that allowed North Korean architects later to combine standard unit plans in a variety of ways. This type eventually proliferated across the nation under the name 'oerangsik'.

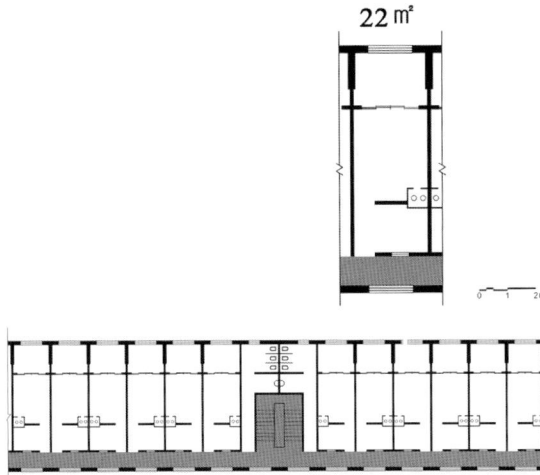

Unit and building plans of single-corridor-access apartment building PUDI 1958 (redrawn by the authors).
Source: Geonchukgwa Geonseol, Sep. 1958

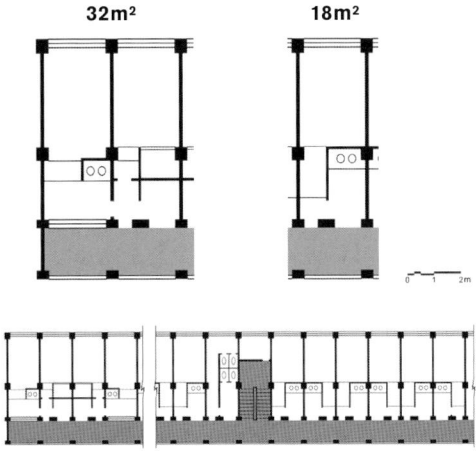

Unit and building plans for single-corridor-access apartment building for Pyongyang Microdistrict no. 62 in 1958 (redrawn by the authors).
Source: Geonchukgwa Geonseol, Sep. 1958

Analysis of a range of published plans reveals that the single-corridor access type, the *oerangsik*, was usually chosen as the most suitable housing model for rapid mass production. It was regarded as the cheapest and easiest housing model, given North Korea's economic and technological circumstances at the time.[14] The North Korean regime did not clarify the model's origin, although it briefly commented on a competition for 2–3-storey urban housing held in 1957.[15] Nonetheless, this plan probably derived directly from the type II plan designed by the DAG in 1956. A comparison of the two plans shows strong similarities. Following the German models, North Korean architects proposed a unit plan with repetitive bays that minimised requirements for materials and workforce.

The single-corridor-access type had three different variants of building plan that were based on the combination of units: one-room flats (studio type), one-room and two-room mixed flats, and two-room flats. The 1958 standard plan (PUDI 1958) consists of one-room flats with bays that are 3.44 metres wide. Repetitive bays are perpendicularly connected to long corridors on up to six floors without a lift. The inhabitants were required to share toilets adjacent to the staircase which, following the German model, complemented the units' small inner space. In comparison to the German model, housing built using the PUDI 1958 plan had long rectangular rooms that could be divided into two parts by sliding doors. This flexibility made it possible to combine units. Two units could be merged to form a single unit by removing partition walls. This method seems to have been intended to solve the immediate housing shortage and simultaneously to prepare for dwelling spaces to be extended in the future.[16]

North Korean architects made great efforts to accommodate diverse family patterns in prefabricated housing. Their efforts led to the creation of a unique building plan that alternated one- and two-room flats on the same floor. The first example can be found in a single-corridor-access building erected in Pyongyang microdistrict no. 62 in 1958. This plan has a one-room flat and a two-room flat placed on different floors. However, as service facilities such as toilets and laundries were gradually included in individual units, the inner space available for rooms became smaller. This problem was particularly serious in one-room flats; accordingly, the service areas for one-room flats encroached on the space of the two-room flats, as in CSDI 1962 A, B. In the latter plans two dwelling units interconnected with one another, meaning that the layout of the service areas did not follow the bay system. Because the service area was the same size in both one-room and two-room flats, its partition walls did not coincide with the bay partitions.[17]

Two-room flats of 40–45 m² accessed by a single corridor gradually became the dominant standard design in North Korea's post-war urban housing. This model underwent a complex process before becoming the most frequent standard plan. North Korean design institutes put forward several proposals, compared their respective merits and drawbacks using models, and selected a single final variant. After this variant had been trialled in real construction, architects adopted it as the standard plan. The plan underwent several modifications during this process. For example, the CSDI 1961 variant of the two-room flat was conceived with identical three-metre bays. However, the layout of the kitchen, storage, toilet, and washroom was insufficiently compact, reducing spatial efficiency. The 1962 standard plan (PUDI 1962) overcame this problem by regularising the size of the service space, repositioning the services, or positioning the staircase more efficiently. Li's book *History of Architecture in Joseon* described this plan as a typical two-room flat.[18] A similar plan reappeared in the 1967 standard plans (CSDI 1967 A, B). These unit plans made a good fit with the *ondol* system and mass production in North Korea. Kim Il Sung also preferred the two-room unit to the other options.[19] For this reason, most flats built in the late 1960s were based on this standard plan.

The three-metre width of a typical bay was only arrived at after North Korean architects had conducted

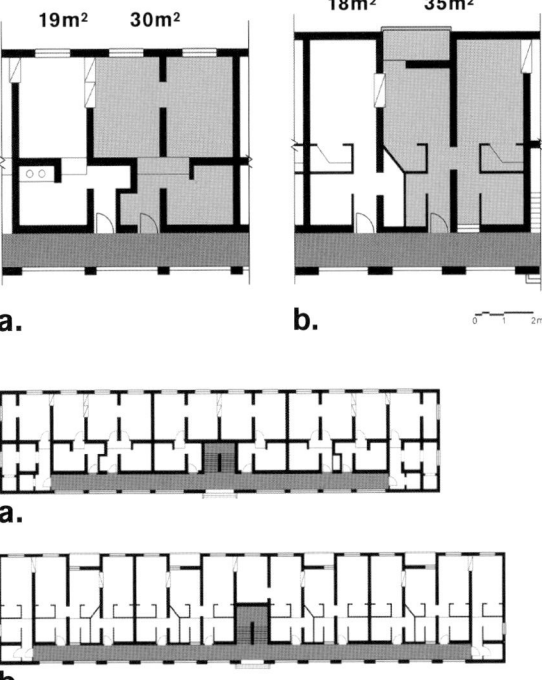

Unit and building plans for the single-corridor access apartment building CSDI 1962 A, B (redrawn by the authors).
Source: Geonchukgwa Geonseol, January 1962

numerous studies. Three bay sizes (2.7 m, 3.3 m, 3.6 m) were compared, largely from the viewpoint of economy and convenience. The three-metre bay won out because it was compact and avoided wasted space in the staircase and corridor,[20] while the prefabricated components were light enough to be lifted by North Korean cranes. Above all, this size had the advantage of creating a compact design for the service area. This typical bay size was applied to both single-corridor-access and staircase-access housing. In the same studies architects reduced the length of the bay size from nine metres (the typical modular size in single-corridor-access housing) to 8.1 metres.

The staircase-access type, copied from the Soviet *sektsiia* plan, was also adopted as an important housing model in North Korea. After undergoing several

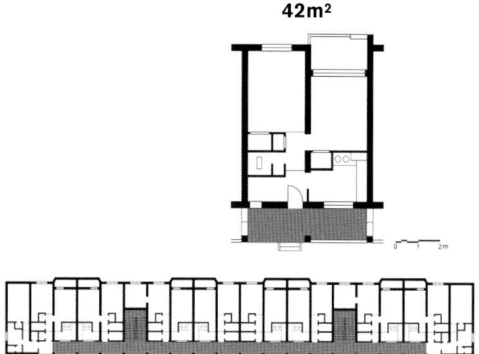

Unit and building plans for single-corridor-access apartment building CSDI 1961(draft) (redrawn by the authors).
Source: Geonchukgwa Geonseol, July 1960

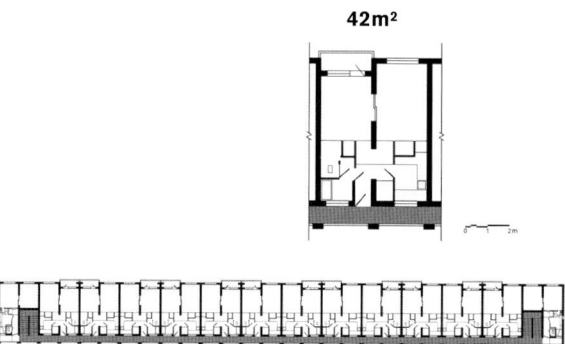

Unit and building plans for single-corridor access apartment building PUDI 1962 (redrawn by the authors).
Source: Geonchukgwa Geonseol, January 1962

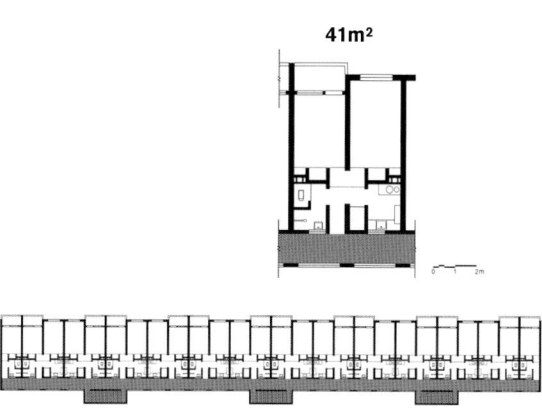

Unit and building plans for single-corridor-access apartment building CSDI 1967 (draft) (redrawn by the authors).
Source: Geonchukgwa Geonseol, June 1967

modifications, the 1962 plan (CSDI 1962 C) was adopted as standard. Comparison with the original Soviet *sektsiia* plans reveals three important differences. First, in a single section containing three residential units, the central longitudinal load-bearing supports (*garojijidae*) acquired an important structural role and determined the spatial direction; this is in stark contrast with the Soviet-style *sektsiia* house, in which the perpendicular partition walls were load-bearing. The longitudinal load-bearing supports made it easier to combine identical units, enhancing the flexibility of unit plans. Second, North Korean flats employed the three-metre-wide system of identical bays that had already been used in single-corridor-access housing. Soviet houses did not have bays with identical widths. Contemporary Soviet mass housing designed and constructed in the Khrushchev era (known as 'khrushchevkas') allowed for a variety of spatial arrangements within units. This meant that bay size remained of secondary importance and varied according to the function of the rooms.[21] The final difference was that unit layouts were designed to accommodate the *ondol*: the kitchen and *ondol* room are adjacent to one another. Compared with the single-corridor-access type, this type of housing was less popular because living rooms could not be oriented toward the south.

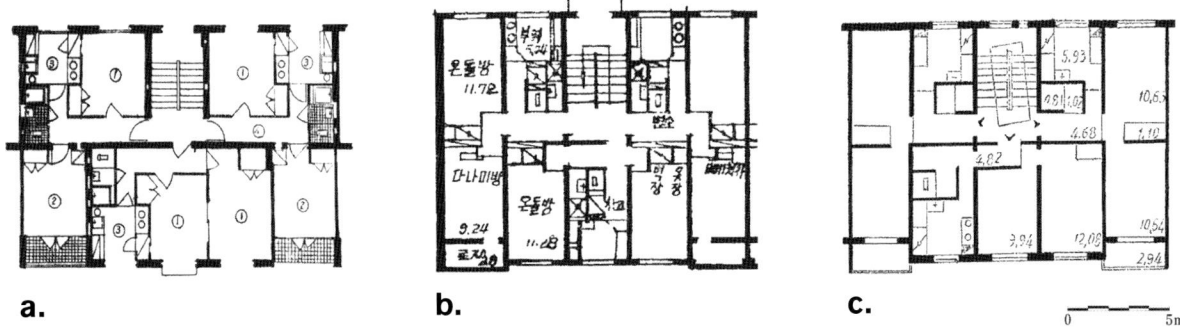

Plans for *sektsiia* type apartments: (a) PUDI 1959, (b) CSDI 1962 C, (c) *sektsiia* type proposed by the Central Standard Design Institute in 1967.
Source: *Geonchukgwa Geonseol*, January 1959; *Geonchukgwa Geonseol*, January 1962; *Geonchukgwa Geonseol*, July 1967

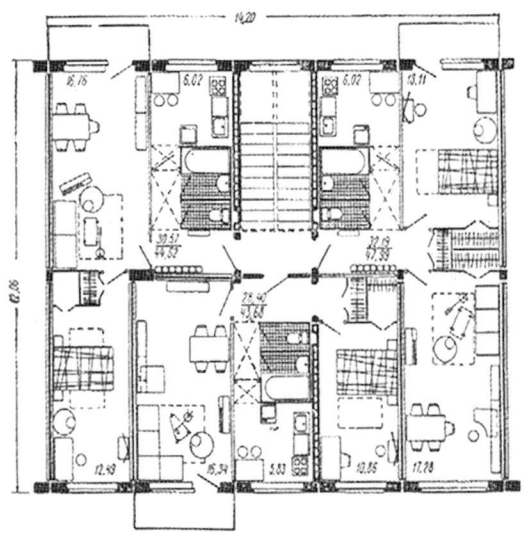
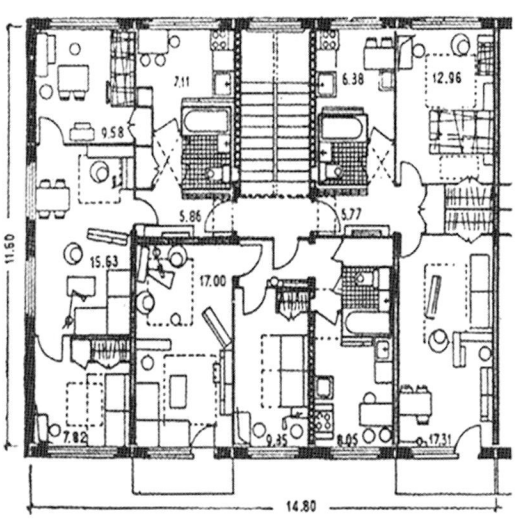

Plans of Soviet mass housing (*khrushchevka*): (a) Type I-355A (1964), (b) Type I-355K (1961).
Source: Meuser Philipp, Zadorin Dimitrij, *Toward a Typology of Soviet Mass Housing Prefabrication in the USSR 1955–1991*, DOM publishers, 2015

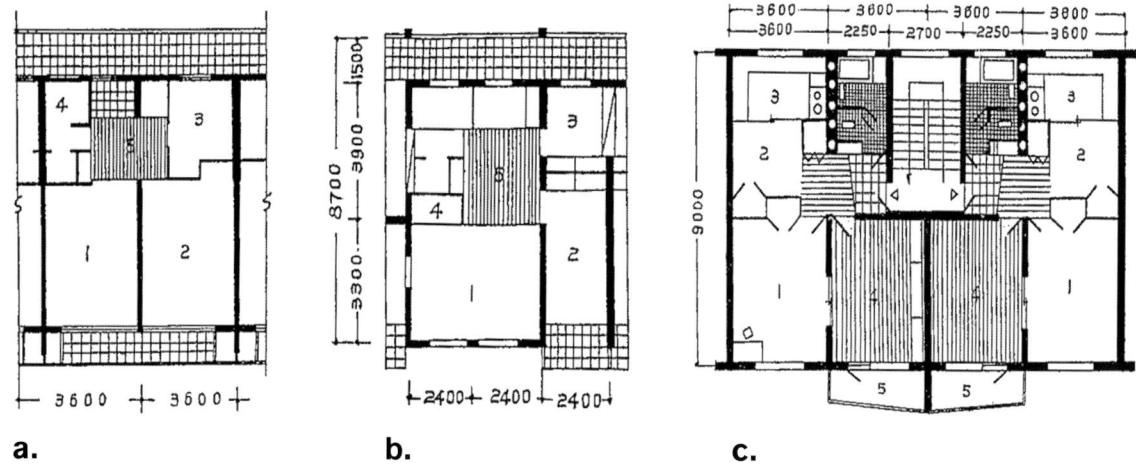

Plans of *sektsiia*-type apartments: (a) PUDI 1959, (b) CSDI 1962 C, (c) *sektsiia* type proposed by the Central Standard Design Institute in 1967.
Source: *Geonchukgwa Geonseol, January 1959; Geonchukgwa Geonseol, January 1962; Geonchukgwa Geonseol, July 1967*

Diversification of standard housing plans

In his speech to the Pyongyang Builders Congress in 1958, Kim Il Sung, who had evaluated the results of housing construction in the previous year, asked participants for qualitative improvements in housing design.[22] In response, North Korean architects developed new standard housing plans to improve both quality of living and economy in housing construction. With respect to the first objective, North Korean architects conducted research into the best habitation size and established a table of standards for the ratio of rooms to family members. A detailed table for housing planning in 1966 shows that one-room flats should accommodate 1–3 persons; two-room flats, 4–7 persons; and three-room flats, 8 or more persons.[23] In conjunction with this spatial distribution, each unit had its own separate toilet, storage space, and kitchen; this meant that shared use of facilities was now eliminated. In addition, the table 'A series of standard housing prospects', published in 1964, proposed nine types of housing that varied in accordance with differences in climate, city size, heating system, orientation, and number of floors. The table subdivided North Korea into four regions based on their winter weather and North Korean cities into four categories based on population.[24] By combining identical bays, North Korean architects could create flexible unit plans to accommodate the above subdivisions.

The proposals for standard plans produced by the Central Standard Design Institute in 1964 should be considered from the point of view of diversification of urban housing. Unlike previous standard plans, these were not drawn up to be directly applied to construction but were proposals based on the use of a central heating system. They included two standard types of apartment building – with corridor access and staircase access – and reflected efforts by North Korean architects to diversify the established standard plan. The most notable change was in the bay width, which was increased to 3.6 metres. In addition, a central-heating system using hot water made a difference to how the interior spaces were laid out. The strong connection between the kitchen and the *ondol* room now began to dissolve. The enlargement of the *jeonsil* (ante-room), which served as a dining room and multi-functional space, was another important

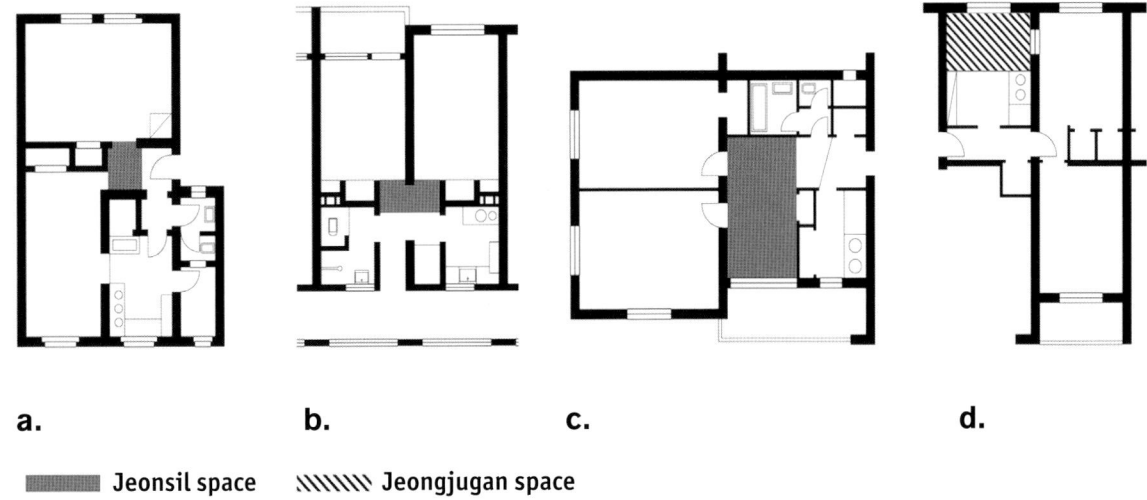

a. **b.** **c.** **d.**

▪ Jeonsil space   ⧸⧸⧸⧸ Jeongjugan space

Development of *jeonsil* and *jeongjugan* spaces: (a) PUDI 1956 B, (b) PUDI 1962 A, (c) CSDI Tower (1960), (D) *sektsiia* plan of Cheonjin City, Hamgyeong Province (1961) (redrawn by the authors).

change. Originally, this space was created to accommodate the *ondol* heating system. It first emerged as a transitional space resulting from the difference in height between the kitchen and the *ondol* room, but it eventually served as a multi-functional service space. Its ambiguous function recalls the traditional *jeongjugan*, a type of extended kitchen range often found in traditional vernacular villages in Hamgyeong Province. Two-bay flats from this time are particularly likely to have this space, a vestigial trace of the traditional space in modern housing. As the transitional area increased in size, it became a prominent space in North Korean flats and a symbol of North Korea's unique lifestyle.

Variation is found not only in bay modules but also in building plans. Sometimes the two basic housing types, staircase-access and single-corridor-access, were combined to create a new housing type. In 1966 the Central Standard Design Institute proposed six types of plan that mixed staircase access with single-corridor access for improved convenience of living.[25] The mixed types addressed problems in the two basic types. A building in the city of Chongjin illustrates how the two types may be

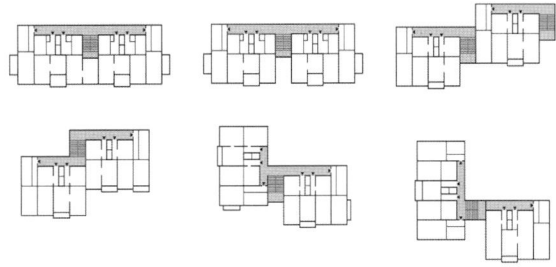

Variations of building plans by the Central Standard Design Institute (redrawn by the authors).
Source: *Geonchukgwa Geonseol*, May 1966

combined. Whereas two of its three units were designed for single-corridor access, the split-level third unit was accessed by a staircase. However, despite having different types of access, all units provided the same conditions with the exception of the location of their balconies. These mixed types were particularly suited to use as corner apartment complexes or on sloped sites.

High-rise housing was adopted to make urban areas more dynamic. North Korean architects sought to break the monotony of what the Germans call 'Zeilenbau'

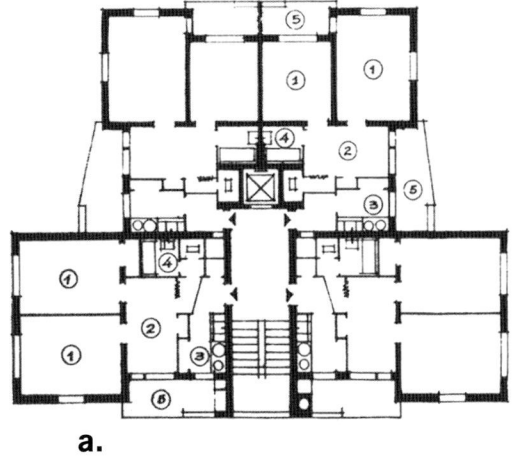
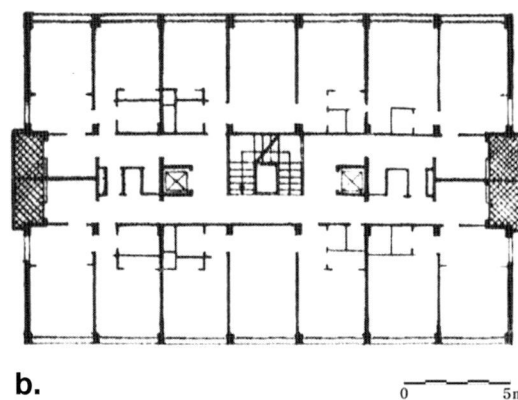

a. b.

Two examples of standard housing in a high-rise apartment in 1960: (a) tower type (CSDI Tower 1960) (b) double-corridor type.
Source: Geonchukgwa Geonseol, June 1960; Geonchukgwa Geonseol, Dec.1960

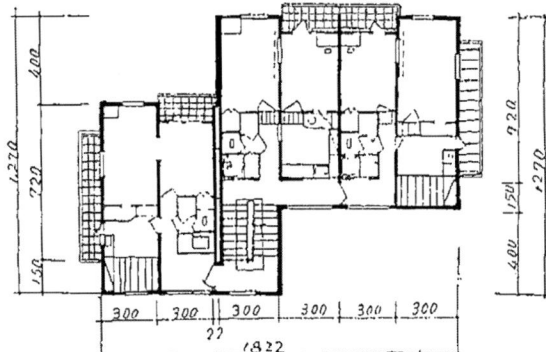

Building plan of tower-type housing in Cheongjin City.
Source: Geonchukgwa Geonseol, January 1965

(linear block-style complexes of flats). To create a sense of rhythm in the skyline, they inserted high-rise towers at intervals. The height of high-rise housing varied by region, but normally the term 'high-rise' refers to buildings with more than six storeys that require a lift. The approach to designing this type of housing was very different from that embodied by the existing standard housing in terms of structure, fireproofing, climatic conditions, and convenience of living. In view of these factors, North Korean architects sought answers to two questions: which building plan is the most suited to North Korea, and how many dwelling units can a staircase service economically and reasonably? In answering the first question, North Korean architects created two standard types in 1960: the double-corridor-access type and the tower type. The double-corridor-access type, however, was not particularly suitable for North Korea, which required natural ventilation during the hot summers and access to daylight in the cold winters.[26] The long dark corridor was also seen by residents as a disadvantage. The tower type was superior with respect to these points and minimised the need for earthworks on uneven ground. For instance, a standard plan produced for high-rise housing by the Central Standard Design Institute in 1960 used the tower type with four dwelling units per floor. A standard plan for tower-type housing created by the Pyongyang Urban Design Institute in 1963 retained this principle, but with larger units.

Technological, Spatial, and Ideological Aspects of North Korea's Mass Housing

The evolution of North Korea's mass housing shows how the new approach to housing design was framed by a combination of three factors: new technologies, spatial layouts, and socialist ideology. These three factors reveal the way in which North Koreans appropriated the socialist way of life.

The *ondol* and the structure of interior space

As the traditional North Korean heating system, the *ondol* had a considerable influence on North Korea's culture of housing design. It gave rise to a unique arrangement of interior space suited to a floor-sitting lifestyle. Spatially, it created a connection between the master bedroom and the kitchen since the furnace performed a dual role as an amenity used in both cooking and heating. The use of the *ondol* in modern housing required fundamental modification of the models imported from the Soviet Union and Eastern Europe; this was a difficult challenge for North Korean architects. The architect Kim Jeong-hui, who claimed responsibility for introducing Soviet models of housing at an early stage of the country's reconstruction, denounced the *ondol* as an old-fashioned custom that North Koreans should abandon along with private ownership and traditional urban structure. He considered it unhygienic, uneconomical, and, above all, nearly impossible to incorporate into multi-storey buildings. In essence, he argued for the creation of a new housing model that rejected the *ondol* and its floor-sitting lifestyle.[27] However, a sudden change of atmosphere came in 1955, when Kim Il-sung praised the *ondol* as the heating system most suited to North Korean living and ordered its installation in multi-storey housing.[28] We do not know the reasons for Kim Il-sung's intervention, but we may speculate that it was the complaints of North Koreans living in Soviet-style housing that led to this change of heart.[29]

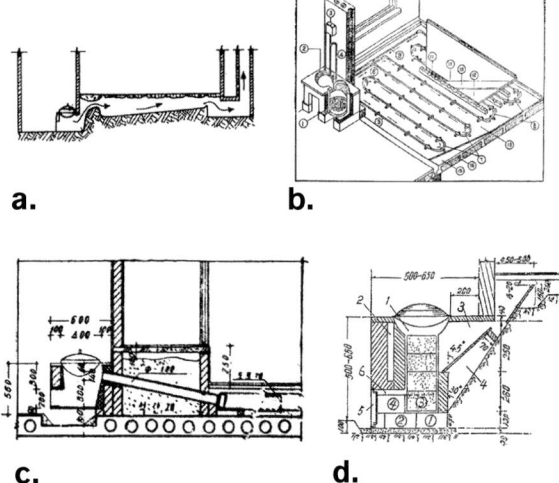

Experimentation with the *ondol* system: (a) traditional *ondol*, (b) *ondol* system using warm water, (c) 'flat' *ondol* system, (d) advanced *ondol* model.
Source: Geonchukgwa Geonseol, Feb. 1958; Geonchukgwa Geonseol, Dec.1963; Geonchukgwa Geonseol, January 1967

In 1956, just after Kim Il-sung's speech, the *ondol* was added to the plans for two-staircase-access apartments (PUDI 1956 A, B). Type A contained a room clearly marked as an *ondolbang*, i.e. a room with traditional under-floor heating. Type B was similar but benefitted from improvements to the heating system and modified access to the kitchen and coal bunker. However, because the traditional *ondol* system was transferred to modern housing that was developing new technology, there was an inevitable difference in levels between the floors in the kitchen and the *ondol* room. The heating equipment, including the hypocaust, requires a space at least 0.6 metres high. Moreover, a chimney must be located opposite the furnace, as in a traditional house.[30] Use of the *ondol* also effectively reduced ceiling height.[31]

Despite the North Korean regime's determination to bring back the *ondol* system, the *ondol* was almost abandoned in the late 1950s because the techniques for inserting it into the prefabricated system were inadequate. As a consequence, early North Korean urban housing had a heating system that used radiators. North Korean architects never stopped developing the *ondol* system, however, despite several technical failures. Competitions were held to find ideas to solve technical problems that sprang from mass production. Diverse experiments were conducted to improve efficiency. In 1958 North Korean architects suggested an *ondol* system using warm water carried in pipes with a diameter of 30 centimetres in the furrows of the hypocaust.[32] In 1961 another creative idea came from the Urban Construction Institute of Pyongyang Construction College, which invented large panels to function as both *ondol* and floor slabs. However, these attempts failed to develop into a system suitable for mass production, so most urban housing in the mid-1960s returned to the early *ondol* system.

Since these technical experiments had encountered difficulties, the emphasis eventually moved to reducing the difference in levels between the kitchen and *ondol* room floors; this led to serious problems in designing the interior spaces.³³ Despite technical developments, floors on different levels were inevitable due to the equipment itself. To eliminate the difference in levels, in 1961 North Korean architects invented a new heating system called the *supyeong* ('flat') *ondol*. This levelled the apartment floors by pouring heated gas into furrows through pipes angled downwards at 30°. In 1966 an *ondol* with a depth of 60 centimetres that was similar to the traditional *ondol* began to be used again in North Korean flats, signifying the failure of efforts to improve the *ondol* system.

Meanwhile, a successful technique invented in the 1960s proved able to circulate heated air into all the rooms of a flat. In 1966 the Hamhŭng Urban Design Institute published an article in an architectural magazine illustrating a variety of *ondol* plans.³⁴ One system for a standard two-room flat conveyed heated air into the second room through a pipe. Hot air circulated under the floor and returned to a chimney beside the stove. The architect made every effort to design rational paths for the heated air. As a result, all the rooms were heated by the *ondol*, and the distinction between the *ondol* room and the *maru* room (a wooden-floored room without heating) gradually disappeared.

The final change in heating systems occurred when a central-heating system was first used in an 18-household block of flats in Pyongyang in 1967.³⁵ The need for individual *ondol* systems disappeared because a newly constructed thermoelectric power plant in Pyongyang distributed hot water to each unit through under-floor panel heating. This change was significant for North Korea's urban housing, which was moving into a new phase at this time, as seen in the plans for CSDI 1964 A and B (see Figure above). The kitchen and master bedroom began to be separated, and the standard unit plan evolved in a totally different direction.³⁶

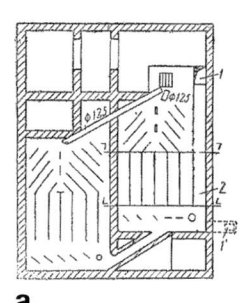 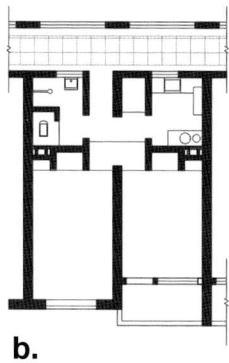

a. b.

Circulation of heated air in the *ondol* of a typical two-room apartment: (a) *ondol* system, (b) PUDI 1962.
Source: Geonchukgwa Geonseol, June 1966

a.   b.   c.

Assemblies consisting of (a) small concrete blocks, (b) large panels, and (c) cubic boxes.
Source: Geonseolja, April 1959; Geonseolja, Nov. 1960; Geonseolja, April, July 1958

Mass-production systems

North Korea's extensive use of mass production resulted in substantial changes in the housing sector. Kim Il Sung's official declaration in 1955 was followed by a rapid increase in mechanisation of housing, from 32.4% in 1957 to 72.6% in 1962.[37] Housing construction in North Korea peaked in 1962, when more than 200,000 household units in both urban and rural areas were built during the course of a single year.[38] This obviously involved the speedy prefabrication of an enormous number of components.[39]

Industrialisation on such a scale gave rise to the myth of 'Pyongyang speed', with one flat being built every 14 minutes.[40] Most media articles and photographs at the time indulged in the reporting of statistics relating to 'how many' or 'how rapid'. In 1958, 20,000 flats were constructed in Pyongyang alone – almost three times the figure specified in the planning goal. Naturally, this industrialisation left its mark on architectural design. Standard plans were created to reduce the number of individual components required and to integrate structures and heating systems into assembly systems.

According to *The Mechanisation of Assembly Operation* (Jorip jageobui gigyehwa), a practical manual published in 1962, North Korean architects used four assembly methods for mass production: assembly of small concrete blocks, large panels, housing units, and cubic boxes. The first stage in the industrialisation of housing involved the assembly of small concrete blocks onsite for elements such as the base, walls, floors, stairs, and roof. The aim, however, was to reduce as far as possible the number of components used in housing construction. So North Korean architects gradually moved towards the assembly of large panels. As a result, whereas the first prefabricated residential building in 1956 consisted of 127 components, two years later, that number dropped to 35 and 30 components for single-corridor-access and staircase-access apartment buildings respectively.[41] Using large panels made it possible to shrink production costs by 12–15% and double construction speed.[42] Builders could build 11 dwelling units in eight hours for six-storey buildings in Pyongyang in 1958; each unit consisted of only six panels. Use of this method spread following a resolution adopted in 1960 by the Party

Central Committee, which sought 'full mechanisation of construction work by making individual components larger and lighter'; this became an advertising slogan in North Korean magazines.

The idea behind using housing units was 'to prefabricate an entire housing unit or half a unit in factories or on construction sites ahead of its installation in a building'.[43] This method was popular in the Soviet Union under Khrushchev. In the 1960s a team of engineers led by the architect Vitaly Lagutenko developed a *khrushchevka*-type apartment unit that incorporated all required services.[44] Despite the fact that a house consisting of such units could be built at great speed, a problem was the need for heavy cranes capable of lifting unit blocks weighing more than 27 tonnes. As a solution, North Korean architects proposed a compromise method called *tongbangbujae*, whereby only key rooms such as the toilet, kitchen, and living room were prefabricated as monolithic boxes prior to being assembled onsite.[45] This method reduced the number of components by between a third and a half compared with assembly using large panels. In 1958, when this system was first introduced, the weight of each cubic box was limited to 4.8 tonnes.[46] *Nodongsinmun*, the official newspaper, proudly boasted that a world record had been achieved in express construction.[47] However, speed of construction was no guarantee of quality. This system revealed many drawbacks after completion, such as poor soundproofing and insulation and a propensity for leaks.[48] Moreover, incorporation of an *ondol* resulted in numerous assembly problems; single components became partitioned components.[49] Use of this prefabrication method led to the width of the standard bay being reduced to almost three metres. In the 1960s, as fabrication technology advanced, the room-assembly method became more systematised and diversified. A single-corridor-access unit from 1964 has diverse sizes for its prefabricated room, lavatory, and kitchen. A two-room flat could be built using only 12 components.

The North Korean regime suffered from a lack of skilled workers and from technological lag in the construction sector. It tried to overcome these handicaps through mass mobilisation, including through the so-called

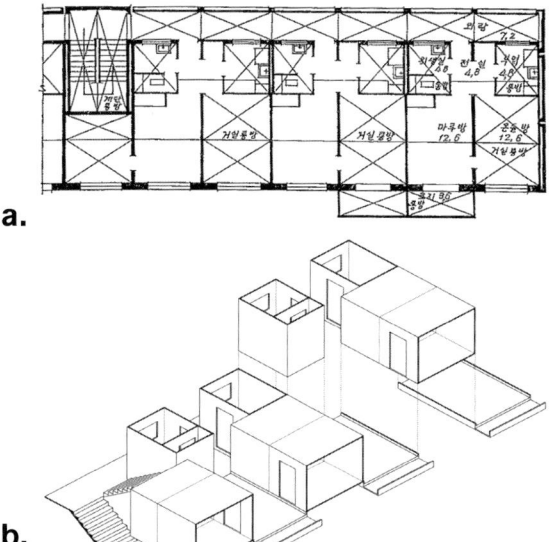

(a) Assembly of *tongbangbujae* for a typical two-room apartment;
(b) an exploded axonometric drawn by the authors.
Source: Geonchukgwa Geonseol, April 1964

'Chollima movement'. Unlike the 'Stakhanovite' movement in the USSR and the 'Great Leap Forward' in China, the Chollima movement was aimed at constructing a large amount of housing within a short amount of time. To accomplish this aim, mass production of housing in North Korea mainly relied on comprehensive standardisation and mass mobilisation.

Large numbers of unskilled workers, including students, housewives, and soldiers, joined in work at construction sites. Office workers were also called upon to roll up their sleeves after business hours. North Korea's regime accordingly employed the simplest possible methods for transporting and assembling components. This approach was totally different from China's, which relied on traditional skilled bricklayers. In North Korea manpower and labour organisation was subordinate to efficiency and assembly procedures. Rapid construction was considered a priority, and the quantity of units constructed by a worker became the yardstick for productivity. The North Korean regime promoted competition between workers by quantifying and comparing required manpower per square metre.

National in form and socialist in content

'National in form and socialist in content' was a slogan that emerged during Stalin's era to explain the policy of indigenisation of non-Russian communities. By the late 1930s, however, there was a notable policy shift in the Soviet Union towards the Russification of government, education, and the media.

After Nikita Khrushchev became First Secretary of the Communist Party in the late 1950s, the trend accelerated. This policy shift in the Soviet Union had a great impact on communist countries in East Asia. In particular, the Soviet Union and China competed with one another for hegemony of the communist bloc. Following the Sino-Soviet split, North Korea's then-leader, Kim Il Sung, developed the ideology of 'self-reliance' in the late 1950s.[50] The emergence of this slogan seems to have reflected North Korea's dilemma in its diplomatic relations with the Soviet Union and China. It also reflected contradictory aspects in North Korea's housing policy, which promoted standardised mass production while simultaneously pursuing indigenisation of Soviet models.

This slogan first emerged in a speech by Kim Il Sung in 1958: 'The housing that we are building must be socialist in content but national in form.'[51] However, analysis of his speech reveals that its original meaning had been changed. Specifically, the emphasis in his speech was placed on the 'socialist in content' idea, rather than on 'national in form'. Explaining the idea behind 'socialist in content', Kim Il Sung said: 'it means the efficient, the cosy, the beautiful, and the solid. That is the construction quality we demand.'[52] Kim Il Sung raised this issue to justify the construction of mass housing in North Korea despite the plan's serious defects, which were due to the unrealistic targets set by the Communist Party. As discussed above, the plan called for the use of cohorts of workers without consideration for professional skills or training; this led to the overall degradation of construction quality.

After Kim Il Sung's speech, a report on 'how to improve the living situations of workers as builders of socialism in a cultured and hygienic manner' was presented at the Central Workers' Council. This stipulated that the giving up of uncultured and unsanitary old customs constituted a great challenge in accomplishing revolution. Moreover, it emphasised that 'all parents should renew themselves as creators of socialist living through a determined fight against old customs in order to bring up their children in the socialist way of life'.[53] Here, we can identify the ideological objective of the housing policy pursued by the North Korean regime: this was a matter of providing comfortable and hygienic dwelling spaces for the 'new communists' whom North Korea's regime wished to form. These new communists were supermen who would selflessly work hard for the new communist state.[54]

Conclusion

Since North Korea's regime had adopted the mass housing system of the Khrushchev era, it faced the burden of dual reform processes: the breaking of old customs and the realisation of a new way of life. From the point of view of the North Korean elites, improvement of workers' living spaces in a cultured and hygienic manner was key to assimilation of the socialist way of life. Whereas the Khrushchevian state battled against a Stalinist, petit-bourgeois consciousness, the North Korean regime believed that a determined battle against old customs could lead to people being re-moulded into living a socialist way of life.

However, the process of this assimilation necessitated collision, compromise, and adaptation. A comparison of standard plans from North Korea's mass-housing programme and the *khrushchevka* shows remarkable differences in the interior space. Whereas living rooms as communal spaces for social activities occupied an important place in *khrushchevka* buildings, such spaces were absent from the standard plans for North Korea's mass housing programme. Instead, a small ante-room (*jeonsil*) was created in front of private rooms. This multi-functional space was closely tied to the use of an *ondol* heating system. The traditional heating system was an important variable because it made a significant difference in how the flat's interior space was organised: the kitchen was directly linked to the *ondol* room.

Moreover, the single-corridor-access type was the most widespread variant in North Korea. That this was the preferred type was primarily due to the relatively low cost of construction, but also to the advantages it gave in surveillance and mobilisation of citizens, which possibly paved the way for the development of a totalitarian state ruled with an iron fist. In fact, North Korea's mass housing was designed to suit the activities of the smallest administrative cell, the so-called 'people's unit' (*inminban*), which usually consisted of 25 to 35 families. The heads of the units served as both distributors of food, fuel, and other necessary goods and strict monitors of residents' behaviour. One of their principal tasks was to turn all households under their authority into 'a 3.15 model home'. This was a kind of living movement that pushed residents to clean the interiors of their houses like palaces and embellish their exteriors like parks. Public amenities in apartment complexes were also utilised as meeting places for people's units. The persistence of the North Korean regime despite serious economic failures is largely due to its monitoring system. In this respect, North Korea's mass housing brings together socialist ideas on residents' everyday life, behaviour patterns, and social organisation.

1. The socialist way of life (*byt* in Russian) refers to every aspect of the daily life, including domestic material culture and family life, which took shape after the Russian Revolution. This term was critically important in communist countries because of its close association with Bolshevik visions of a total revolution in housing.
2. Kim Taewoo, 'Limited war, unlimited targets', pp. 467–92.
3. Joseon Central News Agency (eds.) (Pyongyang, 1961), p. 321.
4. Li Hwa-seon(a) (Pyongyang, 1989), p. 320.
5. The Chollima movement was a campaign of mass mobilisation comparable to the Great Leap Forward in China under Mao Zedong. Beginning in earnest in 1958, the movement aimed to improve labour productivity by means of ideological incentives such as giving the title of 'labour hero' to those who worked hard. As a result, the campaign produced a large quantity of mass urban housing, particularly in Pyongyang: see Balazs Szalontai, *Kim Il Sung in the Khrushchev era* (Chicago, Stanford University Press, 2005), pp. 121-127; Charles K. Armstrong, *Tyranny of the Weak: North Korea and the World*, 1950–1992 (Ithaca, Cornell University Press, 2013), pp. 103–11.
6. The Russian word *sektsiia* literally translates as 'section', 'worship', 'element', 'unit', and 'post-mortem examination'. Urban housing was so named because it consisted of sections, each of which contained several residential units and one staircase.
7. The Ganseoldong and Mangyeongdae housing structures, built in 1949, before the war, were similar to the *sektsiia* type: See Li Hwa-seon(a) (Pyongyang, 1989), p. 288.
8. Harris, (Washington DC, 2013), pp. 47–70. This housing model was largely introduced in satellite countries such as North Korea and China. For the case of China, see Zhang Jie & Wang Tao (Munich, 2001), pp. 124–8, 131–8, 152–168.
9. This institute was founded in 1947 to manage the design of urban projects in Pyongyang. The institute drew up the reconstruction plan for Pyongyang immediately after the ceasefire and contributed to the capital's 'new face' by participating in the design of a series of major districts such as Chollima-geori, Changgwanggeori, Gwangbok-geori, and Tongil-geori.
10. Kim Myun, 'Bimilmunseolo bon gudongdok', pp.94–99.
11. The total amount of East German aid to Hamhŭng was 118,000,000 DM. Armstrong, Charles K. (Ithaca Press, 2013), p. 74.
12. IUA Inquiry, Moscow (1958), 'The Proceedings of North Korea at the Fifth Congress of the International Union of Architects', Bauhaus Dessau Archives, I 010299 D, pp. 23–31.
13. For housing planning by the DAG, see 'Erläuterungsberichte für den Wohnkomplex der Baujahre 1956–1957', Archiv der Stiftung Bauhaus Dessau, Püschel, I_010014_D.
14. The unit cost of construction for single-corridor-access apartments with a traditional *ondol* was 1681 Won, which is comparable to the 1860 Won required for double-corridor-access apartments with central heating. Shin, Sun-gyeong, 'Jutaek geonseol-ui joriphwa-eseo', p. 7.
15. *Pyongyang geonseoljeonsa* (Pyongyang, 1997), p. 250.
16. Ibid., pp. 248–50; Li Hwa-seon(a) (Pyongyang, 1989), p. 369.
17. *Jungang pyojunseolgye yeonguso*, p. 26.
18. Li Hwa-seon(b) (Pyongyang, 1997), p. 60.
19. Kim Il-sung(b) (Pyongyang, 1998), p. 416.
20. *Jungang pyojunseolgye yeonguso*, 'Olhae-e sseul oeryangmich sektsiiahyeong jutaek pyojunseolgyel-eul hago (Standard designs of single-corridor-access and staircase-access housing for this year)', op. cit.; *Jungang pyojunseolgyeyeonguso*, 'Myeochgaji sae jutaekseolgye sian-eul bogo' (A look at new proposals for housing design), op. cit.
21. This housing is similar to the multi-storey building designed by the architect Ivan Zholtovsky and built on Bolshaya Kaluzhskaya Street in Moscow. Zholtovsky's building, which won the Stalin Prize in 1950 and was considered to have foreshadowed the *khrushchevka*, was later published and discussed in the book by Kim Jeong-hui. See Kim Jeong-hui (Pyongyang, 1953), p. 190.
22. Kim Il-sung(a) (Pyongyang, 1998), p. 516.
23. Choi, Chun-yeol, 'Bangsedae biyul-gwa geonseollyang, pp. 31–32.
24. *Jungang pyojunseolgye yeonguso*, *Geonchukgwa Geonseol*, 12. 1964, pp. 32–36.
25. *Jungang pyojunseolgye yeonguso* , 5, 1966, p. 48.
26. *Geonseol daehak geonchukhak gangjwa*, *Geonchukgwa Geonseol*, 1, 1960, p. 23.
27. Kim Jeong-Hui, *Dosigeonseol* (Urban Construction), op. cit., p. 23
28. Li Hwa-seon(a) (Pyongyang,1989), p. 368.
29. Kim Il Sung introduced the *ondol* in November 1955 as follows: 'Since North Koreans have traditionally had an *ondol* room, they

are fond of it. We should install one in multi-storey residential buildings.' (Pyongyang geonseol jeonsa pyeonchanwiwonhoe, ed., *Pyongyang geonseoljeonsa 2* (The Whole Story of the Construction of Pyongyang 2), op. cit., p. 247).
30 Li Hwa-Seon(a) (Pyongyang, 1993), p. 368.
31 The room height was lowered to 2.2 metres in *ondol* rooms and 2.7 metres in *maru* rooms. (*Pyongyang geonseoljeonsa pyeonchanwiwonhoe*, op. cit., pp. 247, 250).
32 *Gyeonggongeopseong Seolgye Yeonguso, Onsu ondol nanbang bangbeop-e daehayeo*, p. 32.
33 Li Hwa-Seon(b) (Pyongyang, 1993), p. 63.
34 *Hamhŭngsi dosiseolgyeyeonguso*, 'Haprijeogin ondol pyeongmyeondeul', p. 3.
35 Joseon Central News Agency (eds.) (Pyongyang: Joseon Central News Agency, 1971), p. 280.
36 Li Hwa-Seon(b) (Pyongyang, 1989), p. 62.
37 *Joseon jungangtongsinsa, Joseon jungangnyeongam* (Annual of North Korea) 1963, op. cit., p. 343.
38 Kim Il-sung (Pyongyang, 2000), pp. 143–4.
39 The number of housing units built from 1954 to 1960 was 771,500, and the number built from 1961 to 1970 was approximately 800,000. Zchang, Sung-Soo and Yoon, Hae-Jung, *Jutaek Forum, 2*, 2000, pp. 82–3.
40 Li Hwa-Seon(a) (Pyongyang, 1989), p. 339.
41 Ibid., p. 367
42 Unknown (Pyongyang, 1962), p. 104.
43 Ibid., p. 109.
44 Harris, Steven E. (Washington, DC, 2013), pp. 75–85.
45 Unknown, *Tongbang jutaek seolgye sian*, p. 20.
46 O, Ik-geun, *Ttohana-ui hyeoksin tongbang panel jutaekgeonseol*, p. 5
47 Ibid.
48 Ibid. ; *Pyongyang geonseol jeonsa pyeonchanwiwonhoe* (Pyongyang, 1997), p. 248; Li Hwa-Seon(a), (Pyongyang, 1989), p. 374.
49 Unknown,, *Tongbang jutaek seolgye sian*', p. 20.
50 Armstrong, op. cit., pp. 108–15.
51 Kim Il-sung(a) (Pyongyang, 1998), p. 305.
52 Kim Il-sung(a) (Pyongyang, 1998), p. 518.
53 Joseon Central News Agency, *Rodong Sinmun*, 27 Dec. 1958, p. 1.
54 Suh Dae-Sook, (New York, 1988), p. 166.

다섯

The Microdistrict-based Approach to Site Planning

Inha Jung/ Kim Mina

During the period following the Korean War, from the mid-1950s to the mid-1970s, the theory of the microdistrict – called *mikrorayon* in Russian and *soguyeok* in Korean – had a strong influence on the formation of North Korea's cities. To facilitate smooth adoption of this model, the North Korean regime constructed several model housing estates based on the microdistrict approach, investigated problems brought to light in this way, and established design criteria that were applicable to all North Korean cities. *Jutaek soguyeok gyehoek* (The Planning of Microdistricts), a book by Li Sun-Gwon and Baek Wan-Gi published in 1963, coordinated the efforts of North Korean architects and planners by identifying 14 large cities in North Korea that built housing based on this approach.[1]

In the aftermath of the Korean War, North Korea's circumstances made microdistricts particularly relevant and important. The country's cities had been destroyed and razed to the ground. The North Korean regime needed an integrated model for large-scale development that not only reflected its political ideology, economic policies, and social institutions but also facilitated housing construction. The microdistrict approach and standardised housing were effectively combined to organise urban space based on the socialist way of life. Similar to the approach based on the neighbourhood unit in capitalist states, the microdistrict approach had both social and spatial-technical dimensions. In addition to envisioning social relationships in self-contained urban communities, the microdistrict approach also included urbanist criteria and design details such as block size, density, population, and the disposition of public amenities. Although these two dimensions – social and technical – are intertwined, they may also have their own autonomous domains; this can make it difficult to fully understand the meaning embodied in microdistrict theory. We therefore address these two domains simultaneously based on the specific situation of North Korean society during the post-war era.

With this goal in mind, it is essential to clarify the process by which the microdistrict approach was applied to North Korean cities. North Korean planners established norms that were put into practice through urban projects; the analysis of this transformation is an important aspect of this study. Additionally, we shall cast light on how North Korea's social framework and everyday life were shaped by urban design. In Foucauldian terms, 'space is a vital part of the battle for control and surveillance of individuals.'[2] In North Korea urban design assumed the dominant role in penetrating the world of domestic life. This erasure of the division between public and private life in North Korean urban and residential spaces created a unique lifestyle that is very different to life in the capitalist world.

The Social Meaning of the Microdistrict Approach in North Korea

Interestingly, discussions of the self-contained urban unit erupted in the 1920s independently of political ideology. The concept of a neighbourhood was not specifically addressed by Western urban planners until the nineteenth and early twentieth centuries. However, as suburban areas around large American cities grew in the 1920s, urban planners began investigating dimensions and amenities for neighbourhood units. This research led to the publication of Clarence A. Perry's paper 'The Neighborhood Unit' in 1929. The Soviet Union explored a similar concept, but its purpose was different, deriving from the comprehensive effort to find settlement patterns compatible with socialist ideology. In the 1920s a new concept of the urban unit called *sotsgorod* (socialist city) emerged as an important principle in industrial cities, and in the 1930s Stalin-era planners created a type of urban block called the *kvartal* (quarter) as an autonomous urban unit. The *kvartal* quickly became established as one of the principal ways to control urban form and density in large cities in the USSR.

However, the Stalinist *kvartal* was incompatible with the kind of large-scale construction needed to solve the deteriorating shortage of housing. The Soviet government therefore changed its housing policy to promote standardisation and prefabrication. Based on this approach, Soviet architects developed an apartment house model known as the *khrushchevka*; this spread throughout countries in the communist bloc, together with the microdistrict approach. At the fifth Congress of the International Union of Architects (IUA), held in Moscow in 1958, delegates approved a resolution that 'planning and construction of housing should be based on the principle of the microdistrict',[3] with the latter's size dependent on realistic economic, geographical, and social conditions. From this moment forwards, the microdistrict approach became a basic principle of city planning in communist countries. According to S. Strumilin, this approach promoted the purpose of a socialist society by supporting collectivised living for workers and releasing women from the drudgery of housework.[4] The microdistrict thus reached beyond its spatial-technical dimensions to achieve cultural and social significance. We can observe these dual dimensions in the microdistricts of North Korea.

Formation of social frameworks
When Soviet forces began amphibious landings in Korea on 14 August 1945 and rapidly took over the north of the country just after the end of World War II, the Korean peninsula divided into two states. Afterwards, North Korean leaders set out to build a socialist state through diverse legal reforms. On 5 March 1946, Kim Il Sung, then the head of the interim people's committee, published a land reform bill legalising confiscation of all land. In the same year the North Korean leaders published a '20-point platform' (*Gangryeong*) intended to serve as a constitution; this clarified the government's character and fundamental mission. These platforms specified equal rights for the sexes, including an eight-hour workday, and reform of the educational system. Due to the Korean War, however, further progress was not made.

The Korean Armistice Agreement was signed on 27 July 1953. The death of Joseph Stalin several months earlier changed the East Asian political landscape. Khrushchev's de-Stalinisation programme put intense pressure on the Stalinist governments of China and North Korea and led to serious conflicts, particularly between the Soviet Union and China. Under pressure from these circumstances, Kim responded to the leadership change in the Soviet Union with sensitivity. When Kim visited Moscow on 20 April 1955, he was encouraged to fundamentally modify his country's existing policies.[5] Thereafter, the North Korean regime changed course, encouraging light industry and agriculture alongside heavy industry. North Korea also began to establish laws and regulations regulating its citizens' everyday life. Such measures mirrored Khrushchev's reforms during the 1950s. The introduction of the microdistrict-based approach to urban planning was thus inextricably linked to the circumstances at the time.

A social framework addressing education, women, labour, status classification, and a monitoring system was developed in approximately 1958. A significant moment in the history of North Korea, the year 1958 was when Kim Il Sung took political power into his hands, preparatory to seizing unlimited power. This is when the Chollima movement began in earnest. Following in the USSR's footsteps, North Korea expedited construction of standardised mass housing, women's participation in economic activities, the establishment of mandatory education, and the distribution of goods. An important element in the formation of these social systems in urban spaces was the planning of microdistricts; these served as a guideline for the mass construction of housing that accompanied the rise of Kim Jong Il in 1973.

To ease the labour shortage it faced during its construction boom, the North Korean regime used women's labour. Classical Marxists of the nineteenth and early twentieth centuries had developed a theoretical framework tying the fight for women's liberation to the struggle for socialism. In line with this notion, the North Korean regime enacted laws regarding women immediately after the state's liberation. In 1957 the North Korean regime introduced a five-year plan that included deploying more women workers on shop floors. This idea was formulated in law in Cabinet Decision no. 84, 'On the deployment of more women's labour forces in economic sectors', published on 19 July 1958.[6] To compel women to participate in every sector of the economy, the North Korean cabinet determined as follows: 1) to increase the proportion of women working in education and public health sectors to over 60% and in other sectors to over 30%; 2) to replace men and employ women in positions in which women can work; 3) to create nurseries, kindergartens, and common laundry facilities using existing public buildings and enterprises to ensure women's participation in social activities; 4) to implement various time-based wage systems so as to extensively employ women in workplaces and to operate kindergartens to suit women's working hours; and 5) to increase the number of women attending colleges, training schools, and vocational schools. The third clause in this decision, which addressed women's housework and provision of childcare facilities, was reflected in microdistrict planning. To reduce demands on women's housekeeping, rice factories, food factories, and domestic workshops were established in microdistricts. This enabled an increase in the female part of the workforce from 19.9% in 1956 to 38.5% in 1964 and 45.5% in 1971.[7]

North Korea's educational system influenced block sizes in the planning of microdistricts. Before the Korean War, North Korea's school system had consisted of a four-year elementary school, a three-year junior middle school, a three-year senior middle school, and a four-year college. However, a bill passed by the Supreme People's Assembly of the Korean Workers' Party on 10 October 1959 modified this system. Senior middle school was replaced with a two-year technical school and a two-year higher technical school. The point of the modification was to prepare for nine-year obligatory education (4 years, 3 years, and 2 years) for all students in 1966.[8] The new system focused on technical education because the deficit of skilled workers was a serious barrier to North Korea's economic development. However, this school system confused the East German architects in charge of rebuilding Hamhŭng, the second largest city in North Korea. Because elementary school in North Korea lasted only four years, there were fewer students to be accommodated than in German schools, which meant that German criteria were not readily applicable to North Korea and had to be adapted.

Since the late 1950s the North Korean regime has tightly controlled the everyday lives of its people by means of diverse social systems. The North Korean regime organised networks to strengthen its ability to control and monitor its citizens through a classification system based on individuals' backgrounds and political tendencies. North Korean totalitarianism was maintained through a number of powerful methods of social control, the most elaborate and intrusive of which was the *songbun* classification system. The *songbun* system divides the country's population into 51 categories – or ranks – of trustworthiness and loyalty to the Kim family and the North Korean state. These categories are grouped into three broad castes: the 'core', 'wavering', and 'hostile' classes. In a speech made in 1958 Kim Il Sung reported that the core, wavering, and hostile classes constituted 25%, 55%, and 20% of the population respectively.[9] Although these proportions have varied over time, the classification system has led to the stratification of urban spaces and living standards.

Control was further reinforced by the central distribution system. In its Cabinet Decision no. 102 of 3 November 1957 'On the National Sole System for Sale of Food', the North Korean regime abolished free sale of food and introduced a comprehensive distribution system for all workers and office employees. The North Korean regime also announced Cabinet Decision no. 82 on 16 July 1958 'On the Improvement of Domestic Commerce';[10] this determined the number and size of commercial facilities by calculating distribution to inhabitants and their needs. The irregularly distributed commercial network was accordingly unified into a national distribution system whereby location was determined through microdistrict planning. Implementation of this centralised distribution system had a severe impact on the everyday lives of North Koreans by preventing residents from choosing where they lived and worked. Homes were assigned to citizens based on their origins and the classification system; they were not permitted to move arbitrarily. Additionally, the distribution of food based on rank and achievement encouraged socialist competition.[11] Many workers formed shock brigades and engaged in competitions to improve quality of production.[12]

The proximity of living and working spaces was one of the key principles of socialist urbanism.[13] In China a work unit called a *danwei* offered its employees lifetime employment and welfare, including public housing and medical care. A typical work unit integrated

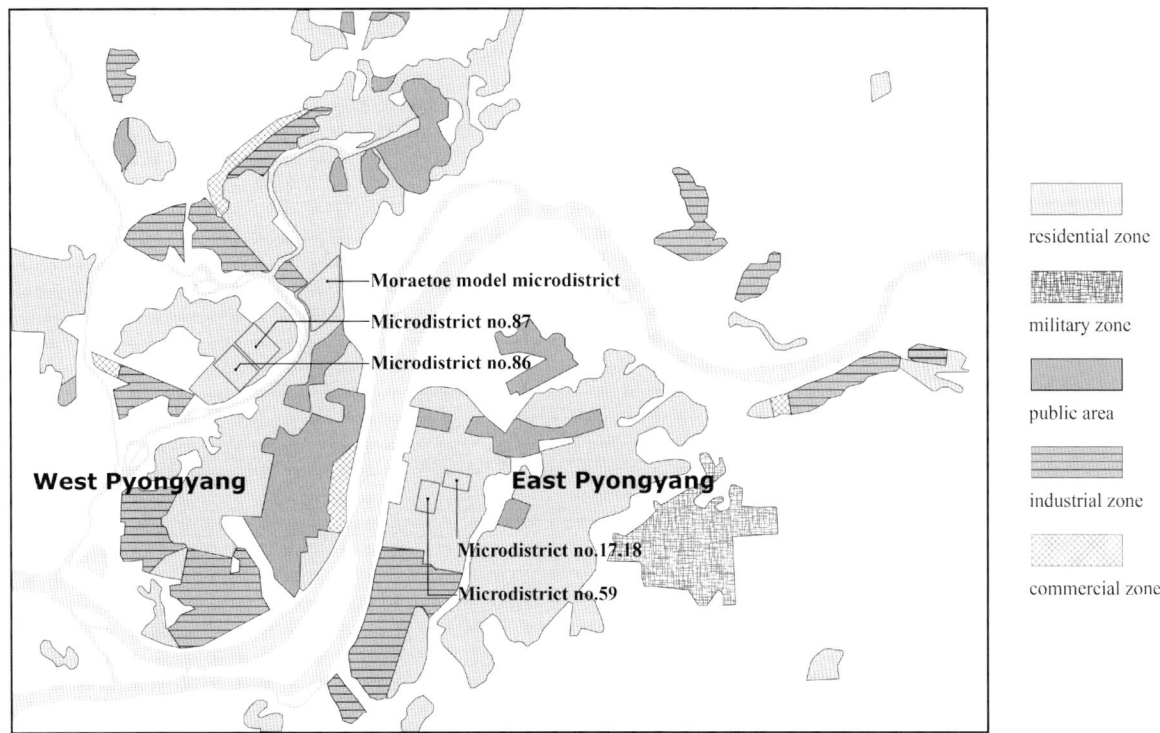

Zoning map and locations of microdistricts in Pyongyang in the late 1960s.
Source: Bukhanui guktogaebal pyeonlam. (1992), p. 168, redrawn by the authors

work, residential, and social facilities in close proximity within one or several walled compounds. This characteristic form had a profound impact on urbanism under Mao.[14] North Korea attempted to maintain the proximity of residential and work spaces without placing them together in a single urban unit as in China. Instead, factories and manufacturing facilities were concentrated in industrial zones, and housing complexes were arranged around these zones. Pyongyang, the capital, retained three industrial zones that had been created in the colonial period. In the 1960s large-scale housing complexes such as Botongbeol and East Pyongyang were intensively developed around these zones, as can be seen in the illustration on this page, which shows Pyongyang zoning maps from the 1960s.

Type no.1

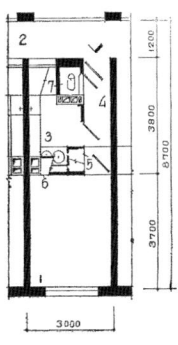

Type no.2

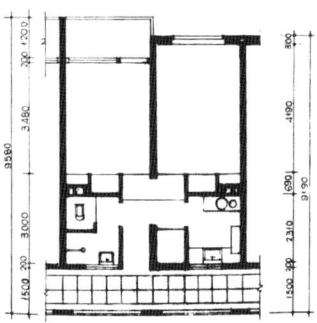

Type no.3

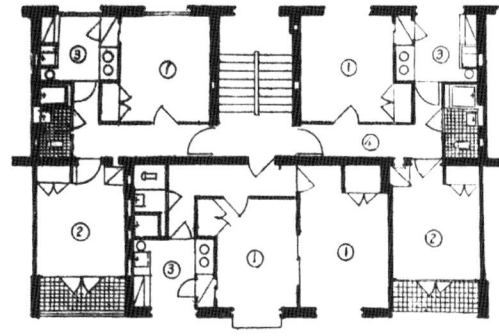

Special house

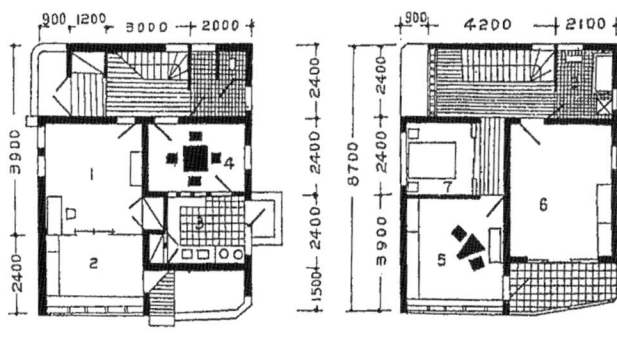

the first floor   the second floor

Categorisation of unit plans based on the classification system.
Sources: Geonchukgwa Geonseol. Jun., (1967), p. 8; Ibid., Feb., (1962), p. 27; Ibid., Jan., (1959), p. 40; Ibid., Dec., (1964): unknown

The Socialist Way of Life and the Birth of a New Communism

North Korea's social framework had many different effects on daily life. Above all, the construction of mass housing fleshed out the socialist way of life with physical form,[15] as the North Korean regime adopted the mass-housing policies of the Khrushchev era. On 31 July 1957 the Soviet government published a new decree, 'On the Advancement of Housing Construction in the Soviet Union', after Khrushchev had announced his de-Stalinisation plan.[16] A core component of Khrushchev's reform, this law marked the beginning of the campaign to deal with the housing crisis. Three months later, the Central Committee of the Korean Worker's Party increased the rate of prefabrication in housing construction to 50%. The North Korean media continued to emphasise standardisation of design, industrialisation of components, and mechanisation of construction,[17] all of which would be important for the construction of 14,000 residential units in Pyongyang and 16,000 units in the surrounding region by 1958.[18] Kim Il Sung's regime mobilised the masses as a way of coping with labour shortages, limited resources, and low-level technology. The Chollima movement and the myth of so-called 'Pyongyang speed' were born in 1958. The movement – similar in purpose and character to the Stakhanovite movement in the Soviet Union and the Great Leap Forward in China – was a campaign of mass mobilisation based on 'volunteer' labour. White-collar workers and students were required to assist in high-speed urban-reconstruction projects.[19]

To improve productivity in this movement, the North Korean regime gave preferential treatment to labourers who surpassed their targets, honouring them with titles such as 'effort hero' or 'republic hero'. This was similar to the Stakhanovite movement in the Soviet Union, where workers who exceeded production targets could become heroes of socialist labour. In this process, labourers soon emerged as a new ruling class, replacing high-ranking officials purged during the August Faction Incident.[20] Strong incentives for hard labour were tied to housing. Following the North Korean land reform of 1946 that confiscated land and prohibited its ownership, North Koreans were only able to rent homes of determinate sizes. These were assigned based on the classification system and the renter's status, and rent was paid monthly. Until the late 1980s, when high-rise apartments first appeared in North Korea's large cities, four housing types were available: types 1 and 2 for common workers and office workers, type 3 for middle-grade officers, and special houses for high-ranking and high-profile officers.[21]

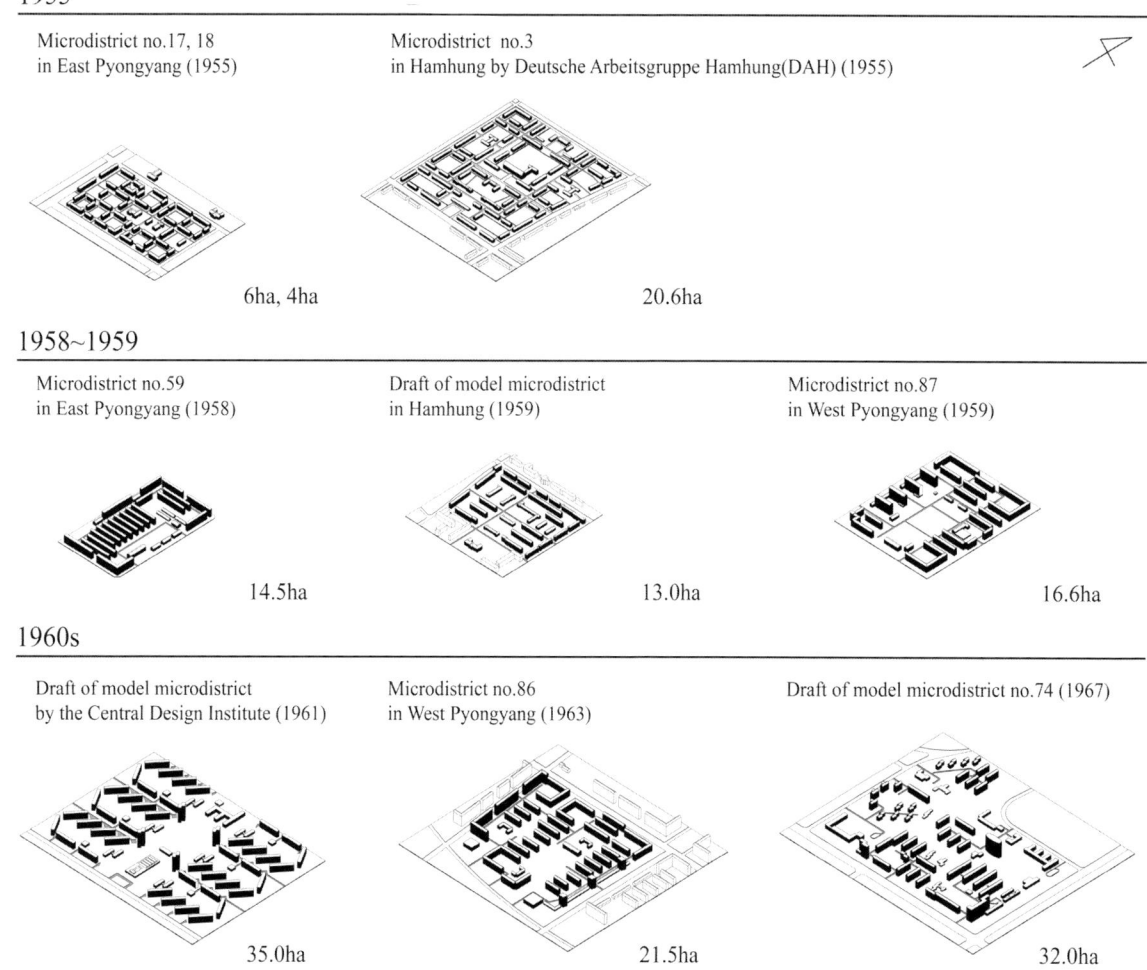

Large microdistricts in North Korea from the mid-1950s to the 1960s (redrawn by the authors).

Like the incentive system, residential space was a tool used by the North Korean regime to promote social control. This goal permeated everyday life through the 'people's unit'. The people's unit was a basic social group consisting of more than 15 households in which collective and private life coexisted.[22] Staircases in apartment buildings usually served as the boundaries separating units.[23] The head of each unit was the distributor of food, fuel, and necessities and was also a strict monitor of residents' behaviour. This person was also in charge of mobilising people for social and national events. Because North Koreans occupied the same housing for long periods of time, it was important to maintain positive, interactive relationships within a unit.[24] People's lifestyles in these units were completely different from those in neighbourhoods or administrative units in capitalist cities; this was a system which allowed the North Korean surveillance system to operate at the level of micro-control. The formation of the people's unit subdivided the microdistrict into primary residential units (*chogeup saenghwal danwi*); meeting places for purposes of ideological education were added. This development also explains why the single-corridor-access apartment was the preferred type of housing in North Korea.

The North Korean regime continued to produce ideological propaganda that concealed social problems and made its own totalitarian system sustainable. Rapid construction had numerous negative side effects. Although standardised mass housing greatly helped in solving the housing shortage, it made the cityscape of North Korean cities very homogeneous; these houses' residential interiors were incongruous with traditional ways of life. To alleviate problems caused by the extreme pace of construction, Kim Il Sung 'promoted enhancement of the quality of overall socialist construction as the most important task' and advocated for intensification of ideological education since he believed that old capitalist thoughts and vestigial feudalistic ideas were what was preventing construction of housing fit for the socialist era.[25, 26] Kim Il Sung's arguments also applied to the North Korean government. Its cabinet resolved that the 'cultural, hygienic, and techno-economic management of rapidly constructed cities can meet requirements for citizens' housing and cultural life.'[27] The Central Committee of the North Korean Federation of All Occupations insisted that 'parents should raise their children in the communist way of life by reforming themselves into thoroughgoing communists through a single-minded struggle against old customs inherited from the previous generation.'[28]

Everyday spaces were accordingly required to be cultural and hygienic and reflect the socialist way of life: fitting homes for a generation of new North Korean communists who would be supermen labouring selflessly for the new communist state. As a result, North Korea's social system succeeded in raising a thoroughly obedient human type. Visitors to North Korea today are struck by how North Koreans' reality is entirely trapped within a liar's box.[29] Deprived of any chance to choose another reality, North Koreans struggle to be faithful to the present.

Planning of, and Technical Criteria for, Microdistricts in North Korea

The origin of the *mikrorayon* (microdistrict) in the Soviet Union can be traced to dissatisfaction with the Stalinist *kvartal*. There were serious problems with these 5–6-hectare traditional urban blocks. Because public amenities could only be economically provided to 6000–8000 inhabitants per block, the existing blocks – which accommodated only 4000 residents – were too small. Moreover, children walking to schools in different blocks had to cross potentially dangerous roads. Another drawback of Stalinist housing districts was their inefficient use of land: roads occupied 20–25% of the land area.[30] The microdistrict offered solutions to these problems. After the fifth congress of the International Union of Architects (IUA) in July 1958, North Korea and other communist countries officially accepted the microdistrict as a basic unit of urbanism.

The microdistrict approach was introduced to North Korea through two channels: the Soviet Union and East Germany. The first mainly involved North Korean students who had studied architecture and urban planning in the Soviet Union; upon their return, these students brought with them the newest planning theories. One such was Kim Jeong-Hui, who played a leading role in drawing up plans for Pyongyang in the 1950s. A look at North Korean architectural magazines in the post-war era shows that Soviet urban-planning theories were translated into Korean immediately after being published. In the case of East Germany, the German Work Team Hamhŭng (Deutsche Arbeitsgruppe Hamhŭng, DAG) was despatched to Hamhŭng in 1954 after the East German Politburo agreed with then prime minister Grotewohl that assistance was needed to reconstruct Hamhŭng.[31,32] Grotewohl appointed his own son, Hans Grotewohl, an architect, as head of the DAG to direct this project. The next year, 143 East German experts, including city planners, architects, engineers, economic specialists, and master craftsmen, landed in Hamhŭng.[33] Equipped with modern machines and tools, this autonomous work brigade began to rebuild the entire city, including its housing, office buildings, streets, and all other necessary infrastructure.[34]

Originally planned as a ten-year project from 1955 to 1964, the reconstruction of Hamhŭng had its prorgamme reduced to eight years when all East German experts were withdrawn in 1962.[35] During the first four years (1955–1958), the East German architects constructed 5193 household units and urban structures in Hamhŭng and Hungnam.[36] Their approach to designing housing estates followed the Bauhaus tradition with additional strong influence from Soviet methods and practice. The plans also reflected the specific local situation. Konrad Püschel, a student of Wassily Kandinsky at the Bauhaus, was the head of city planning for the Hamhŭng project from 1955 to 1959.[37] In Hamhŭng Püschel paid close attention to traditional Korean city forms and spatial relationships: instead of modernity affecting tradition, 'tradition finds a new context in our society.'[38] According to a report by the DAG, the East German architects and planners drew attention to the economic importance of standard criteria for building-to-land ratio and housing density and transformed the East German standard criteria into criteria suitable for North Korea.[39] The main differences, they believed, came from environmental factors such as climate, geography, soil, and specific social conditions, such as large families.[40] However, after bruising debates with Kim Il Sung and North Korean planners over construction methods and costs, the DAG's experts began pulling out of housing construction in North Korea in 1958, and the East German government decided to sharply reduce its aid to North Korea in 1960.[41]

Photo of construction site for Microdistrict no. 3 in Hamhŭng.
Sources: Bauhaus Dessau Archives (unknown)

Photo of construction site in Hamhŭng.
Sources: Bauhaus Dessau Archives (unknown)

Table 1.

Living floor area	Number of inhabitants	Density (person/ha)		Size of microdistrict (ha)		School
		2~3story	4~5story	2~3story	4~5story	A 10-year, 20-class school/ a 7-year, 14-class school
Under 6 m²/person	12,000	450	700	32-34	22-24	Two rotations of people's school and one rotation of middle schools
Over 6 m²/person	8~9,000	300	470	32-34	22-24	One rotation of all schools

Table 1. Li Sun-Gwon's proposal for microdistrict sizes, based on diverse variables.
Source: Geonchukgwa Geonseol Feb. 1958, p. 20, redrawn by the authors

Microdistrict size

It was not until East German architects produced their reconstruction plan for Hamhŭng that schools became a central factor in the design of North Korean housing estates. The architects selected schools as their criterion for calculating numbers of residents and the size of housing estates.[42] One specific problem, however, was that the two countries had different school systems. Until 1959 North Korea's system comprised four years of elementary school, three years of junior middle school, and three years of senior middle school.[43] German architects accordingly assumed seven years (elementary school plus junior middle school) to be the equivalent of German elementary school. However, due to the deficit of school buildings, the North Korean regime had introduced a three-shift rotation system, tripling the number of students studying at each school. If a three-shift rotation system and seven-year school were assumed, the sustainable population for a microdistrict would be approximately 3000 and its size vary from 8 to 36 hectares, depending on building height.

This standard is clearly documented in the report submitted by the North Korean delegation to the fifth meeting of the International Union of Architects (IUA) in Moscow in July 1958.[44] According to the report, 'our aim is to build self-contained residential blocks and neighbourhood units. In some towns this principle has already made considerable headway. The dimensions of a residential block depend on the number of school-age children accommodated in a single school. On this basis the population of a block varies from 3000 to 3500.'

Subsequently, North Korean experts introduced various other ideas regarding the size of microdistricts. Like experts in the Soviet Union, they were concerned that the previous block-centred plan made it impossible to place schools and kindergartens in a rational way, division into recreational areas and public spaces would be difficult, and building orientation would be unattractive.[45] Instead, they thought it of urgent importance to establish a rational scheme, standards, and methods tailored to the local situation. Li Sun-Gwon's article 'On a Rational Method of Housing-section Construction Using Standardised Design' first explored methods of calculating the size of a new microdistrict. Li Sun-Gwon suggested using three variables: living space per person, building height, and number of students in an elementary school.[46] However, Kim U-Ho's article 'On Architectural Density in

Table 2.

Geographical conditions	Standard height of buildings	Number of inhabitants	Size of microdistrict (ha)
flat, virgin site surrounded by four roads	4~5 story	10,000	30
an uneven site surrounded by green space on two or three sides	2~3 story	4,000~8,000	20~40
a downtown area	integration of existing small blocks (4-12 ha) into microdistrict		

Table 2. Classification of microdistricts in accordance with geographical conditions.
Source: Geonchukgwa Geonseol, Dec.1961, p. 21, redrawn by the authors

Microdistricts' suggested a different method of calculation. He referred to microdistricts no. 31 in West Pyongyang and no. 23 on Stalin Street, both of which consist of six-storey buildings. Here, the sizes of the microdistricts were expected to be different. According to Kim, if a ten-year, 20-class school were erected, the microdistrict would have a population of 7400 and be 11–12 hectares in size.[47] These were smaller and denser than other microdistricts because Kim based his calculations on microdistricts in downtown Pyongyang. It became clear that a key criterion in planning a microdistrict should be the number of residents supported by its school. However, the Central Design Institute, which was under the umbrella of the National Construction Committee, determined that there should be three types of microdistrict. Each would be tailored to geographical conditions such as site size and shape, topography, geology, and location.[48] The Central Design Institute drew up a model based on the first of the three microdistrict designs: 35 hectares with an anticipated population of 10,800. This was an economical design, with 15% lower construction costs and 40% less paved road area than the Stalinist block-centred model.[49]

When Li Sun-Gwon and Baek Wan-Gi published *The Planning of Microdistricts* in 1963, they synthesised various discussions about the size of microdistricts. To ensure convenient and comfortable living conditions for residents, a school for 880–1200 pupils and a 350-place kindergarten could, they believed, become the standard size for microdistricts. Under these guidelines, it would make most sense for a microdistrict to cover an area of 15–20 hectares and accommodate 5000–7000 inhabitants – smaller than under previous calculation methods.[50] However, a microdistrict of less than 10 hectares would be too small to guarantee convenience for residents. Reducing construction costs was another important factor. Because the construction costs of paved roads, water supplies, sewer systems, and heating systems depended on the size of the microdistrict, it was essential to find a suitable balance among these requirements.[51] Considering requirements such as residents' convenience, working conditions, transportation, the economics of urban construction, city size, and building height, they therefore concluded that a microdistrict covering 15–30 hectres and housing 5000–10,000 inhabitants would be most suitable for North Korea, as demonstrated in contemporary North Korean cities. Statistically, the average size of microdistricts in 14 cities (Pyongyang, Hamhŭng, Chongjin, Wonsan, Sariwon, Sinuiju, Kaesong, Kanggye, Haeju, Hyesan, Songrim, Nampo, Kimchaek, and Sinpo) is 15–25 hectares with building heights of 4–5 storeys.

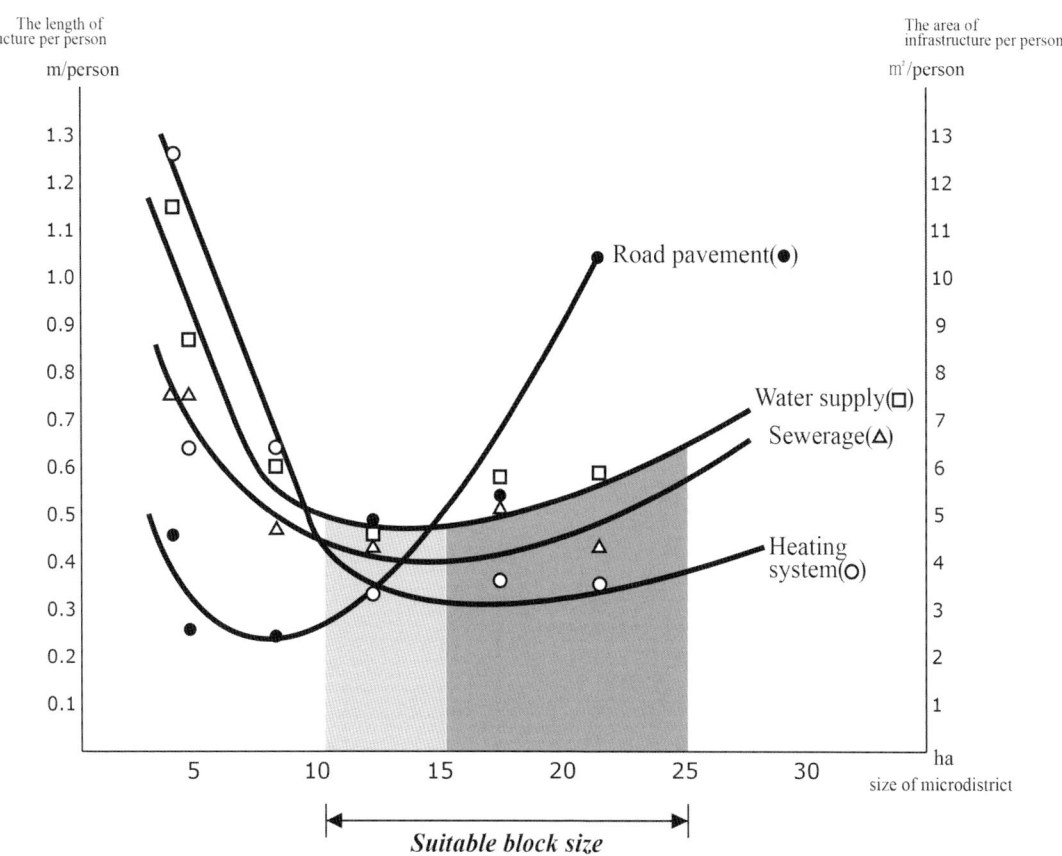

A graph showing how to determine the appropriate size of a microdistrict.
Source: Li, Sun-gwon and Baek, Wan-gi, Jutaek soguyeok gyehoek. 1963, p. 43

Building layout and transportation

Just as determining the ideal size of a microdistrict presented challenges, so did designing block layouts. Here architects had to consider a combination of cityscape, housing type, structure height, distance between buildings, and transportation. In Kim Jeong-Hui's *Urban Construction*, published in 1953, how buildings were positioned in a city block was heavily influenced by Stalinist-era principles. Buildings were located on the perimeters of traditional urban blocks (*kvartaly*, or 'quarters'). According to Kim, this arrangement was convenient for residents, protected the interiors of urban blocks from heavy traffic, subordinated individual buildings to the overall composition of the cityscape, and avoided buildings becoming isolated.[52] This type of site layout dominated reconstruction plans for North Korean cities in the mid-1950s,[53] as can be seen in the initial layouts for Pyongyang and Hamhŭng.

However, this approach changed when microdistricts no. 17 and no. 18 in East Pyongyang were planned in 1955. These districts adhered to the perimeter layout of traditional urban blocks, but with one difference: the new layout left the blocks' corners open, making the blocks' inner courtyards more accessible. The Hamhŭng housing complexes designed by East German architects in 1955 had a similar layout. Open block corners allowed the buildings to have 3.0–3.5-metre-wide roads inside the block, providing access to each household. However, as these roads became longer, this led to increased construction costs and created dangers for children.[54] Both of these problems conflicted with the original goals for microdistricts.

From 1958 to 1961, a different layout dominated microdistrict construction. This approach used the 'Zeilenbau' style of row housing as a replacement for the previous arrangement based on the urban block. Microdistrict no. 59 in East Pyongyang shows that although the block perimeter continued to consist of five-storey buildings so as to create a consistent cityscape, the inside of the city block underwent significant changes. Unlike the previous block layout, in which the courtyard was surrounded by four buildings, the new layout used parallel rows of four-storey apartment buildings aligned east-west. This change occurred after the single-corridor-access apartment building (*oerangsik*) was widely adopted as standard. The introduction of prefabrication also influenced this new microdistrict layout. All units in microdistrict no. 59 were built using one of four standard plans; this simplified the construction process and reduced the time and labour involved.[55] However, the high density of the long, monotonous parallel buildings failed to produce harmony in the urban context. The distance between buildings also failed to satisfy requirements. The model microdistrict no. 86 in Daetaryeong, the microdistrict no. 87 in West Pyongyang, and the model microdistrict erected in 1959 in Hamhŭng also shared this layout but solved these problems by incorporating variety in how the buildings were arranged.

Finally, yet another microdistrict layout was introduced between 1961 and 1967, this time using apartment buildings that were eight to 12 storeys high – as seen in the 1961 proposal for model microdistricts by the Central Design Institute.[56] Although not used immediately, this was subsequently implemented in model microdistrict no. 74. From this point forwards, the practice of fringing the perimeter of a microdistrict with buildings was abandoned.[57] Instead, buildings were aligned obliquely in rows. This change was a consequence of microdistricts' increasing population density and the construction of high-rise buildings. To break up the monotony of the block layouts, North Korean architects aimed to design more open and more diverse cityscapes. Despite not all rooms having equal sunlight, this layout was more visually appealing. The more open arrangement influenced the road systems inside the city block: street networks changed so that primary residential units could be directly accessed only by arterial roads. This arrangement reduced road length, which lowered construction costs and resulted in buildings being arranged more freely around primary living units. A proposal for a model microdistrict in 1961 consisted of six primary residential units, an organic arrangement of buildings, and inner streets that were directly accessible from outside the microdistrict. This design made it possible to build microdistricts on sloped suburban land.[58]

(a) Perimetric blocks :
The detailed drawing of city center in Hamhung

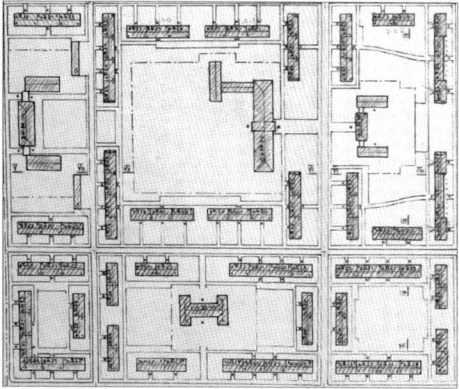

(b) Open corners :
Microdistrict no.3 in Hamhung developed by DAH

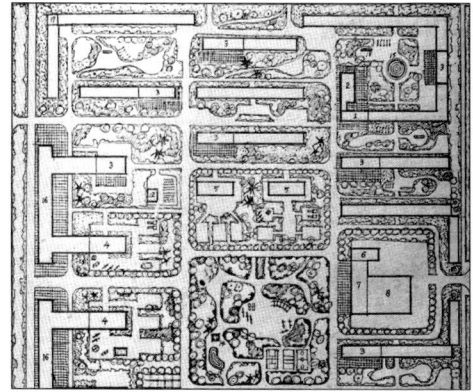

(c) Parallel rows :
Microdistrict no.87 in West Pyonyang

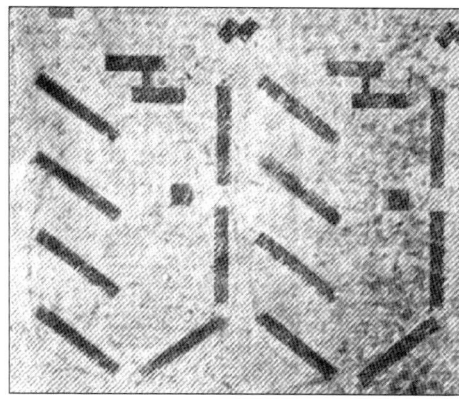

(d) Oblique alignment :
The draft of model microdistrict developed by Central Design Institute

The building layout of microdistricts.
Sources: Bauhaus Dessau Archives (unknown); ibid., (I_010014_D); Geonchukgwa Geonseol. Feb.1959:9; Ibid., Dec.1961, p. 21

(a) Distributed commercial facilites
: Microdistrict no.59 in East Pyongyang

(b) Added family restaurants
: Microdistrict no.87 in West Pyonyang

(c) Intergrated public buildings
: Draft of model microdistrict developed by Central Design Institute

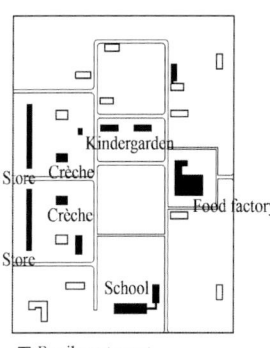
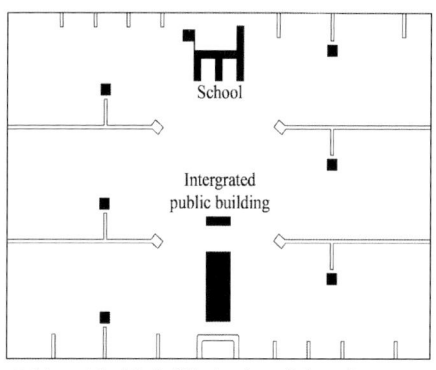

Organisation of service networks in microdistricts (redrawn by the authors).

Organisation of service networks

The organisation of service networks in North Korea's microdistricts changed over time. Among the first service facilities to be planned were networks of shops, the number and size of which were decided based on the distribution and needs of residents. This decision was announced in Cabinet Decision no. 82 on 16 July 1958 'On Improving Domestic Commerce'.[59] It was implemented on an urban scale by Pyongyang Urban Design Institute. There were two types of commercial network: general stores selling industrial products and branch stores selling groceries and everyday necessities. One general store was assigned to every 20,000 people. These stores were situated at a maximum radius of 400 metres from housing, meaning that they could be reached after a journey of no more than six minutes on foot. One branch store was assigned to every 5000 people. Branch stores were situated within a maximum radius of 300 metres or a 4–5-minute trip on foot from houses. This meant that each 15-hectare microdistrict had two branch stores and there was one general store per two microdistricts.[60]

Another point of contention was whether service facilities were to be located in their own buildings or on the ground floor of residential buildings. Planners viewed independent buildings as preferable to ground floors in that they allowed a more flexible organisation of interior space and were safer for children. Although it was recommended that large facilities should occupy independent buildings, convenience stores could be located on the grounds floor of ordinary houses.[61] This principle can be seen in microdistrict no. 59 in East Pyongyang, designed in December 1958. Although microdistrict no. 59 had no general store due to its small size, it had two branch stores selling everyday necessities and groceries. These stores were independent buildings and formed the centre of the microdistrict, along with educational facilities, baths, and clothing co-ops, all of which were clustered near schools.[62] However, once this plan had been built, problems were revealed: the school was next to major roads, which made it difficult to guarantee children's safety, and the microdistrict's centre was open only on one side and so did not have an organic connection with the services network.

Another focus in implementation of microdistricts' service networks was effective use of women's labour. In this context the communal canteen emerged as an important feature of service facilities. Calculating the canteen's size presented a challenge since planners had to consider the traditional family system. During the initial development phase, when East German planners were in charge of site planning of housing complexes in Hamhŭng, family size was considered an important factor.[63] Thus the East German planners proposed a variety of unit types to accommodate families of different sizes. Families with 4–6 members accounted for 46.3% of the anticipated population of a microdistrict, and families with nine members accounted for over 5%; this meant that large families had to be taken into account during early planning. Accordingly, although a communal restaurant was included in the 1955 plan for microdistrict no. 3, it was intended to play only an auxiliary role in providing meals to residents. This planning method was continued in the model microdistrict designed by Hamhŭng Urban Design Institute in February 1959. Two restaurants with a total area of 900 m² were situated on the ground floor of a building at the centre of the district.[64]

However, this plan was modified three months later, most notably with regard to the size of the families to be accommodated. The new plan reduced the habitable area of each home and increased the number of residents in such a way that most families were to be accommodated in one-, two-, and three-room apartments. Large families were split up into single occupants or nuclear families. This meant that urbanisation in North Korea in the 1950s broke up traditional family culture. Accordingly, the role of the communal dining room in microdistricts increased in importance. Later, two 660 m² restaurants were built in addition to the first restaurant, which had a floor are of 1215 m².[65]

This approach was continued in subsequent projects. For model microdistrict no. 87 in West Pyongyang, Pyongyang Urban Design Institute added a food factory and a family restaurant to the existing educational and commercial facilities. The food factory processed vegetables and grains, saving labour for households and providing family restaurants with ready-to-use ingredients. One factory would be built at the centre of each microdistrict with 5000–6000 inhabitants. The family restaurant would provide residents with meals, using ready-to-use ingredients from the factory. North Korean planners expected that 50% of residents would use these restaurants, especially the elderly and families with children. Based on this prediction, a family restaurant, located on the ground floor, was included in every two residential buildings.[66]

In the 1960s service facilities in microdistricts tended to occupy part of another building. At the National Builders Congress in April 1961, Nam Il, then vice prime minister and chief of the National Construction Committee, cited the resolution issued by Kim Il Sung as the basis for four important decisions in the construction sector.[67] These affected the design of service networks in microdistricts. In May 1961 the National Construction Committee established the principle that public buildings should be built to accommodate a number of different but similar functions.[68] It also determined that primary residential units should be placed around these integrated buildings. This change of approach informed the plan for a model microdistrict published by the Central Design Institute in December 1961 in which the microdistrict consisted of an integrated public building and six primary residential units. The building's ground floor accommodated a family restaurant, a shop selling semi-prepared oods, and rooms for hygiene instructors from the people's unit; the second floor contained workshops for domestic manufacturers.[68]

Table 3.

Inhabitants of city	Hierarchy of city			
	Microdistrict	Residential District	Residential Zone	City
Small cities with 10,000~30,000 inhabitants	Microdistrict with 5,000 inhabitants			City
Large cities II with 100,000~200,000 inhabitants/ middle cities with 30,000~100,000 inhabitants	Microdistrict with 5,000-100,000 inhabitants	Residential District with 20,000-30,000 inhabitants		City
Extra-Large cities and Large cities I with over 200,000 inhabitants	Microdistrict with 5,000-100,000 inhabitants	Residential District with 40,000-50,000 inhabitants	Residential Zone with 100,000-150,000 inhabitants	City

Hierarchical division of urban spaces in accordance with number of inhabitants.
Source: Li, Sun-gwon and Baek, Wan-gi, op.cit, p. 105

Residential districts and urban centres

The microdistrict approach was soon applied on a larger scale: that of the residential district (*Jutaek Guyeok*). The context for this expansion was provided by the Soviet Union. 'When the third Party programme was published and the 22nd Party Congress indicated the path to communism in 1961, a new driving force was the impending communist future.'[70] To foster a proto-communist consciousness among the population, it was necessary to supply efficient service facilities needed in everyday life by grouping them in accordance with frequency of use. The ultimate goal was to realise an ideal socialist city, creating a self-contained community clustered in several microdistricts. North Korea, however, did not accept Soviet ideological rhetoric, including the 'bright communist future'; instead, it emphasised economy in housing construction.

This trend was reflected in a speech given by Nam Il in 1961 which suggested a wide range of technical innovations for housing units on the urban scale. Specifically, Nam Il stressed the following: 1) a hierarchical division into city, county, and ward on the basis of development potential and regional character; 2) widespread application of microdistrict planning to reduce construction costs for infrastructure; and 3) rejection of the current practice of aligning buildings along streets, with the aim of lowering the cost of urban construction and maintenance.[71] The purpose of these measures was to anticipate everything necessary for urban construction and to avoid waste in construction projects. Accordingly, urban planners reconsidered existing designs and drew up new plans to reduce construction costs.

Many options were considered to reduce financial waste; the emergence of the residential district concept was one of them. If service networks expanded from microdistricts into larger urban areas with similar proportions, expenditure on land and construction would be wasted. Service networks therefore began to be designed based on exact calculations of their frequency of use and capacity. In residential districts service facilities could be put into three categories: 1) those that were used daily and located in microdistricts, 2) those that were used regularly and located within a 750–1000-metre radius of the centre of a residential district, and 3) those that were used by all residents of a district.[72]

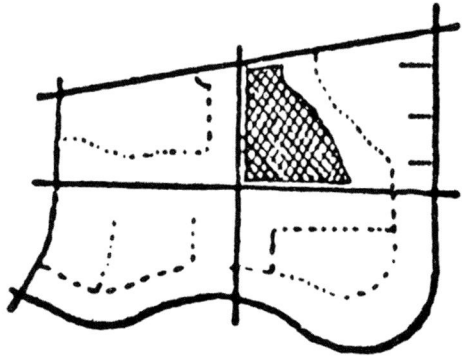

a. A planar solution

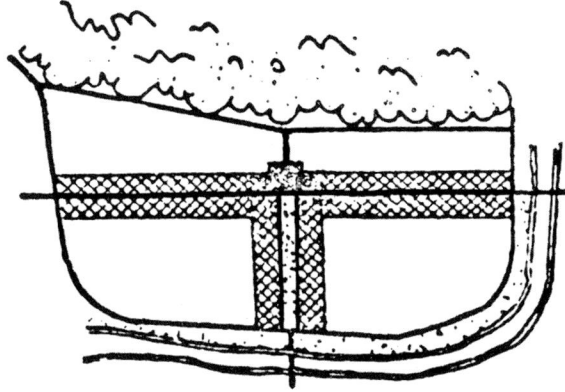

b. A linear solution

The two approaches to the design of the residential district centre.
Source: Li, Sun-gwon and Baek, Wan-gi, op. cit., p. 110

The population of a residential district varied in accordance with a city's category. The National Construction Committee put North Korean cities into five categories based on their geographical condition, character, size, and development potential; specific building heights and layouts were planned based on these categories.[73] In the light of this classification, North Korean urban planners defined a residential district as consisting of four to five microdistricts.

When planners designed the centre of a residential district, they took one of two approaches: a planar solution in which all cultural and residential functions and light industry were concentrated at the centre of the district, or a linear solution in which all facilities were arranged along arterial streets. North Korean planners who emphasised the relation between streets and service facilities preferred the latter to the former.[74] From this time forwards, North Korean designers began taking into account the relation between streets and service infrastructure when designing a microdistrict. Economic factors played a major role, as shown in Hamhŭng Urban Design Institute's explanation for its modification of a proposal for a model microdistrict published by the Central Design Institute in December 1961.[75] Although the design assumed that one side of the microdistrict would border an arterial city street, the original proposal did not take this detail into account. Hamhŭng Urban Design Institute therefore suggested approaching microdistrict planning as part of the planning of an entire city and organising service networks based on the hierarchy of roads. If any side of a microdistrict faced an arterial street, regularly used service facilities should be constructed on that side. Residential districts and urban centres could be created in this way.

This approach to urban design was implemented in the 1962 plan for Botongbeol in Pyongyang.[76] Development of the area around Bonghwa Street began during the period of the Five-Year Plan. In the first phase the architects constructed five-storey buildings around Bonghwa Street; later, they expanded the surrounding areas into model microdistricts no. 86 and no. 87. Thus the four microdistricts in this area formed a residential district. This pattern of urban development spread into other cities, such as the Munsu area of East-Pyongyang,[77] the central area of Nampo city,[78] Haeangeori in Wonsan,[79] and the centre of Sinpo.[80]

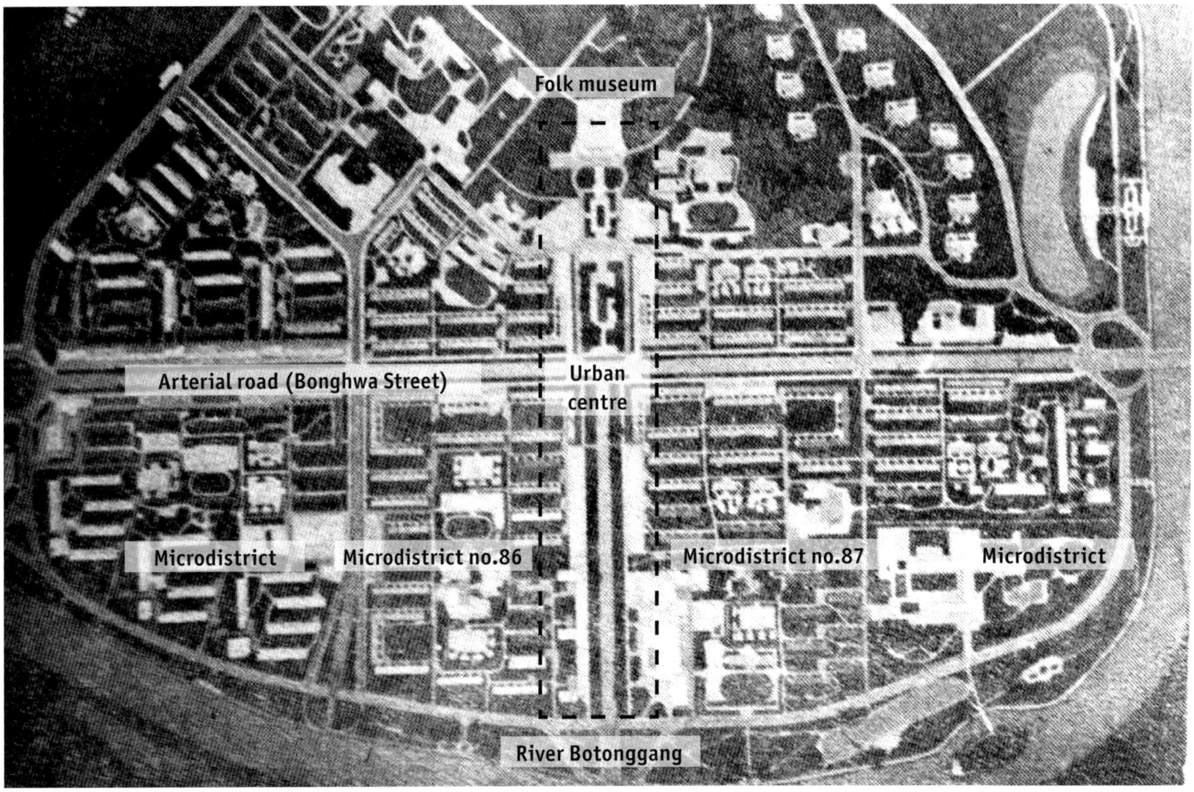

Plan for Botongbeol in West Pyongyang.
Source: Geonchukgwa Geonseol, Aug.1962, p. 34

Construction site for a Botongbeol microdistrict.
Source: Rodongsinmun. 26 Dec.1959, p.3

Conclusion

From the ceasefire that ended the Korean War in 1953 to the present time, North Korea's urban planning can be divided into three different periods. The first lasted from 1953 to the mid-1970s, when Kim Jong Il emerged as heir to the country's founder, Kim Il Sung. The second lasted from the mid-1970s to the mid-1990s, when North Korea was smitten by a great famine known as 'the Arduous March'. The third began in 2000 and is still ongoing. In each of these periods the paradigm for urban planning underwent a complete change. The microdistrict approach profoundly influenced the formation of urban space in North Korea during the first period, just as it reflected North Korea's unique social systems.

North Korean urban planners introduced the microdistrict approach, studied its advantages and disadvantages, and made it a reality. Although North Korea's social institutions were insufficiently established, microdistrict planning embodied them in the physical world by applying diverse design methods and criteria to everyday life. This played a crucial role in determining the size of self-contained urban units and the distribution of service networks in urban spaces. Moreover, microdistrict planning contributed to control of the everyday lives of North Koreans. In particular, since Kim Il Sung's regime embraced the idea of a Stalinist totalitarian state from the late 1950s forwards, urban space turned into a surveillance matrix that eradicated individual privacy. North Korean urban space thus functioned as a well-oiled machine that dominated people's morals and behaviours, thrusting political power and ideology into the most microscopic areas of daily life.

However, when Kim Jong Il became involved in official duties in 1973, he tried to alter the established urban structure by erecting audacious monuments. Not having the charisma of his father, Kim used his interventions in architectural and urban projects as a demonstration of his political capabilities.

In the process emphasis was placed on the visual order of urban form; this led to abandonment of the microdistrict-based approach. Instead, large numbers of high-rise towers were constructed to disrupt the visual monotony, and housing estates on a scale larger than that of the microdistrict or residential district were intensively developed around arterial roads. Nevertheless, the microdistrict approach survived in a more advanced form after the great famine in the mid-1990s. Internally, the planning methods of the 1970–80s were criticised because they led to serious problems with respect to road widening and orientation of buildings. Kim Jong Il and North Korean planners therefore looked for a new way to develop the existing microdistrict idea, adding the concepts of environmental conservation and the smart city. Since 2000 a number of urban projects in North Korean cities have reflected this change.

1. Li, Sun-gwon and Baek, Wan-gi (Pyongyang, 1963), pp. 36–37.
2. Elden, Stuart and Crampton, Jeremy W. (Hampshire, 2007), p. 2.
3. Smith, Smith, and Mark B. (Illinois, 2010), p .117.
4. Strumilin, S. 'Family and Community', p. 15.
5. BaekJunggi, 'Soryeon-ui hanbando anjeonghwa', pp.194–195.
6. Hwang, Ae-ri, 'Bukhan-ui yeoseong nodongjeongchaek', p. 28.
7. Park, Young-ja, 'Bukhan-ui yeoseong nodongjeongchaek', p. 137.
8. Gwon, Seonga, 'Bukhan-ui gyoyugkwajeong jeongchaek', p. 269.
9. Collins, Robert (Washington, 2012), p. 4.
10. Joseon Central News Agency, 'Guknae sangeob-eul gaeseon', p. 1.
11. Jeong, Yeong-cheol, 'Bukhan-ui sahoetongjewa jojigsaenghwal', pp. 122–123.
12. Park, Soo-heon, 'Stalin chejewa soryeonsahoe', p. 280.
13. Bater, James. H (Beverly Hills, 1980), p. 29.
14. Lu, Duanfang (Abingdon, 2006), p. 48.
15. The socialist way of life (*byt* in Russian) involves every aspect of daily life, including domestic material culture and family life; the term *byt* appeared after the Russian Revolution. This term was critically important in communist countries because of its close association with Bolshevik visions of a total resolution of the housing question.
16. Kim, Nam-sub. 'Khrushchevui lusyopeuui jutaek jeongchaek', pp. 217–218.
17. Park, Geum-cheol, 'Gibon geonseol saeop-eul gaeseonhal', p. 3.
18. Joseon Central News Agency, 'Jeolyakhayeo 2mansedae-ui', p. 2.
19. Armstrong, Charles K. (Ithaca, 2013) p. 103.
20. Yoon, Cheol-gi, 'Bukhancheje-eseo gyehoekgwa', p. 249.
21. Lee, Hang-gu. 'Bukhan-ui naemak 28', pp. 254–257.
22. Gang, Jiyeon. 'Uli inminban', pp. 161–162.
23. Ibid., 159.
24. Cha, Munseok and Kim, Ji-hyeong (Seoul, 2008), p. 100.
25. Kim Il-sung(a),'Geonseol-ui jil-eul', p. 519.
26. Ibid., 521.
27. Joseon Central News Agency, 'Dosi gyeongyeong saeobeul', p. 2.
28. Li, Hyo-sun, 'Geunrojadeul-ui saenghwaleul', p. 2.
29. in his 2015 documentary film *Under Sun* Vitaly Mansky, a Russian documentary maker, gave a rare glimpse behind the heavy curtain of secrecy in North Korea. *Sun Without You, There Is No Us: My Time with the Sons of North Korea's Elite* is a piece of non-fiction by Suki Kim, a Korean American writer, published in 2014 after she had taught for two terms at Pyongyang University of Technology.
30. State Committee of Civil Engineering and Architecture (Hawaii, 2004), pp. 85–86.
31. DAG documents can mostly be found in two archives: 1) Bundesarchiv, Berlin-Lichterfelde, DC20-630,DC20-1326,DC20-1327,DC20-1328,DC20-1426; 2) Bauhaus Dessau Archives, I_010001_D ~ I_010310_D (photo albums, reports, letters),I_1001612_D,I_1001413_D,I_1001311_D,I_1001312_D,I_1001314_D, I_1001413_D,I_1006318_D,I_1006319_D (drawings).
32. Kim, Myun, 'Gudongdok-ui dae bukhan', pp. 366–367.
33. Bundesarchiv Berlin-Lichterfelde. Bericht Über die Durchführung, p. 2.
34. Hong, Young-sun (New York, 2015), p. 60.
35. Rüdiger, Frank (Aachen, 1996), p. 113.
36. Bundesarchiv Berlin-Lichterfelde, Jahresabschlußbericht der Deutschen, p. 181.
37. Armstrong, *Tyranny of the Weak*, p. 74.
38. Ibid., p. 77.
39. For details, see Bauhaus Dessau Archives (b).
40. Bauhaus Dessau Archives, Für den Entwurf von, pp. 12–13.
41. Hong. op.cit., pp. 78–80.
42. Ibid., pp. 3–7.
43. Choi, Yeong-pyo (Seoul, 2006), p. 225.
44. IUA Inquiry Korea, pp. 2–4.
45. Li, Hyo-su, 'Dosi gyehoek-eseo pyojun seolgye-e', pp. 7–9.
46. Li, Sun-gwon, 'Pyojun seolgye-e uihan jutaek', p. 20.
47. Kim, U-ho. 'Soguyeok jojikeseoui geonchuk mildo-e daehayeo' , p. 37.
48. Gukgageonseol wiwonhoe, 'Dosi gyehoekeseo soguyeok', p. 20.
49. Ibid., p. 21.
50. Li, Sun-gwon and Baek, Wan-gi (Pyongyang, 1963), p. 44.
51. Ibid., p. 43.
52. Kim, Jeong-Hui (Pyongyang, 1953), p. 193.
53. Kim, Suk-ja, 'Ganggye-siui', p.3 ; Kim, Suk-ja, 'Sariwonsiui', p. 3.; Kim, Suk-ja, 'Bokgu geonseoldoeneun', p. 3.; Oh, 'Bokgugeonseoldoeneun', p. 3.
54. Li, Sun-gwon and Baek, Wan-gi (Pyongyang, 1963), p. 82.

55 Li Hwa-seon(a) (Pyongyang, 1989), pp. 347–348.
56 Gukgageonseol wiwonhoe, 'Dosi gyehoekeseo soguyeok', p. 19.
57 Kim, Bong-su, '74ho sibeomjutaeksoguyeokgyehoek', p. 29.
58 Jungangseolgye yeonguso dosigyehoeksil, 'Dosi jubyeonui gyeongsajiwa', p. 7.
59 See note 10 above.
60 Baek, Wan-gi, 'Pyongyangsi jutaek soguyeok-eseoui', p. 28.
61 Ibid., 29.
62 An, Ryang-ok, 'Dongpyeongyang jungangbu jutaek', p. 24.
63 Bauhaus Dessau Archives, 'Erläuterungsberichte für den Wohnkomplexe', pp. 10–23.
64 Yun, Changbong, 'Mobeom jutaek soguyeogui geonseol', p. 14.
65 Yun, Changbong, 'Hamheungsi mobeom jutaek soguyeok-ui', p. 24.
66 An, Ryang-ok, 'Daetaryeong mobeom jutaek', pp. 7–11.
67 Nam, Il, 'Sae hwangy-eonge jeokeunghage', pp. 2–11. The decision was as follows: 1) innovate construction projects, pursue cost savings, and construct more buildings; 2) enhance the level of planning; 3) consolidate material and technical bases; and 4) continue to thoroughly embrace the spirit of Cheonsanri and develop communist ideological education.
68 Gukgageonseol wiwonhoe dosigyehoegguk, 'Dosigyehoeg bumuneseo 3wol', p. 23.
69 Gukgageonseol wiwonhoe, 'Dosi gyehoekeseo soguyeok', p. 22.
70 Ilic, Melanie and Smith, Jeremy (eds.) (New York, 2009), p. 30.
71 See note 67 above.
72 Gang, Chunmo, 'Dosigyehoek-eseo sangeopmang-ui haprijeok pochi', p. 24.
73 Guggageonseol wiwonhoe, 'Dosigyehoeg bumuneseo 3wol', p. 21.
74 Li, Sun-gwon and Baek, Wan-gi., *Jutaek soguyeo gyehoek*, p. 110.
75 *Hamhŭngsi dosiseolgyeyeonguso dosigyehoeksil*, 'Soguyeokgyehoekeun dosi chonggyehoekui', p. 18.
76 Unknown, 'Botongbeol-ui o-neulgwa', p. 34.
77 Kim, Yeong-bok, 'Munsudong gwangjang mit juyogarogeonchk ggyehoek', pp. 23–24.
78 Kim, Sunkwan. 'Namposi-ui juyo garo hyeongseong', pp. 24–27.
79 Jeong, Myeong-geun, 'Wonsansi haean geori', pp. 46–48.
80 Han, Jong-ok, 'Sinposi jungsimbuui geonchuk', pp. 25–27.

여섯

Socialising Rural Space in North Korea

Inha Jung / Shin Gun-soo

In 2014 Kim Jong Un, North Korea's young leader, sent a message to the National Meeting for Heads of Work Cells (*bunjojang*) stressing that the 'Theses on the Socialist Rural Question in Our Country' (commonly known as 'the Rural Theses'), which had been drafted by Kim Il-Sung, his own grandfather and the nation's founder, were perfect theory and practice for the countryside.[1] This means that the Rural Theses, penned in 1964,[2] continue to function as the backbone of North Korea's socialist ideals. Consolidating socialist ideology through nationalisation of land and collectivised agricultural management, the Rural Theses aimed to increase agricultural production, eradicate backwardness in the countryside, and abolish the opposition between city and countryside.[3] Based on these principles, the North Korean regime launched intensive rural reforms. The landscape in the North Korean countryside today is the result of these reforms.

Rural planning and policy in socialist countries is not easy to grasp conceptually or practically because there are dynamic interplays between idealist theory and reality, tradition and progress, collectivism and individual privacy, and standard models and local variations. The Rural Theses established an ideal of a socialist countryside directly managed by the state. The North Korean government wished to realise this ideal by constructing model villages. Deviations from the plan, however, occurred as the Rural Theses confronted practical challenges. Nowadays, state-run farms representing socialist ideals and small-sized workplaces reflecting real conditions co-exist in the North Korean countryside. Tracing the origins of the formation of the unique landscape in the North Korean countryside, the present piece of research attempts to elucidate crucial factors in the decision-making process for settlement planning and housing in post-war North Korea; it focuses on the relationship between socialist ideals and the rural economy that underpins the transformation of rural space in North Korea.[4]

Together with settlement planning, the current investigation looks closely at how dwellings in North Korea's countryside have been transformed. The North Korean regime actively promoted urban living as the most progressive form of settlement and tried to introduce the urban way of life and its production systems into the countryside. However, these attempts at transformation, which were mainly political in nature, clashed with the traditional rural way of life, leading to the emergence of new housing types. A close look at rural settlement models and standard housing designs in North Korea reveals that the country passed through three stages of development, each of which is closely connected with different sizes of settlement and dwelling space.

The transformation of North Korea's countryside in the 1960s is important in understanding the post-war modernisation process in North Korea because rural settlements and housing were primarily constructed during this time, and the transformative pattern reveals a different trajectory than that found in the Soviet Union, China, and other communist countries. Chronologically, the socialisation of rural space in North Korea commenced one generation later than in the Soviet Union. At the ceasefire that brought an end to the Korean War, the urbanisation rate was only 17.7%. Rural reform in North Korea was closely associated with urbanisation; notably, the rate of urbanisation in North Korea reached approximately 50% in 1970. Moreover, industrial facilities had been completely destroyed during the Korean War; this hindered the mechanisation of agricultural production in the post-war era. Due to the underdevelopment of industry in the 1950s, the Soviet Union objected to the rapid socialisation of the countryside in North Korea.[5] This social and economic background explains the unique context in which the North Korean regime established relationships between the countryside and the city.

The socialisation of rural space in North Korea was also influenced by the political response of Kim Il-Sung's regime to changing conditions in the communist bloc in the 1950s and 1960s. In February 1956, at the 20th Party Congress in Moscow, Khrushchev launched a campaign to correct what he viewed as the most harmful legacies of the Stalin era. He instructed all Communist parties worldwide to eliminate Stalinist-style 'cult[s] of personality' of the leader, to pursue a policy of peaceful co-existence with the capitalist world, and to shift economic resources from heavy industry to consumer goods. Each of Khrushchev's mandated policy changes clearly posed a serious threat to Kim Il-Sung.[6] Accordingly, Kim Il-Sung pursued his own strategy for survival. His unique style of government appeared to master the difficult situation. He applied his method to management of agricultural production, organising rural space as a tool by which to sustain totalitarian dictatorship. In this regard, this study of rural space in North Korea can help to make clear the structural relations inherent in North Korean society.

Agricultural Cooperativisation in North Korea

Land reform and the emergence of agricultural cooperatives

The socialisation of rural space prompted North Korean peasants to drastically change not only their production methods but also their lifestyles. Typically, this socialisation was accompanied by a change in land ownership. In 1946 the Provisional People's Committee for North Korea instituted a land reform that led to a fundamental shift in who owned the nation's land. All land was confiscated and handed over to peasant farmers. Landlords were allowed to keep only the same amount of land as the peasants who had formerly rented their land, thereby creating a far more egalitarian distribution of property. After the armistice that brought an end to the Korean War in 1953, the 6th Plenary Session of the Party Central Committee decided that all types of farm should be agricultural cooperatives [*nongeop heopdong johap*]; this inevitably led to the emergence of socialist collective farms.[7] The socialist farming system in North Korea was established relatively easily because the Korean War had dismantled the landowner class and pushed peasants out of villages; this contrasted with the Soviet Union and China, where collectivisation of farms was only completed after the eruption of numerous social conflicts.[8] Economically, North Korea's reforms led to collectivisation of the means of agricultural production. In other words, agricultural production managed by individuals or families on freely distributed land was transformed into collective production overseen by cooperatives. This change greatly affected rural space in North Korea because the North Korean way of life had to be reorganised in accordance with the new system of production. The North Korean regime began to remodel rural space in earnest at this time.

What is the most appropriate rural unit for the collectivisation of agricultural production? This was the most important question in the socialisation of North Korea's countryside. In the early days, the North Korean regime applied the Soviet rural model in order to strengthen its agricultural platform. In the process it had to enlarge its agricultural cooperatives to make agricultural management more rational and efficient. To accomplish this goal, the regime changed the existing administrative hierarchy – consisting of *do* (province), *gun* (county), *myeon* (district) and *ri* (village) – in order to determine the optimal unit for distributing agricultural products and maintaining a self-supporting economy. The *myeon* was abolished. In its place the core administrative unit was now the *ri* (village), whose size corresponded to the size of an agricultural cooperative. Small agricultural cooperatives formerly managed by *myeons* were integrated into independent and self-sufficient cooperatives at the level of the *ri*. Thus the North Korean government simplified its complex administrative system. The number of agricultural cooperatives accordingly fell by one fifth in just one year with no corresponding overhaul of the service infrastructure.[9] Cooperativisation based on the *ri* as core administrative unit made a fundamental difference in villages because it involved reorganisation of the entire rural space. Cabinet decision no. 105 announced this change upon conclusion of the plenary session of October 1957. Following this decision, the North Korean regime published a standard plan and guidelines for the planning of rural settlements; it also made preparations for the construction of a model village.[10] The government proposed designs for 55 types of industrial facility and 15 types of educational, cultural, and public-health facility and amenity that were necessary in the planning of large villages.[11] The 500-farmhouse Yongho Agricultural Cooperative in Sukcheon County, built by integrating five scattered villages in a hilly area, was one of the state-managed model villages. Its boundaries were fixed to avoid encroachment on farming land. This increase in the size of a village represented a rejection of conventional rural structure and portended a reorganisation of North Korea's rural space, while showing the new direction taken by North Korea's rural policy, which now aimed to endow the countryside with urban features.

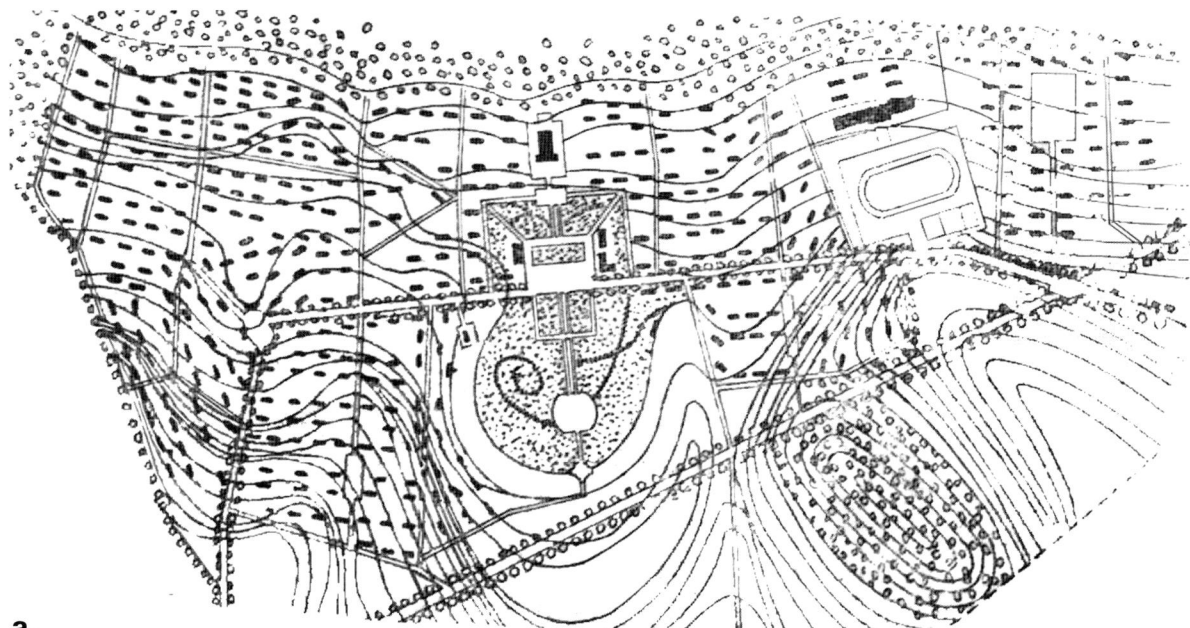

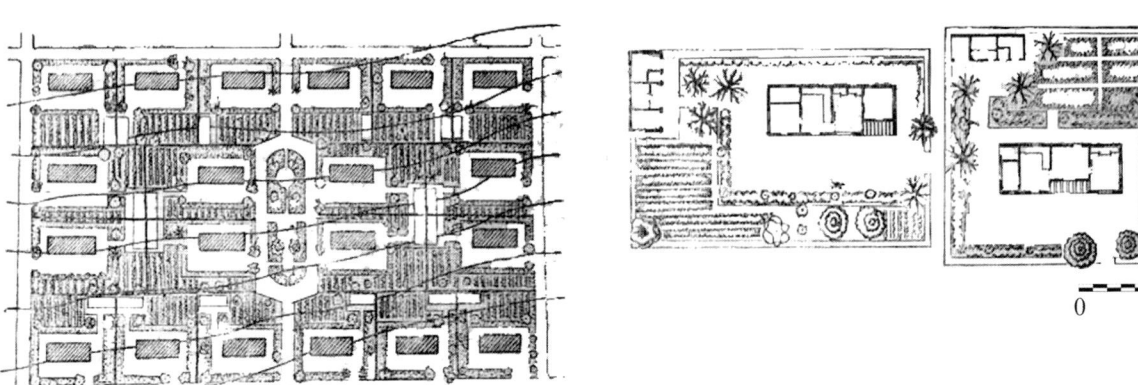

Village plan (a), site plan (b), and unit plans for the Joseon-Soviet Goodwill Agricultural Cooperative (*Josso chinseon burak*).
Source: *Geonchukgwa Geonseol*, July 1958

The Spatial organisation of agricultural cooperatives
The average size of agricultural cooperatives was enlarged to 300 households. These cooperatives were much larger than traditional rural communities and small cooperatives (consisting of 20–30 households and 80 households respectively) when cooperativisation concluded in 1957.[12] The form of this organisation was influenced by the Soviet collective farms known as *kolkhozy*.[13] The Soviet Union was the first country to socialise rural spaces, which led to the establishment of collective farms (*kolkhozy*) and state-run farms (*sovkhozy*) from 1927 forwards. The collectivisation of rural life continued until the 1940s. North Korea adopted this Soviet model at an early stage of its cooperativisation.

The Joseon-Soviet Goodwill Agricultural Cooperative (*Josso chinseon burak*), established in Gangseo County, South Pyeongan Province, in 1957, shows planning methods that were typical for rural settlements and housing. The idea was that the village should accommodate 413 households. Farmhouses were regularly laid out in designated locations without regard for geomorphic variations. The architects distributed the necessary amenities based on the site size, number of residents (681 persons), and working conditions.

Unlike the site planning for the village, which resulted in a modern grid and zoning system, individual house plots were designed and positioned on roads in a conventional manner. The size of each plot was 350–450 square metres. The parts of a plot that were not used for building were used for vegetable gardens (*teotbat*) or service facilities.[14] This combination is characteristic for farmhouses in North Korea. Because the North Korean regime prohibited private plots and private production in principle while allowing agricultural products only for consumption, each household generally cultivated the surrounding vegetable gardens exclusively for its own food supply. This attempt at village organisation and private plot distribution led to the first major change in the North Korean villagescape.

Rural housing in agricultural cooperatives
The adoption of Soviet models in the 1950s brought North Korea difficulties in designing rural homes to suit its own way of life. Traditional Soviet rural houses did not work well in North Korea. Moreover, by the mid-1970s, Soviet architects were simply transferring urban housing standards to rural areas. They did not recognise the need 'to design homes to suit the economic situation of rural families' or 'to harmonise with local topography and culture.'[15]

It was in this situation that North Korean architects began devising new standard housing plans concurrently with cooperativisation. The first new houses built in the North Korean countryside imitated existing rural housing for the sake of speedy reconstruction after the Korean War. The first standard plans for rural housing in 1957 created seven types of houses taking into account local conditions such as geography and climate.[16] The site plan for the village reflected these conditions: each house in the village was designed to have identical orientation, access, and size. The *ondol*, the conventional and traditional heating system, was incorporated in the house's layout as a key feature. This explains why the kitchen was posiitoned in the centre of the house. Normally, annexes were located on one side of the kitchen and two *ondol* rooms were located on the other side. The traditional gabled roof with large eaves blocked both sunshine and rain. Windows were typically small because North Korea has cold winters. Wooden terraces called *toetmaru* were built onto the front of bedrooms for the sultry summers. These designs all derived from existing vernacular houses.[17]

In addition, several attempts were made to experiment with new housing models in the countryside.[18] However, since the architects had also to focus on economical use of materials, these attempts rarely went much further than construction of a prototype. Nevertheless, based on sources available to it at the time, the CIA concluded, 'North Koreans also may have been inclined to overlook deficiencies in other consumer areas when they saw the improvements in

Village plan (a), site plan (b), and unit plans for the Joseon-Soviet Goodwill Agricultural Cooperative (*Josso chinseon burak*).
Source: *Geonchukgwa Geonseol*, July 1958

housing.'[19] A closer look at the statistics reveals that this conclusion is persuasive. 600,000 housing units were built from 1954 to 1960, 800,000 units from 1961 to 1969, and over 1,000,000 in the 1970s. By 1976 North Korea had constructed new housing for almost three fourths of its urban and rural households – a notable accomplishment.[20]

The Chongsan-Ri Movement and the New Socialist Countryside

The ideal rural model and a shift in rural policy
In the 1950s aid from the Soviet bloc was clearly crucial for North Korea's reconstruction. 'According to Soviet reports, over the course of the DPRK's [North Korea's] Three Year Plan of 1954–56, grants from Soviet-bloc countries provided 75 percent of all capital investment, while aid and loans from these allies financed 77.6 percent of imports and 24.6 percent of the state budget.'[21] However, financial aid began to decline following Nikita Khrushchev's secret speech denouncing Joseph Stalin, which provoked the 1956 August Incident (*Palweol jongpa sageon*) in North Korea.[22] The North Korean regime had to develop its own method of survival. Kim Il-Sung began to steer his country in a different direction, which led to North Korea making a marked-shift away from the Soviet sphere of influence. He promoted the Chongsan-Ri movement, together with the Chollima movement (1958),[23] as a national strategy to address rural issues.

The Chongsan-Ri movement originated from an instruction handed down by Kim Il-Sung at a plenary session of the Central Committee in December 1959. While establishing a new rural policy, Kim Il-Sung visited Chongsan-Ri Cooperative Farm, staying there for 15 days in February 1960. During this visit he developed North Korea's agricultural policies. After his initial visit, he visited the farm 38 more times over eight months, suggesting principles and methods for creating the conditions and environment for socialist living.[24] As a result, Kim Il-Sung's unique governing style, known as 'on-the-spot guidance' (*hyeongji jido*), was implemented using his principal methods to find solutions to local problems. As the North Korean leader became involved in issues relating to rural space, North Korea's countryside entered a new phase. Furthermore, after the regime successfully completed a five-year reconstruction plan in 1960, Kim Il-Sung gained the confidence to focus on rural issues. The following April, the North Korean government decided to construct 600,000 housing units in the countryside over 5–6 years.[25] In his New Year's Speech for 1962, Kim Il-sung stated that 'one of six goals in the first Seven-Year Plan is to construct 200,000 housing units, half of which is to be rural housing.'[26] Together with construction of rural housing, systematisation of agrarian management fundamentally changed the character of rural space in North Korea.

Changes in North Korea's rural space were closely related to political ideology, which sought to create a city-like countryside. The planning of the Chongsan-Ri Cooperative Farm showcased the intentions behind this policy. This farm is famous for its model village, which implemented a system of scientific and mechanical farming.[27] This farm continues to be one of the important sites for foreign visitors to visit. Chongsan-Ri Cooperative Farm consisted of 300 households, meaning that it was smaller than the Joseon-Soviet Goodwill Agricultural Cooperative village. Two- and three-storey houses were built in the lower areas, and single-storey houses were built in the higher areas. A clinic, nursery, and public bath were clustered together, and orchards were located on the mountain behind the village. A small park was planned at the centre of the village, which was similar in form to North Korean cities.[28] This kind of rural village was diagrammatically illustrated in a cartoon in *Chollima* magazine. The large, plain-type village was not easily distinguishable from regional towns and had almost no rural character: it was well planned and equipped with all necessary service facilities, including a nursery, a kindergarten, a worker's club, a restaurant, and a shop; it also had collective sanitary infrastructure, including sewage pipes, central heating, and water supply. In the cartoon the magnifying glass directed at the three-storey apartments reveals the propagandist intentions of the North Korean regime. Here we see residents reading newspapers on balconies in the manner of city-dwellers and chatting around birdcages in mimicry of an urban life of leisure. This village also contained single-storey farmhouses, but the magnifying glass only hinted at their existence, displaying merely part of a typical farmhouse with auxiliary storage and traditional roofs and vegetable gardens. Other farmhouses were not included in the rendering.[29] The North Korean regime intended to reduce the cultural and other gaps between the countryside and the city and to reorganise rural space by introducing an urbanised rural model. However, this intention was difficult to realise in reality.

① Revolutionary history memorial hall
② Revolutionary history memorial stone
③ Study room for Kim Il-sung's idea
④ Historical buildings
⑤ Office
⑥ Training centre for agricultural science and technology
⑦ Cultural centre
⑧ Dormitory
⑨ Shops
⑩ Administrative committee building of cooperative farm
⑪ Garden for children
⑫ Restaurant

Satellite photo of Chongsan-Ri Cooperative Farm (a) and the current state of the Central District (b) from Google Maps, 28 July 2016.

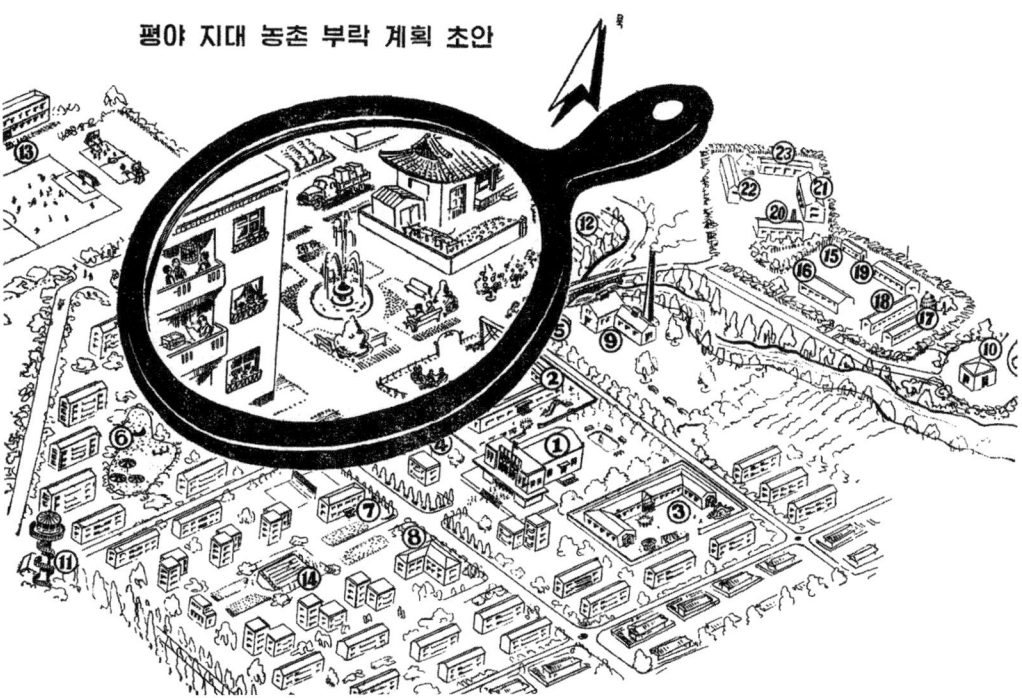

A cartoon illustrating a plain-type large village.
Source: Chollima, Feb.1964

6. Socialising Rural Space in North Korea   147

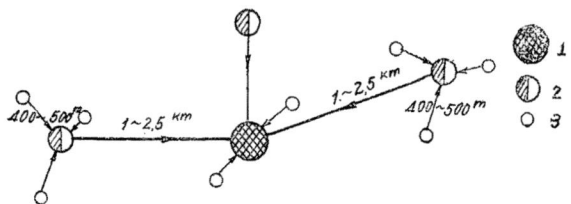

A diagram for service infrastructure connecting scattered settlements.
Source: Geonchukgwa Geonseol, Jan. 1962

Organisation of work units and service networks

The North Korean regime encountered many barriers to disseminating its ideal model. The most challenging problem was that many villages were on too small a scale: North Korea is essentially a mountainous country, and farmers had to live close to their arable land since they usually could not spend time commuting. This meant that the situation evolved into the opposite of what the North Korean regime intended. The size of the work units changed after Kim Il-Sung's on-the-spot guidance in Chongsan-Ri. The cooperative farms were subdivided into work-group settlements (*jakeopban burak*) for 70–100 persons. The work-group system was cemented by the introduction of incentives to farmers who exceeded the scheduled amount of work, i.e. above and beyond basic allocations (called *jakeopban udaeje*), to enhance their work efficiency. Using this system, the work-group settlements could function as independent units and could even combine group and individual profits. This in effect meant a new socialist framework for collective living that differs from the framework for the agricultural cooperative and takes shape through spatial organisation. Unlike the huge settlements that the Soviet Union and China organised as labour units, North Korea's rural space featured scattered small villages that were connected to one another.

These were the circumstances in which planners were asked to come up with the best way to install efficient service networks in scattered small villages. The planners examined realistic options to meet this challenge: as opposed to large plain-type villages, which could have efficient service networks, scattered small villages did not lend themselves to the installation of public service networks in an organic way. In 1962 the North Korean regime therefore created a rational model to connect scattered small villages with service networks.[30] This model subdivided cooperative farms into three types of work-group settlement and linked them using service networks. The central work-group settlement (*jungsim burak*) had administrative, cultural, and educational facilities for all the cooperative members. An ordinary work-group settlement (*jakeopban burak*) had only a small office, a nursery, and a kindergarten. Whereas the central and ordinary work-group settlements were separated by a distance of over 1–2.5 kilometres, auxiliary work-group settlements (*bojo burak*) were created to resolve inconveniences in the use of public services. The auxiliary settlements were within 0.4–0.5 kilometres of each other and were equipped with public facilities such as a propaganda office, a people's school, a bathhouse, a barbershop, a laundry, and a food kiosk. Except for the central farming settlement, each settlement was intended to contain 20–50 households and was partitioned into rectangular plots following the geographical contours of the site. A shared well was dug within 50 metres of every 2–10 households. The plot size shrank to 240–300 square metres; the buildings faced south or southeast.[31] The faming settlements in principle used service facilities collectivelyas in urban areas, but the rural space was distributed over a wide area – unlike distribution in urban areas. From this point forward, North Korea's rural policy was directed into two categories: the formation of a few large, urbanised villages on the one hand and, on the other, scattered settlements connected by diverse facilities. This trend reflects North Korea's geographical features and production system.

New types of rural housing

Chonsan-Ri village served as both a representative model village and as a standard housing prototype in the era of Kim Il-Sung. An aerial view of Chongsan-Ri

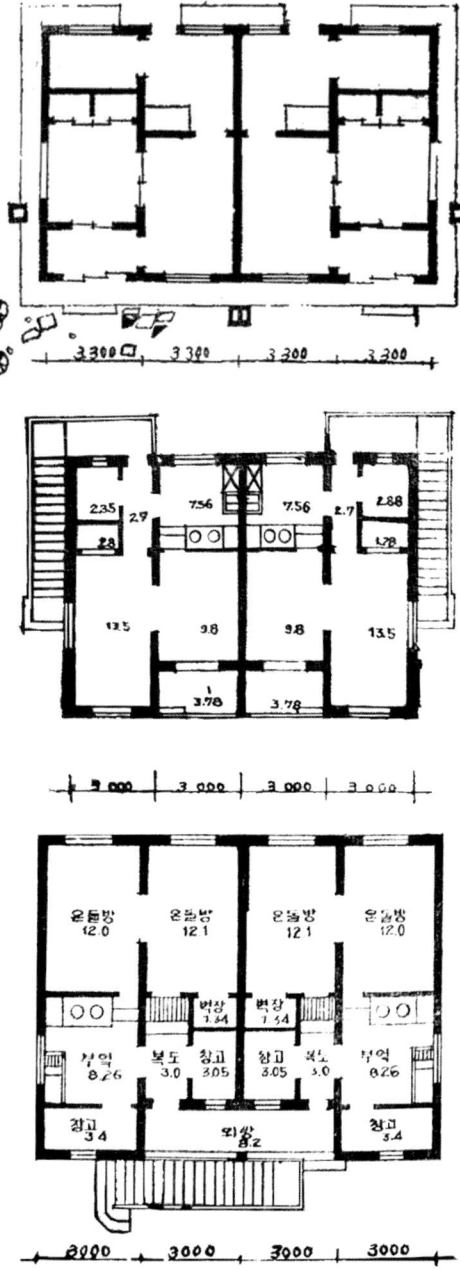

Unit plans for single-storey (a) and two-storey (b, c) prefabricated rural housing.
Source: Geonchukgwa Geonseol, Dec. 1960

Cooperative Farm shows two different patterns of rural housing: row houses and 2–3-storey apartment houses. These patterns resemble plans by the Central Design Institute and Pyongyang Urban Design Institute, the institutions in charge of designing urban housing. 'A proposal for standard rural housing by prefabrication', published by the Central Design Institute in December 1960, describes this situation and suggests two types of rural housing: a row house with two households and a two-storey apartment house with four households. Construction materials for this housing were saprolite blocks and bricks. As opposed to plans for agricultural cooperatives, which were modern modifications of traditional vernacular houses, these plans more closely resembled typical urban housing. For this reason, the warehouses required for rural living were separate from the kitchens. These houses were not provided with

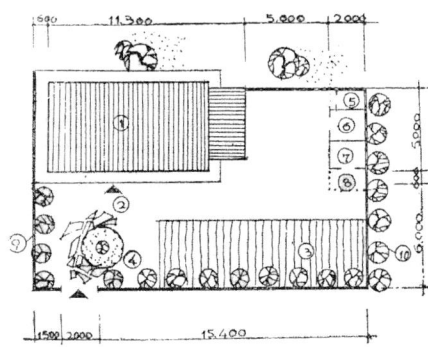

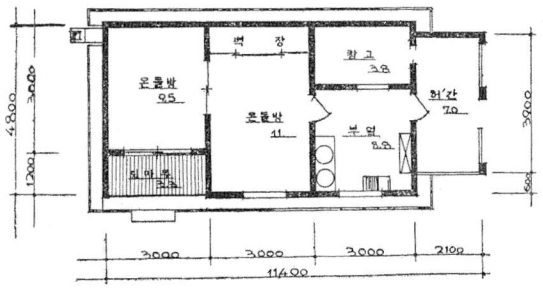

Unit plans for a one-building, one-household detached house.
Source: Geonchukgwa Geonseol, Jan, 1962

vegetable gardens. With these types of housing plan the North Korean regime tried to implement 'cultured and hygienic', its slogan inculcating modernised socialist living. It failed, however, to construct any actual houses except for the model village. Above all, private plots in designs for rural housing became sensitive to farmers' wishes. Farmers desired traditional tile-roofed houses, and their farming methods did not suit the new housing.

The difference between standard housing plans and the realities of working life in the countryside became an important issue when the North Korean regime attempted to urbanise the countryside. Recognising the difference between rural and urban lifestyles, *Nodongshimmun*, an official newspaper in North Korea, published editorials on this issue stating 'we have to improve the standard plan of rural housing in a way that suits peasants' real life and rural management.'[32] More specifically, *Nodongsinmun*, the official newspaper of the Central Committee of the Workers' Party of Korea, argued that the one-building, one-household policy – as opposed to multi-storey apartment buildings – should serve as the principal planning principle, although two-household buildings would be permitted as a possible scenario. It also indicated that only public buildings should be multi-storey.[33] In view of this argument, Kim Il-Sung revisited Chongsan-Ri on 2 December 1961 and revised the standard plans to reflect Korean housing traditions. The revised plans were for single-storey dwellings reflecting the peasant way of life; these commonly retained a warehouse and barn near the kitchen. The kitchen was at the centre of the house, and the large barns were annexes. To maximise construction efficiency, the module for the kitchen and bedrooms was designed to be three metres wide, but the barn was 2.1 metres wide. The choice between these two types depended on the shape and location of the site. For flat land, a row house containing two households was usually employed because the plot permitted both a vegetable garden and a front yard. On sloped hilly sites, by contrast, one-building, one-household housing was more advantageous because it could utilise all the surrounding space for vegetable gardens.³⁴

Rural housing in North Korea still consists primarily of these single-storey dwellings, each of which has one bedroom, a living room, a kitchen, and a storage area and accommodates, on average, two families. Although many are relatively primitive and built with local materials, rural dwellings erected since the war are considered modern by Asian standards.³⁵ The preference for independent row houses in North Korea's countryside contrasts starkly with Chinese rural housing. A rural settlement in Dazhai, a model village in Mao's China that is closer to the ideal of the people's commune on the smallest scale,³⁶ developed two-storey barracks-like housing. Under the strong influence of the Dazhai model, Qinyong village had similar terraced houses, divided into identical units expressing the physical sameness and social equality of all inhabitants.³⁷ Compared to the Chinese models, North Korea's rural houses were more independent, a result of the peasants' desire to have their own private plots.

The Rural Theses and dual rural spaces

In February 1964 Kim Il-Sung announced the principles of his rural policy. His Rural Theses remain in force until the present day. Reflecting on the rural policies that had been implemented until that moment, the Rural Theses set out three basic principles for resolving rural problems under the socialist system: comprehensive adoption of the revolutions of technology, culture, and ideas; industrial assistance for agriculture and urban assistance for the countryside; and the fulfilment of national ownership of rural property through the application of advanced enterprise management to agriculture. The North Korean regime continuously pursued a socialist model based on national ownership, as stipulated by Article 23 of North Korea's Socialist Constitution; this led to the promotion of a state-run farming system in all regions.

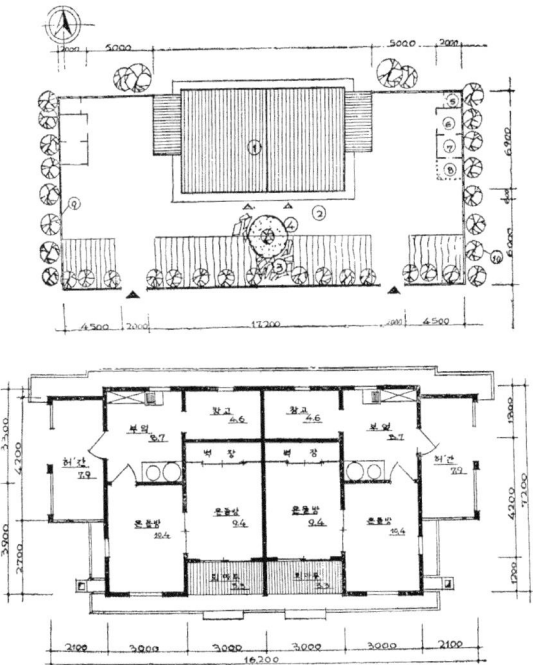

A one-building, two-household row house.
Source: Geonchukgwa Geonseol, January 1962

However, this ideological approach conflicted with the spirit of Chongsan-Ri, which emphasised the congruence of rural space with reality through 'on-the-spot guidance'. Whereas the Chongsan-Ri movement tried to solve issues in North Korea's countryside 'on the spot', the Rural Theses suggested a long-term vision based on the promise of the introduction of full mechanisation. The North Korean government accordingly stressed that 'the ownership of cooperatives must be ceaselessly converted into ownership by the entire people.' On the basis of these principles, the government aimed to urbanise rural areas and regarded the countryside, peasants, and agriculture as objects for improvement.³⁸ Thus the Rural Theses led to the bifurcation of North Korea's rural planning policy into the realistic and the ideal; this had an enormous impact on the organisation of rural space.

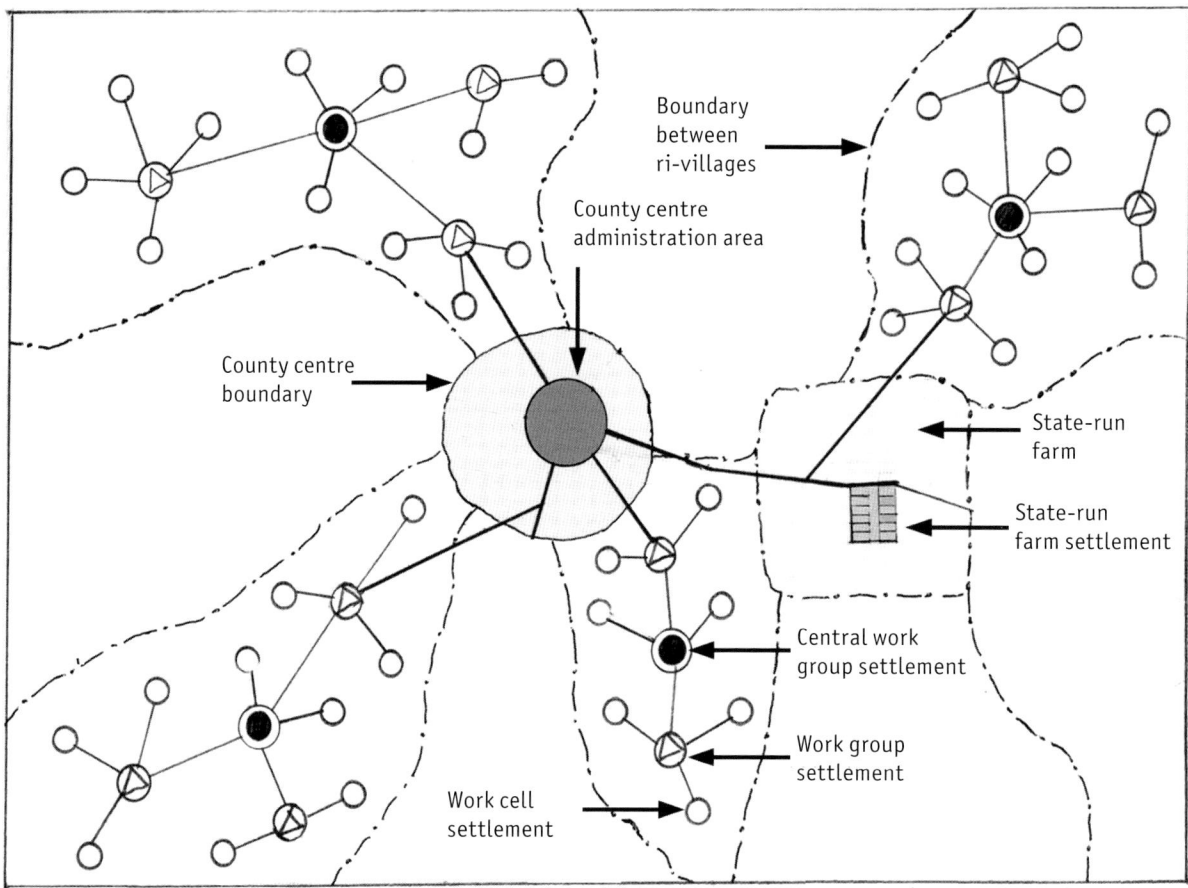

Spatial organisation of a county (gun) in North Korea.
Source: map.ngii.go.kr

Larger administrative units
In parallel with the Rural Theses, the North Korean regime added two spatial units to the existing administrative system: a large unit regarded as an intermediate step to achieving the desired level of state ownership and a small unit that was necessary to flexibly adapt to rural realities. The Rural Theses emphasised the role of the county (*gun*) as an administrative unit linking cities and towns with the countryside and introducing an urban management system to the latter. Whereas the county became the basic unit of regional administration, the village (*ri*) – the existing administrative unit that corresponded

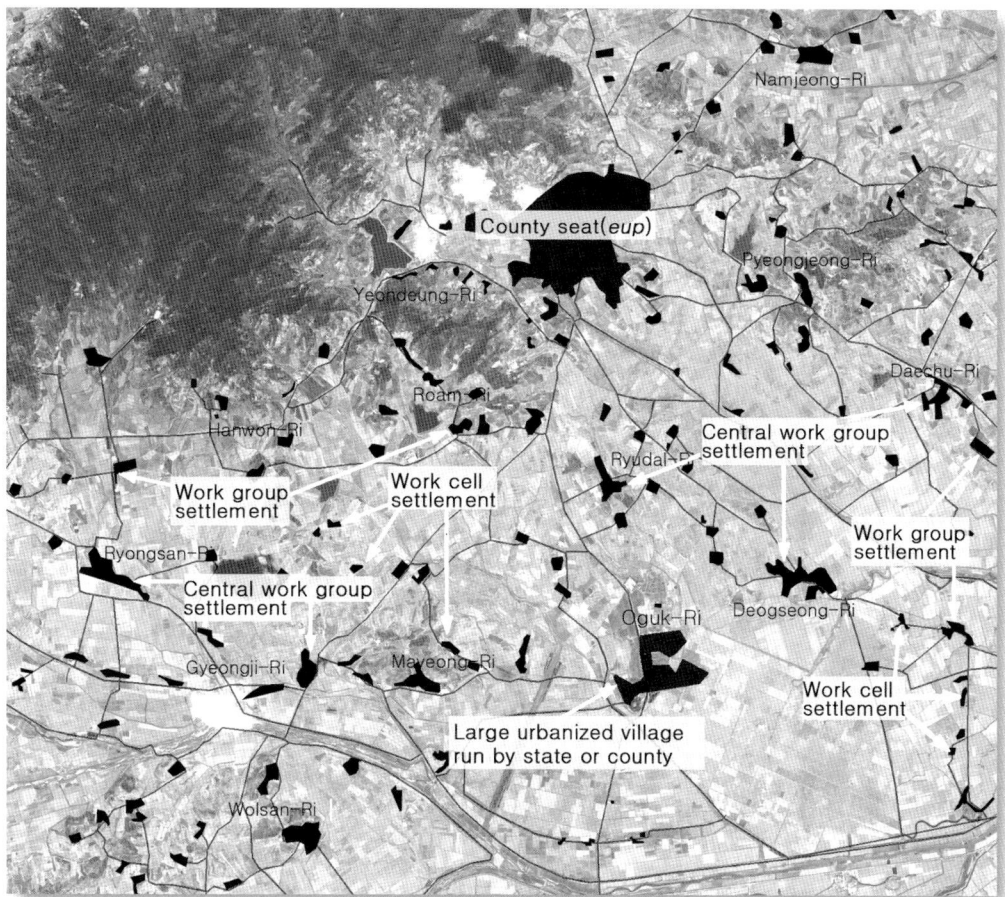

Based on the Rural Theses and diagrams for village planning from *Nongchon burak gyehoek*, and spatial organisation of Anak-gun.
Source: map.ngii.go.kr

to the cooperative farm village – played a role as the basis for production and distribution by cooperative farms. The new measure attempted to diminish the role of *ri*-based self-sufficient farms; instead, the production and distribution systems were to be controlled at the county level. The county was large enough to accommodate service facilities for a population of at least 30,000 people. Moreover, the county-run construction unit took charge of building in the rural space.[39]

Kim Il-Sung considered it essential to urbanise the countryside. The county centre (*eup*) consisted of non-agricultural production areas and political, economic, and cultural centres that were responsible for managing the entire county area.[40] The county centre also had an industrial character: daily necessities were produced here, and national industries could be accommodated here if necessary.[41] As a semi-independent base in the countryside, the county centre was a hub of production and consumption. In view of its urban/industrial character, the Rural Theses gave the county centre a special role in all aspects of socialist rural life.[42] The lifestyle of people who lived in the county centre was no different from that of urban workers. The county includes two types of area: agricultural production areas and non-agricultural production areas.

Townlike large villages and small work units

Together with county centres, large villages and small work settlements were scattered over North Korea's rural space; they demonstrated considerable differences in size. Large villages included a variety of service facilities and had an urban character in terms of building size and population density.[43] Farms in large villages fell into three categories: state-run farms growing specific agricultural products that were important to the state; county general farms, which occupied a position between cooperative farms and state-run farms; and model farms, which benefitted from urban space and elements of entrepreneurship on a county level. These types of village were difficult to clearly differentiate and had several things in common: a larger size consisting of about 1000 households; political propaganda facilities positioned at their centres; and possession of service networks including farming offices, shops, and educational facilities.

A perfect model of an urbanised village was Changdong-Ri village, which was built on a plain. The North Korean regime integrated 11 small villages into one 500-household central village and two 400-household auxiliary villages. Changdong-Ri central village was like a microdistrict built in a rural area. Its northern section possessed a large square surrounded by administrative and cultural facilities. In its southern section, single-storey service buildings ran along a central street; accompanying them were high-rise apartment buildings. This large village suggested an ideal model based on transformation of the poor countryside into an urbanised environment through the support of the state and the Party.[44] Changdong-Ri also included two cooperative farms, a state-run farm, and a mine.[45] Since the scale of this village was large enough to include several work-group settlements, it had a strong urban character. The government could manage it directly; enterprise management could be employed; and the everyday life of residents largely depended on its service network. The village's urban structure was similar to that of the county centre, which included regional industrial plants. In this case an ideal rural village in

	Changdong-Ri village	Oguk-Ri village	Yonglim-Ri village	Ohyeon-Ri village
Village layout (Village centre in dashed-line rectangle)				
Building date	1965	1974	1974	After 1962
Number of households	500	1300	1000	About 7–800
Housing types	2–4 storey corridor-access-type (*oerangsik*) and staircase-access-type (*sektsiia*) apartment buildings	Basically, 2-storey houses. 3–4-storey houses with service networks	3–4-storey houses: 40%, 2-storey houses: 60%	2–3-storey houses on flat land. Single-storey houses on sloping land
Village centre				
Service facilities	Room for studying the thoughts of Kim Il-Sung, propaganda centre, farm office, culture club, shop, nursery, kindergarten.	Room for studying the thoughts of Kim Il-Sung, propaganda centre, farm office, culture club, shop, nursery, kindergarten, elementary school, middle school	Room for studying the thoughts of Kim Il-Sung, propaganda centre, farm office, culture club, shop, nursery, kindergarten, elementary school, middle school	Room for studying the thoughts of Kim Il-Sung, propaganda centre, propaganda room for studying science and technology, farm office, culture club, shop, nursery, kindergarten,

Table 1. Plans for four prestigious large villages in North Korea.
Source: Li Hwa-Seon, Joseongeonchuksa 3 (History of Joseon Architecture 3); Jianzhu xuebao, 3 (1978)

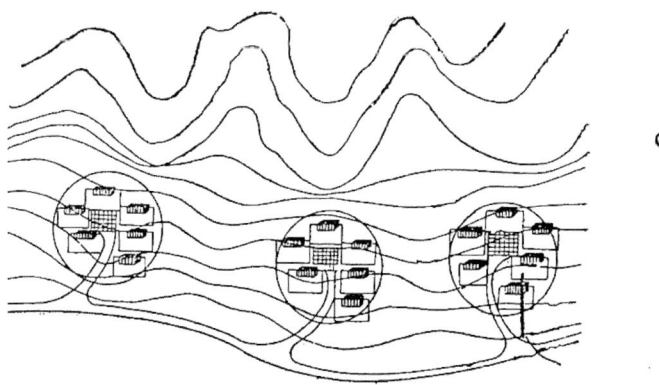
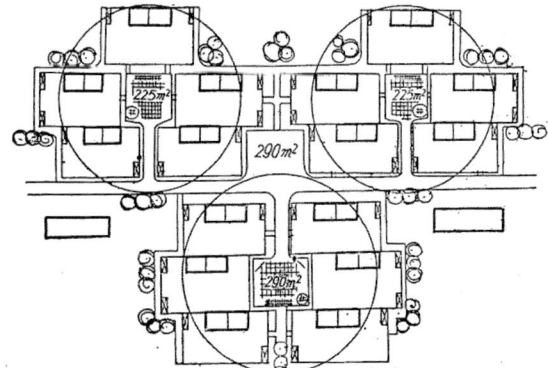

Clustering of work-cell settlements.
Source: Geonchukgwa Geonseol, May 1967

North Korea meant that peasants worked in an enterprising manner and enjoyed a rural life that resembled the life of urban labourers. Accordingly, the urbanised large village including state-run farms, county general farms, and cooperative farms showcased urban life in the countryside. In the 1970s similar model villages were constructed in Yonglim-Ri and Oguk-Ri, but these types of village never became widespread (see Table 1). Their role was limited to cultivating specific crops on about 10% of the total quantity of cultivable land.[46]

In addition to the emergence of large villages, another basic unit that appeared at this time was related to the changing work units. One year after the Rural Theses, North Korea adopted a work cell called the *bunjo*, a smaller division of the existing work group (*jakeopban*). These work cells were responsible for the attainment of annual agricultural production goals and provided the basis for the government's estimates of yields for each year. The work-cell responsibility system (*bunjo chaegimje*) was implemented in 1966 and – together with the work-group preference system – became the backbone of food distribution in North Korea. The work cell led to the emergence of an equivalent rural space, consisting of 5–13 households. The smallest settlements (*bunjo burak*) were inserted into the existing service network. Because the spatial conditions of rural settlements and the distance between work-cell settlements varied depending on geography and the production environment,[47,48] the North Korean regime revised the existing model to make it more flexible. Architects devising house layouts conducted extensive research into topographical contours and connections with other settlements.[49] The shapes of the smallest living units were largely based on organising various clusters of rural houses.[50]

This spatial organisation was different from that in China, where rural space was dominated by peoples' communes. The communes integrated rural society's administrative and economic functions to promote a self-sufficient labour unit consisting of 4000–10,000 inhabitants. A substantive difference, however, between China and North Korea in organisation of rural space is that China could create such large rural settlements, which were advantageous for labour-intensive farming, whereas North Korea was unable to generate particularly large production organisations due to the size of its population and the nature of its agricultural economy. In North Korea it was more important to connect scattered, small work-unit settlements into networks.

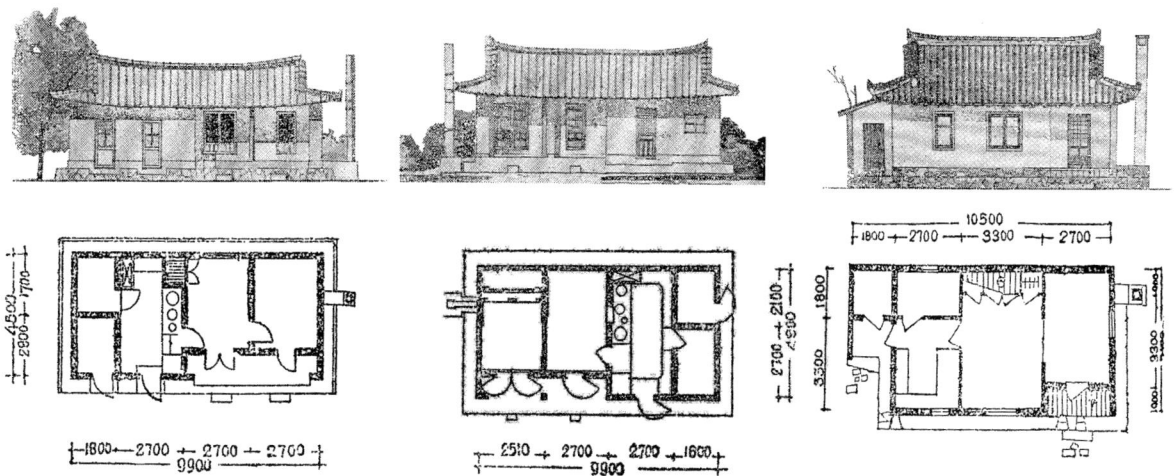

Unit plans and elevations for rural housing, as they appeared at the National Exhibition of Standard Design.
Source: *Geonchukgwa Geonseol*, January 1966

Continuity and change in rural housing

North Korea's rural housing reveals a similar contrast. Standard housing in agricultural production areas largely amounted to single-storey detached houses or row houses containing two households. In most of these types of rural housing the traditional layout of rooms was retained more or less unchanged throughout the 1960s.[51] Drawings for housing for a national exhibition of standard design (1965) show a number of common features: a layout based on one kitchen and two rooms, the central role of the kitchen in the overall residential space, an annexed barn and warehouse, a conventional heating system, and a modular design. The floor plan was simple for the sake of prefabrication, but the roof form remained complex because local peasants preferred the traditional hipped or half-hipped roof. The Central Standard Design Institute suggested a more economical simple gable roof for row houses containing two households. The bay in the kitchen and rooms was three metres wide; in the service facilities, 2.7 metres. A wooden floor (*toetmaru*) was built onto the front of the rooms. Since most rural housing was single-storey, rural dwellers did not have to confront the structural and heating problems faced by city-dwellers. As a result, construction methods did not affect floor plans.[53] In addition to shared rural spaces, rural houses were characterised by private and familial living space. The latter included vegetable gardens, which were very important for everyday food. Despite their traditional appearance, these houses were linked to the service network of production, distribution, and management.

By contrast, rural housing in urbanised large villages added urban features. Multi-storey apartment buildings provided living spaces that differed from those in the single-storey rural housing of the late 1960s. North Korean architects imported two urban housing types, the corridor-access type (*oerangsik*) and the staircase-access type (*sektsiia*),[54] from standard urban housing. The effective spatial compositions and heating systems used in these housing types were directly applied to rural dwellings. The model house in Changdong-Ri is the best example of this application. This house's kitchen area has been reduced to approximately five square metres, being smaller than the 7–8 m² of the typical 1960s house; its layout is quite unlike that common in rural living, and there is no independent vegetable garden. This means that its rural residents faced the public domain directly, with no intermediate space.

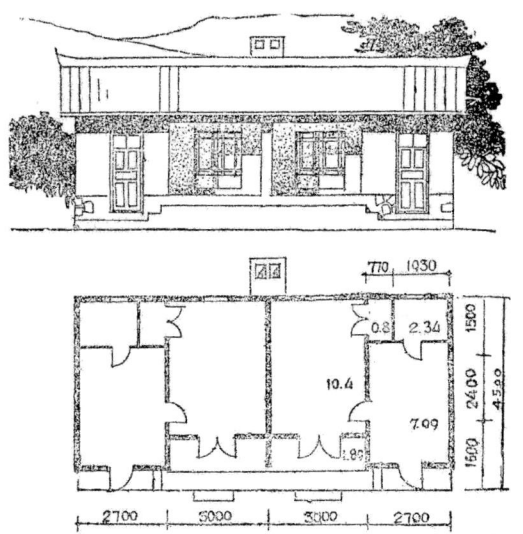
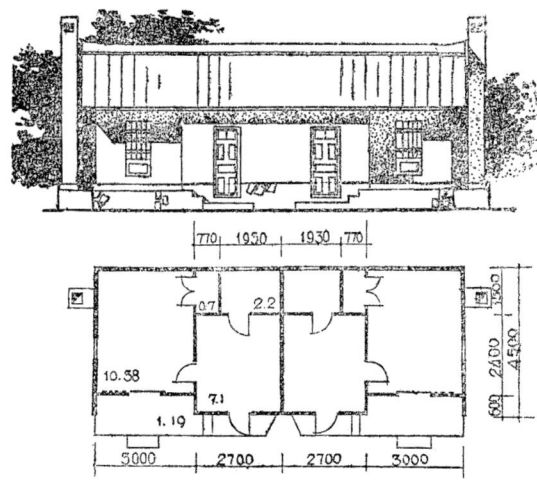

Unit plans and elevations for row houses containing two households (1966).
Source: Geonchukgwa Geonseol, March 1966

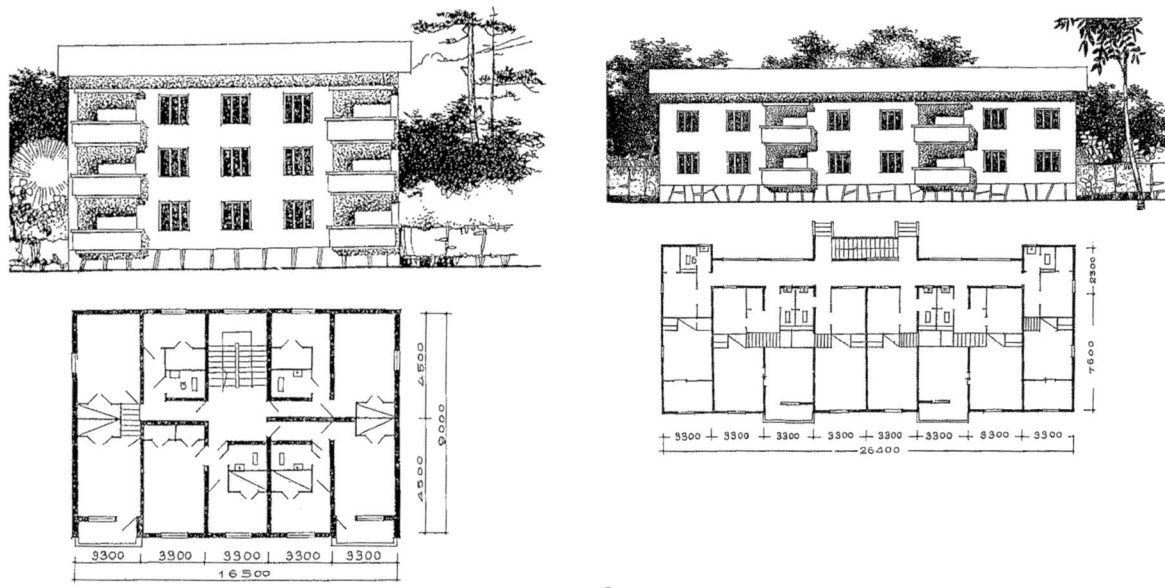

a. b.

Unit plans and elevations for corridor-access (a) and staircase-access (b) apartment buildings at Changdong-Ri village.
Source: Geonchukgwa Geonseol, March 1965

Conclusion

After the Korean War the North Korean government adopted the Soviet model for organising rural settlements. It quickly recognised however, that the Soviet model did not work in real life. North Korea accordingly pursued its own strategy for organising rural space. The North Korean regime began to pay attention to the specificities of rural reality after Kim Il-Sung's visit to Chongsan-Ri amid the Sino-Soviet split in the 1960s. In the Rural Theses the regime set out basic principles for solving rural problems under the socialist system.

As a result, rural space in post-war North Korea was restructured to form two different types: large urbanised villages and scattered work units. Unlike other communist countries which created many difficulties for themselves by uniformly imposing the urban system on their countryside, North Korea pursued unique strategies in socialising life in the countryside. Several factors were at work here. First, rural transformation in North Korea coincided with the reconstruction of the post-war era; this accelerated the process of reorganisation. Due to the low level of industrialisation, there was a deficit of various kinds of machinery; production therefore mainly depended on manual work. In addition, the country's mountainous geography divided arable land into relatively small parcels, which increased commuting times from home to workplace. To ensure optimal distances, North Korean planners proposed more flexible networks connecting small settlements. These are important factors to which the North Korean government gave serious consideration when restructuring rural space. These approaches worked effectively to enhance living standards in North Korea. Nevertheless, the North Korean government did not abandon the socialist ideal of urbanising the countryside. Model villages clearly demonstrate the North Korean government's intentions. Large urbanised villages were created to link towns with small settlements and to bring an urban atmosphere into the countryside.

Housing design in the North Korean countryside was determined by a different set of factors to those which shaped settlement planning; these factors included the traditional way of life, local materials, the system of mass production, and private subsidiary plots. New types of housing were created. The government failed in its intention to introduce multi-storey apartment buildings into the countryside; such houses were constructed only in large urbanised villages. Instead, single-storey row houses for two families became the most common type of rural housing. These houses' interior space shows a modification of the traditional wooden-floor-room-kitchen sequential layout. To rationalise the construction process, this housing type introduced standardised bays sharing an outer wall with another unit. Above all, private subsidiary plots allotted to inhabitants played an important role in improving the quality of life in North Korea.

Rural space in North Korea today consists of a small number of urbanised large villages, scattered small work-unit settlements connected by service networks, and two-family row housing. This organisation of rural space reflects socialist ideology, agricultural production systems, and the traditional way of life. This means that rural space in North Korea has not been organised in accordance with one dominant model but rather through a number of overlapping interventions. State-run farms representing the socialist ideology were created as model villages, but, as time passed, turned into villages dedicated to the cultivation of specific crops. Self-sufficient work unit settlements belonging to *ri*-based cooperatives shared production and distribution through a well-organised network of services. This system was maintained substantially unchanged until the North Korean famine, known as the Arduous March, in 1994 – 1998, after which the agricultural production and distribution system collapsed.

1   Kim Jong-un, (Pyongyang, 2014), p. 1.
2   At the 8th Conference of the Party Central Committee held in February 1964, Kim Il-Sung presented his 'Theses on the socialist rural question in our country', first published on 26 February 1964 in *RodongSinmun*, a North Korean official newspaper.
3   Kim Il-sung (Pyongyang,1965), pp. 5–6.
4   There are some earlier studies on rural settlements and housing in Korea and China: Kim, Young-Jae, Jang, Bo-Hye, and Han, Dong-Soo, Kim, Young-Jae, Jang, Bo-hye, and Han, Dong-soo, 'Saheojuui gukgaui nongchochurake gwanhan yeongu'; Lee Wang-Kee, O Young-sik, 'Bukhanui nongcho maeulbaechi mit jugeogyhoeke gwanhan yeongu'; Cha Jiade, Gao, Chengzeng, Xie ruosong, 'Chaoxian nongcun jumín dian guihua shejì'. However, these studies commonly lack rigour in explaining North Korea's rural settlements and housing.
5   Seo, Dong-man (Paju, 2010), p. 128.
6   Weathersby, Kathryn (Washington DC, 2008), pp. 11.
7   For more detail on agrarian reform in North Korea, see Lim Ki-beom (Pyongyang, 1992), pp. 13–29; Korean Institute for National Unification (Seoul, 2009), pp.195–199.
8   Communings, Bruce (New York, 2005), p. 440.
9   The number of agricultural cooperatives reached 13,309 in 1957, when cooperativisation was almost complete, but fell to 3843 due to small cooperatives merging in 1958 (Joseon Central News Agency (Pyongyang, 1959), p. 190.)
10 Joseon Central News Agency (Pyongyang, 1958), pp. 68–69.
11 Li Hwa-seon(a) (Pyongyang, 1993), pp. 359–360.
12 Kim Seung-jun, op. cit., pp. 182–183.
13 For more on the *kolkhoz*, see Nove, Alec (Harmondsworth, 1972), pp. 303–305, 333–339.
14 Kim Jong-Deuk, 'Josso chinseon nongeop hyeopdong', pp. 42–44.
15 Pallot, Judith (Washington, DC, 1993), pp. 212, 222.
16 Pak Im-tae, 'Nongchon geonseol-eseo geodun seonggwawa gwaeop', p. 23.
17 According to Joo Nam-Chul, there are six types of traditional housing on the Korean Peninsula. Two of these, the Pyong-An Province type and the Hamgyeong Province type, are common in North Korea. The first type was largely built in the plains of Pyong-An Province, and typically has a layout with a kitchen and two rooms in a row. The Hamgyeong Province type, which is found in the northeast of the cold region, consists of a kitchen, a *jeongjugan* (a type of extended kitchen range), and double strings of rooms in a grid pattern (Joo Nam-Chul (Seoul, 2006), p. 75). North Korea's architects depended on these types when designing rural housing.
18 To construct multi-storey housing using cheap local materials, architects experimented with the use of lespedeza bicolour to save steel and developed arched ceilings to save concrete.
19 Hunter, Helen-Louise, (Connecticut, 1999), p. 190.
20 Ibid., p. 187.
21 Van Ree, Erik, pp. 57–58.
22 The August Incident involved the attempted removal of Kim Il-sung by two opposite fractions, the Soviet-Korean faction and the Yanan faction. The attempt failed despite support from the Soviet Union and China; the participants were arrested and executed. This political struggle left North Korea with no factions capable of challenging Kim Il Sung.
23 The Chollima movement was a campaign of mass mobilisation which began in earnest in 1958. The movement aimed to improve labour productivity and produce a large quantity of mass urban housing, particularly in Pyongyang. For details of the relationship between the Chollima movement and mass urban housing, see Shin, Gunsoo and Jung, Inha, 'Appropriating the socialist way of life: the emergence of mass housing in postwar North Korea', pp. 170–175.
24 Specifically, the Rural Theses clarified the Chongsan-Ri spirit as follows: cooperative managers work for the public interest; they help civilise the people and transform them so as to build a communist country. The Chongsan-Ri method involves coordination between upper and lower institutions to solve problems based on understanding of local conditions.
25 Kim Il-sung, 'Nongchon munhwa jutaeg-eul', pp. 181–183.
26 Kim Il-sung, 'Sinnyeonsa' (Pyongyang, 1963), p. 2; Kim Il-sung, 'Joseon Rodongdang je4cha daehoe' (Pyongyang, 1962), p. 35; Jungang pyojunseolgye yeonguso, 'Nongchon munhwa jutaek geonseol-eul ganghwahagi wihayeo', p. 11.
27 Joseon Central News Agency, 'Chongsan nongeop hyeopdong johap-ui munhwa jutaek geonseol-e chaksu', p. 1. These houses were implemented as discussed in the newspaper, and North Korea prmoted the village in propaganda as an important rural model.
28 Pyongyang, the North Korean capital, has an urban centre with vast public spaces and green areas such as Kim Il-Sung Square and Moranbon Park.
29 Unknown, 'Deouk aleumdawojineun uli nongchon maeul', p. 118.
30 Kim Gwang-yun, 'Nongchon burak gyeohek bangdo', pp. 16–18.
31 Kim Ryong-chul, 'Nongchon burak gyehoek-eseo daeji jojiksang', pp. 51–53.
32 Editorial, 'Nongchon munhwa jutaeg geonseol', p. 1.
33 Kim Byung-ik, '60man dong-ui nongchon munhwa jutaeg geonseol', p. 2.
34 Pyonganbukdo dosiseolgye yeonguso, pp. 10–12.
35 Hunter, Helen-Louise, *Kim Il-song's North Korea*, op. cit., p. 201.
36 Zhao, Chunlan, PhD dissertation, Catholic University of Leuven (KUL), 2007, p. 264.
37 Jing, Xie and Wu, Deng, 'Socialist Architecture in Mao's Model Village', pp. 293–327.
38 Kim Il Sung, 'Urinara sahoejuui nongchon munjee gwanhan teje', op.cit., p. 6.

39 In general, the province building committee offered standard housing plans, and the *gun*-run construction team decided on the construction method and possible materials.
40 In the rural administrative reform of 1961, North Korea's regime decided that the *gun* is the centre of agricultural management: see Kim Il-sung, Cabinet Decision no. 157 (22 December 1961), (Pyongyang, 1962), p. 191.
41 Kim Cheol-su, 'Gunsojaeji gyehoek', no. 10, 1963, pp. 33–35 and no. 11, 1963, pp. 39–41.
42 Kim Il-sung, 'Urinara sahoejuui nongchon munjee gwanhan theses', op.cit., pp.16–18.
43 Lim Ki-beom, op.cit., pp. 117–126. North Korea's urbanised rural villages are similar to the agro-towns proposed by Nikita Khruschchev, who took the lead in the second socialisation of Soviet farms. Because North Korea and the USSR had the same ideological goal, many of the agrarian-reform strategies, such as mechanisation, amalgamation of living units, labour-intensive methods, etc., were shared. For Soviet agricultural reform, see Auri C. Berg (Toronto, 2012).1
44 Li Hwa-Seon(b), (Pyongyang, 1993), pp. 56–58.
45 http://www.cybernk.net/infoText/InfoAdminstList.aspx?mc=AD0101&ac=A0217017[accessed 25/07/2016].
46 Kim, Young-hoon, 'Bukhan nongeopnongchonui byeonhwa', p. 3.
47 For organisation of agricultural working areas, see Kim Gwang-yun, 'Nongchon saengsan jiyeok gyehoek-e daehan uigyeon', pp. 10–15.
48 Kim Gwang-yun, 'Seohaean pyeongjidae nongchon bulag-ui haplijeok, pp. 32–35; Kim Byeong-Heon, 'Hwanghaebugdo jigu nongchon burak gyehoek', pp. 22–23.
49 Kim Ryong-Chul, Kim Duk-Gi, Hong Don-Sik, Ryu Pae-Yun, Kang Ryong-Sun, Kim Gi-Hong, (Pyongyang, 1991), pp. 19–22.
50 For details on clustering of rural housing, see Kim Tae-Ro, 'Nongchonmaeul gyehoek-eseo jutaek-eul', pp. 33–35; Pyeongyang dosigyehoek yeonguso 'Nongchonmaeul gyehoek-eseo mukkeumsik jutaek baechi bangbeop', pp. 22–24. For details on further systematisation from the early 1990s, see Kim Ryong-Chul, Kim Duk-Gi, Hong Don-Sik, Ryu Pae-Yun, Kang Ryong-Sun, Kim Gi-Hong, op.cit., pp. 48–60.
51 Li Hwa-seon(b), op. cit., p. 54.
52 There are studies on roof types and structures in several volumes of the magazine *Geonchukgwa Geonseol* (Architecture and Construction), 1966–67.
53 Gunsoo Shin, Inha Jung, op.cit., pp. 170–175. For details on the construction method for rural housing, see Yang Jin-Young, 'Gyeongpan jolipsik nongchon jutaek sigong', pp. 18–20; unknown, 'Junggongsik junghyeong block-e uihan nongchon munhwa jutaek-ui jolipsik geonseol', pp. 20–21; unknown, 'Nongchon munhwa jutaek geonseol-e doibhal leuggolsik byeoppan-eul gusang', p. 21.
54 For the two prestigious urban housing types, see Gunsoo Shin, Inha Jung, op.cit.

일곱

The Planning of Gwangbok Street New Town in Pyongyang

Inha Jung / Kim Mina

This chapter focuses on the planning process for Pyongyang Gwangbok Street New Town so as to identify the planning concepts that shaped North Korea's new towns under Kim Jong-il. New towns in the Kim Jong-il era were developed in a manner that was absolutely unique. In modern cities we find no other case where a political leader has directly intervened in urban planning in order to make political propaganda for his ideology. His intervention reminds us of Albert Speer's Berlin project. Kim Jong-il was a key player in the design of major residential complexes constructed after 1973, when he was appointed successor to his father, Kim Il-sung. Kim Jong-il's political ambition was the main driving force in his intervention. For North Koreans, Kim Il-sung was a charismatic leader who commanded absolute obedience during his anti-Japanese movement, the foundation of North Korea as a socialist country, and the successful reconstruction of cities destroyed during the Korean War. Kim Jong-il, whose official career began in the 1970s, had no opportunity to build charisma of such magnitude. Construction projects for new towns and large residential complexes were accordingly regarded as achievements showing off his qualities as successor to his father. The production of revolutionary operas to glorify Kim Il-sung's past and the socialist system had the same purpose.[1] For this reason, planning methods for the residential complex in Pyongyang underwent fundamental changes after Kim Jong-il began to exert his political power. The most significant considerations were not residents' convenience, economy, or welfare, but how the cityscape was perceived from specific viewpoints. Architecture was regarded as a physical device with which to construct a showcase; through it Kim Jong-il attempted to visualise the unique identity and political ideology of North Korea.

One of the most important characteristics of urban and housing planning in the Kim Jong-il era was emphasis of visual effects. This was totally different from the design approach taken in the Kim Il-sung era, which had been dominated by planning based on the microdistrict. The latter planning process had been entirely shaped by statistical data such as distance, population, and construction costs.[2] In the Kim Jong-il era, on the other hand, not only Pyongyang but also major cities in the region followed new principles.[3] Kim Jong-il 'sought an open as opposed to closed pattern in urban planning, so as to break the conventional monotonous streetscape, and attempted a revolutionary transition in the creation of architecture.'[4] With respect to building layouts, visual effects along arterial streets became more important than functionality. In 1991 Kim Jong-il published *Geonchuk yesullon* (On the Art of Architecture), which repeats similar arguments. Gwangbok Street is a particularly clear example of the drastic change in housing and urban planning after the 1970s as political power shifted from Kim Il-sung to his son, Kim Jong-il. This study sets out to investigate the case of Gwangbok Street New Town with the following objectives. First, we need to identify Kim Jong-il's aesthetic principles, which played a key role in planning Gwangbok Street New Town. Second, it is necessary to identify the discursive framework guiding North Korean architects and urban planners who supported Kim Jong-il's ideas. Lastly, this study will review the impact of the Soviet Union on changes in urban planning in North Korea in the post-Khrushchev era.

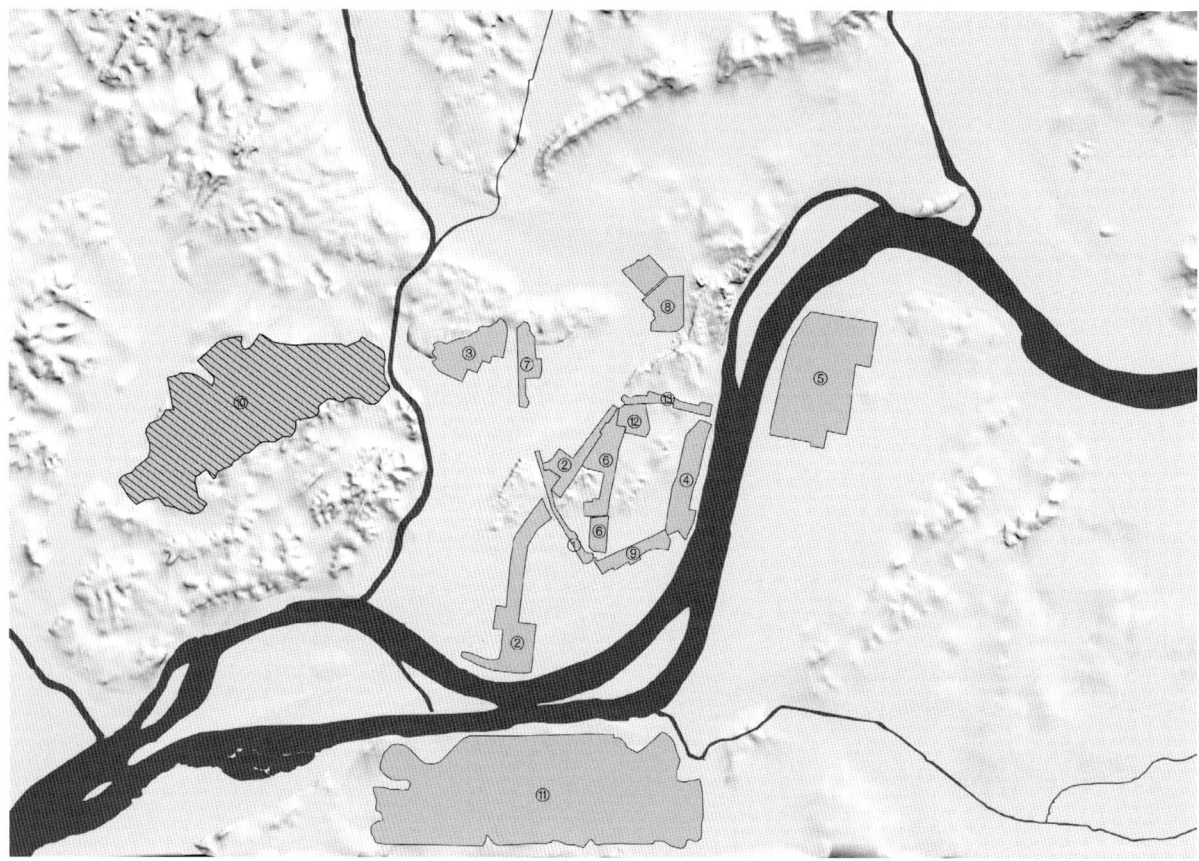

Apartment complexes in Pyongyang built in the era of Kim Jong-il.

Kim Jong-il's Aesthetic Principles in North Korea's Housing and Urban Design

During the reign of Kim Jong-il, 13 large housing estates were built in Pyongyang. The construction of these new estates transformed Pyongyang's cityscape. Some of these housing estates, such as Gwangbok Street and Tongil Street, were almost as large as new towns. In the early stage, Kim Jong-il's interventions were modest; they became bolder with the passage of time. Gwangbok Street marks a climax; at this point Kim Jong-il's aesthetic was firmly established, together with the Juche ideology. Gwangbok Street New Town is unique and special because the key criterion in the planning of these residential complexes was a dictator's taste.

	Street name	Duration of construction	Area of site	Height of tallest building	Number of household
1.	Seoseong	Early 1970s	(unknown)	15 storeys	(unknown)
2.	Chollima	Stage 1: early 1970s	approx. 80 ha	15 storeys	(unknown)
3.	Rakwon	Stage 2: mid-1980s	(unknown)	30 storeys	4500
4.	Seungri	1975	approx. 60 ha	20 storeys	3000
		1975	approx. 70 ha	15 storeys	(unknown)
5.	Munsu	Stage 1: 1980–1982	approx. 40 ha	30 storeys	1700
		Stage 2: 1982–1983			
6.	Changgwang	Stage 1: 1980	approx. 40 ha	30 storeys	1730
		Stage 2: 1982	(unknown)	45 storeys	2400
7.	Gyeongheung	Early 1980s	approx. 30 ha	41 storeys	(unknown)
8.	Buksae	1984–1987	approx. 30 ha	27 storeys	(unknown)
9.	Yeonggwang	1985	approx. 70 ha	25 storeys	(unknown)
10.	Gwangbok	Stage 1: 1985–1989	approx. 400 ha	42 storeys	20,000
		Stage 2: 1990–1992			30,000
11.	Tongil	Stage 1: 1989–1993	approx. 800 ha	25 storeys	20,000
		Stage 2: 1992–1993			30,000
12.	Mansudae	2008–2009	approx. 20 ha	18 storeys	(unknown)
13.	Changjeon	2011–2012	approx. 40 ha	45 storeys	(unknown)

The concept of *hyeongseong* and three aesthetic attributes

The term *hyeongseong* was used in North Korea in the Kim Jong-il era for many different categories of design ranging from architectural design to urban planning. This is a key concept in Kim Jong-il's book *On the Art of Architecture*. 'Architecture and *Hyeongseong*', the third and key chapter of this four-chapter book, deals with the principles of architectural creation. We also see this word used repeatedly in architectural magazines published in North Korea at this time to describe the architecture, housing, and urban design of the period. *Hyeongseong* covered a wide spectrum of design and planning for individual buildings, streets, districts, and cities. Furthermore, when combined with other words, the meaning of the term expanded. *Hyeongseong* forms compound words such as *geonchuk hyeongseong* (architectural design), *geori hyeongseong* (street formation), *bongsamang hyeongseong* (arrangement of the service network), *dosi hyeongseong* (urban planning), architectural *hyeongseong* (design) theory, main *hyeongseong* (composition) space, and three-dimensional spatial *hyeongseong* (formation). A precise understanding of this term's meaning in specific contexts is important for comprehension of Kim Jong-il's aesthetic system.

First of all, since a design proposal for a building is called a '*hyeongseong* proposal' in North Korea, the term *hyeongseong* is similar to 'design' but not equivalent to it. This is because its meaning changes depending on context. For example, while 'entrance *hyeongseong*' in a housing estate indicates scenic composition including the arrangement of the buildings, '*hyeongseong* centre' refers to nuances relating to the centre of the planned area. At the same time, this word always implies aesthetic concepts such as grandeur, diversity, unity, and three-dimensionality. In this respect, it is also connected with the emotional response generated by scenes in urban space. Such abstract rhetoric was rarely used in the era of Kim Jong-il's father. Writings on urban planning in the Kim Il-sung era

Kim Jong-Il with North Korean planners in front of a model of Gwangbok Street.
Source: Lee, H. & Lee, H., 1990

argued that planning should be conducted in a scientific manner; according to Kim Il-sung, this meant that they should be 'socialist in content'. Accordingly, North Korean planners did their best to create an effective and functional plan. In the process microdistrict planning was adopted as the dominant approach. From this it is clear that the term *hyeongseong* was important to the process of establishing Kim Jong-il's aesthetic approach.

When Kim Jong-il used the term in his book, his main focus was on architectural form. He believed that architectural *hyeongseong* should form the core of the creative process. Kim sometimes used this term when talking about cities. For example, *dosi hyeongseong* (urban formation) does not mean a simple arrangement of buildings or the regulation of their height; it is a part of architectural creation. An urban architect should consistently place buildings in the city centre; this can complete the *hyeongseong* (formation) of urban architecture.'[5] An architect who knows how to create genuine architecture is defined as 'one who forms cities' by revealing the characteristics of buildings so that harmony can be achieved in the arrangement of buildings throughout the city.'[6]

7. Planning of Gwangbok Street New Town in Pyongyang   167

Kim Jong-il's arguments were comprehensive and ambiguous; North Korean architects and city planners, however, had to interpret them in a practical, applicable way. In the process the three attributes of unity, diversity, and three-dimensionality emerged as the key criteria in city formation. Once these aesthetic concepts were accepted, they became dogma in North Korean urban planning and have been repeatedly used to explain specific urban plans. For instance, elucidating the layout of buildings in the plan for the second stage of Chollima Street, the architect Cha Cha-young stated: 'the most important thing in the street formation is to guarantee unity, diversity, and three-dimensionality.'[7] Furthermore, he stated: 'unity, diversity, and three-dimensionality must be achieved in street formation in order to enhance the inherent emotional power and artistic quality of the architectural form. This way, the entire city can be beautifully harmonised, and grandeur and splendour can be guaranteed.'[8]

Of these three qualities, unity was defined in Kim Jong-il's *On the Art of Architecture* as 'a property that binds and harmonises various architectural elements with a unified system and order.'[9] This property appears not only in city and street formation but also in an overall architectural design, including the decoration of individual buildings, their relationship with nature, etc. In order to address the issue of unity in architectural design, each part and element had to be harmoniously combined in congruence with the overall order. In the formation of a street or cityscape, it was important to establish major and minor elements and establish a good relationship between the two.[10] In pursuit of this idea, North Korean architects and planners tried to create a sense of formal rhythm by setting up a hierarchy among buildings and differentiating the height of dominant and subordinate buildings. These characteristics were clearly reflected in the residential complexes planned in the early days of the Kim Jong-il era, e.g. Changgwang Street and Rakwon Street. In the latter cases unity is created by the buildings along main streets, where there is a rhythmic alternation of low, long buildings and tall, slender ones.

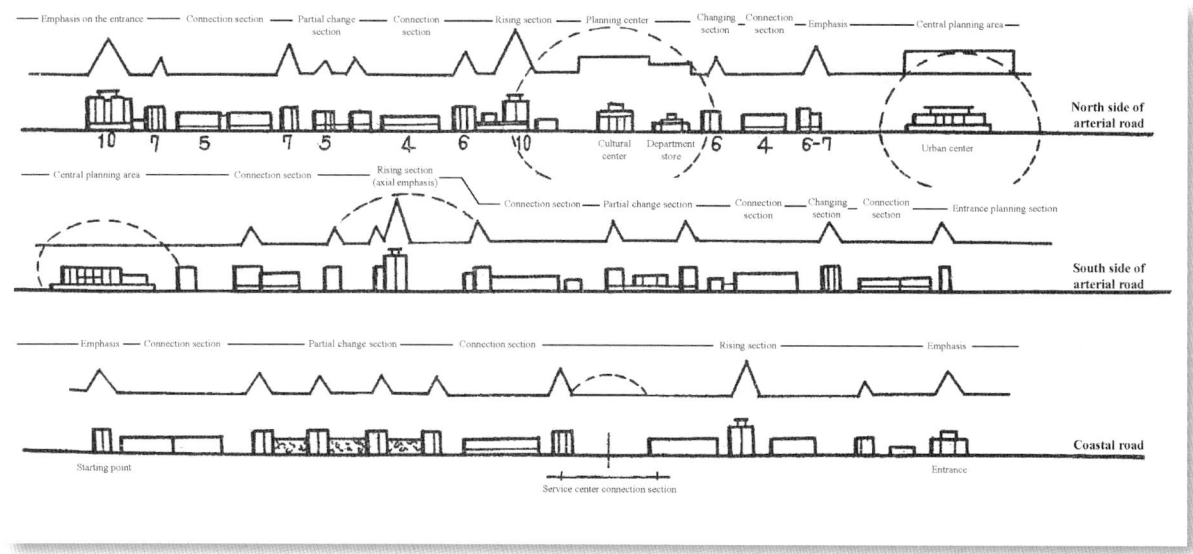

Diagram showing rhythmic unity of street formation.
Source: Kim, Cheol-su, 1992

Model and aerial view of Nakwon Street.
Source: (Up) Li, Hyeon-deok, and Li, Hyeon-bok, 1987, (Down) Google maps, 2018

In the urban planning of the 1980s, however, this early principle changed as diversity and three-dimensionality came to be more strongly emphasised. Diversity was mainly regarded as non-recurring, clearly distinguishable form. Prior to Gwangbok Street, architects made restrained attempts to introduce diversity by, for instance, adding round or arc-shaped balconies to box-like buildings.[11] However, after high-rise towers with a polygonal unit plan had been erected on Gyeongheung Street, architects explored the towers' visual effect on the scale of the city plan. They made the most of the irregularity of the convex and concave shapes on Gwangbok Street, where the soaring towers look bold and bulky – precisely the expressive effect sought by Kim Jong – and their overlap contributes to diversity and three-dimensionality in urban space.[12]

Afterwards, the concept of diversity was explored in two different approaches on Gwangbok Street. One approach was to insert polygonal towers to give the urban ensemble formal diversity as seen from the outside. For example, high-rise towers with cylindrical, pinwheel, polygonal, S-shaped, and stepped forms were erected in the main part of this housing estate. The other way was to create a long linear building type which partially transformed the existing staircase-accessed houses. These 15–20-storey-high buildings offer a range of different views from different standpoints and serve as a foil to the high-rise towers, being lower than the latter but 200–300 metres long. Similar building types were explored in the 1970s in the Soviet Union.

Three-dimensionality was considered the most important planning factor when designing the street formation for the Kim Jong-il housing complex. Gwangbok Street was seen as a new model based on a three-dimensionality that overcame the monotony of existing residential complexes. To draw out the three-dimensionality visually, Kim Jong-il speculated over how the large apartment buildings would look at each important site. To make Pyongyang's major streets seem full of life and vitality, he wanted the grand buildings on them to be arranged atypically to enhance their three-dimensionality.[13]

This idea led to an increase in building heights on housing estates. In the era of Kim Il-sung, average building height had been 6–8 storeys at most. In the time of Kim Jong-il, however, there was a leap to 20 storeys in 1975 Rakwon Street, 30 storeys in Changgwang Street, 40 storeys in Gyeongheung Street, and 42 storeys in Gwangbok Street. The surge in building height was a conscious effort on the part of Kim Jong-il and North Korean architects to accentuate the effect of three-dimensionality in urban form. Kim Jong-il used scale models of cities to control building height. After viewing the models, he would issue further specific instructions to his architects.

Three viewpoints based on distance
Kim Jong-il wanted Pyongyang's major streets to come across as places full of vitality and grandeur. To this end, he asked architects to research how urban images could be enhanced through propaganda photos taken with different distances between viewer and object. Views of urban space can, he claimed, be put into three categories: close-, middle-, and long-range. 'As we approach buildings from a great distance,' he said, 'we gain a lively appreciation of the plastic effects of their details and finishing materials and come to perceive their size as larger and larger.' For this reason, he stressed, 'it is necessary to accurately measure plastic effects from close up, middle distance, and long distance, to consider how to enhance plastic effects as seen from a given distance, and to investigate a new design approach based on these views.'[14] This suggestion was realised in the photo albums of Gwangbok Street New Town. After construction of the new town had been completed, the North Korean government issued a number of photo albums to promote Kim Jong-il's achievement. Analysis of these photos shows that the viewpoints of the urban space surrounding Gwangbok Street are limited to three types, namely close-up, middle-distance, and long-distance.

The photographs of Gwangbok Street were taken so that the shapes and outlines of individual buildings could be immediately grasped. The photographs were usually taken at eye level. Since they were shot while looking up

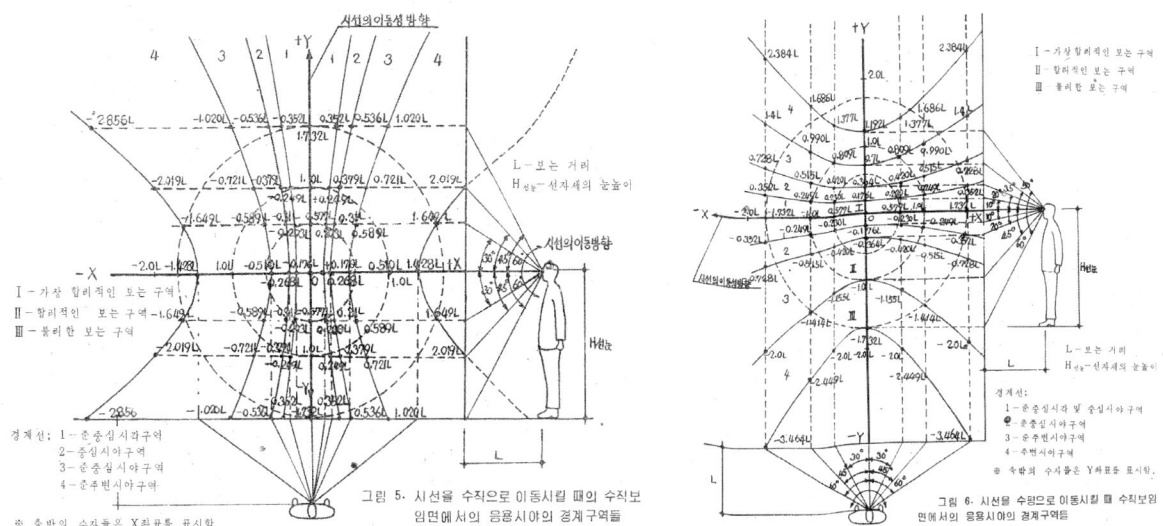

Illustration showing the proper range of a view according to distance.
Source: Bang, Cheol-ung, 1992

at the top of a building from the ground, it was possible to emphasise the height of the towers: distorted perspectival effects intentionally highlighted the buildings' glanderous shapes. However, the close-range photographs do not clearly reveal the three-dimensionality of all buildings that was so important to Kim Jong-il. In most of the photo collections, close-up photographs of Gwangbok Street are restricted to high-rise apartment buildings.

In mid-range views efforts were made to underline the three-dimensionality of urban spaces through the relationship between buildings. Kim Jong-il instructed North Korean architects to overlap similar-sized buildings. In the second stage of the planning of Chollima Street, he stated that 'a city must look three-dimensional by the use of overlapping high-rise buildings.'[15] Thus 'the overlapping of 20-, 25-, and 30-storey towers can express the grandeur of a city.'[16] This idea developed into the 'clustered layout' on Gwangbok Street. 'In the past,' Kim Jong-il argued, when the overall urban impression and skyline was being determined, 'buildings were positioned side by side along streets.' He was not satisfied with this approach. Instead, he claimed that 'an indented layout of small and large buildings, and the overlapping of small and large buildings can provide streets with a three-dimensional "hyeongseong". In particular, street formation using a clustered layout can help streets look majestic.'[17]

An additional technique in enhancing a street's three-dimensionality was to use low-rise service-facilities buildings. This method was preferred because such buildings can both serve as buffers that unify irregular building forms and, as a result, reduce visual disorder. 'Service-facilities buildings constructed in a row beneath high-rise apartment buildings,' asserted Kim Jong-il, 'can make a street look three-dimensional because they do not obstruct the pedestrian's field of vision.'[18] Accordingly, a common approach to photographing Gwangbok Street was to use a diagonal composition with a focus on the service-facilities buildings.

In the planning of large-scale residential complexes in North Korea, the long-distance view was considered important – as is clear from diverse panoramic shots of Gwangbok Street in propaganda photo albums. In long-distance views, residential complexes were photographed

7. Planning of Gwangbok Street New Town in Pyongyang

from a high angle not only because this produced a legible overall view, but also to reveal the city's rhythmic skyline and give the photograph a sense of stability. The reason why irregular buildings are arranged around the main road in Gwangbok Street is that they strengthen the impression of three-dimensionality in a long-distance view. In a long-distance view of a residential complex with an irregular arrangement of buildings, the varied clustering of the large buildings is more noticeable compared to in a mid-range view, while giving the residential complex as a whole a certain unity. The effect of the overlapping buildings is to make the density of the entire city seem higher than in actual fact. If a panoramic view is photographed with a natural landscape in the background (e.g. the Daedong River, Mount Daeseong, Mount Hyeongje, etc.), this suffices to give an impression of a 'socialist city as utopia' or 'urban housing in a park', an impression which is in stark contrast with that made by capitalist cities.

Close-range, mid-range, and long-distance views of Gwangbok Street.
Source: Meuser, Philipp, vol. 1, 2012, pp. 15, 30, Han, Beom-jik and Li, Bok-u, 1991

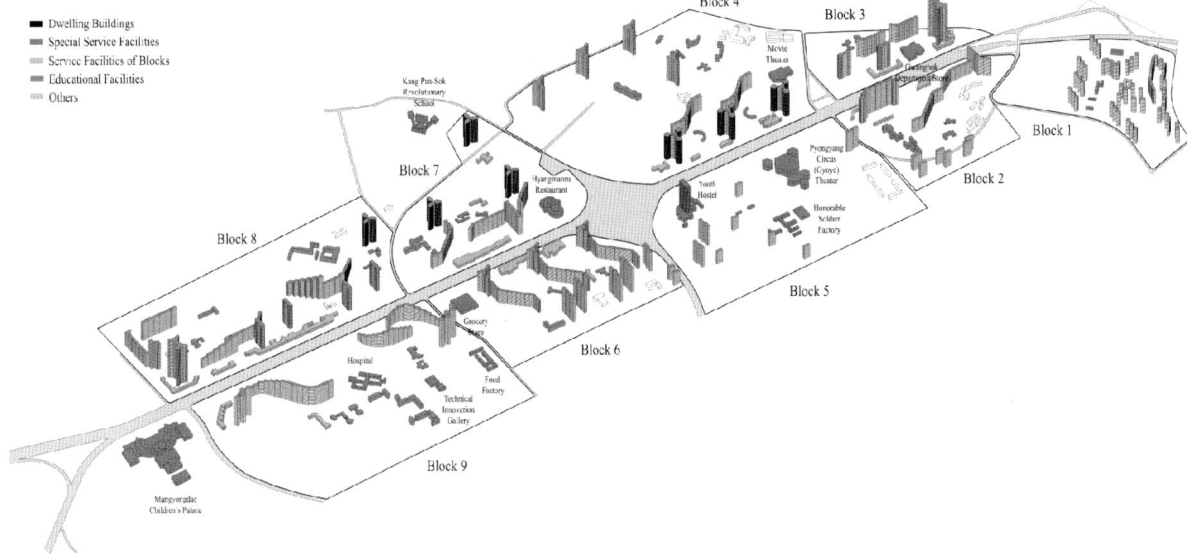

The layout of Gwangbok Street.
Source: Li, Hyeon-deok, and Li, Hyeon-bok, 1987, redrawn by the authors.

Planning Method for Gwangbok New Town

Background

Gwangbok Street in Mangyongdae, a western outskirt of Pyongyang. has emerged as the main site of the Pyongyang Festival. Even though there are no high mountains here, people avoided this area as a place in which to live due to its lack of rainfall. The scarcity of rain left farming undeveloped, and Mangyongdae remained for a long time filled with hills and woods. Even when North Korean government incorporated the area into the city of Pyongyang in September 1959, urbanisation did not take off. Moreover, since Mangyongdae was the birthplace of Kim Il-sung, North Koreans recognised it as a holy site, preserving its green spaces despite its proximity to downtown Pyongyang. This changed when the Pyongyang Festival sparked large-scale development in the area. Stadiums were constructed along Cheongchun Street perpendicular to the River Daedong, and a large housing estate was erected on Gwangbok Street.

Birds-eye's view of Gwangbok Street.
Source: Li, Hyeon-deok, and Li, Hyeon-bok, 1987

Originally built as accommodation for participants in the 13th World Festival of Youth and Students in 1989, Gwangbok Street was allocated to Pyongyang citizens after the festival ended. At this time, the North Korean regime was trying to prevent South Korea hosting the Summer Olympics of 1988. It failed. In 1981, when the choice of host city was finalised, the North Korean government decided to hold the 13th World Festival of Youth and Students as its response to the Summer Olympics. Due to its ideological rivalry with South Korea, North Korea went to all lengths to make Gwangbok Street a showcase project; this included trying to create a unique city form such as had never been seen before in the world. Gwangbok Street is accordingly the most political of the various housing complexes developed by North Korea after the mid-1970s. After acquiring confidence in 'our style of street formation' through the experience of developing Rakwon, Chollima Street, and Changgwang streets, among others, Kim Jong-il went all out to show what he could do in Gwangbok Street.

The North Korean government developed this area on a grand scale in preparation for the Pyongyang Festival, turning it into a new show town in the vicinity of Pyongyang. With a total area of 416 hectares, the new town accommodates 35,200 households along the six-kilometre-long Gwangbok Street. The development process had two stages. The first stage was from 1986 to 1989 and provided housing for 25,000 households. The second construction stage, from 1990 to 1992, added accommodation for 10,200 households.[19] Compared to the five new towns around Seoul, this complex is low-density. It is is a fifth the size of Bundang New Town (1963 hectares) and a little smaller than Pyeongchon New Town (510 hectares). The average building-to-land ratio is 7.6% and the floor-area ratio is about 80%. Density of population is approximately 340 persons per hectare, half that of Bundang New Town (614 person/ha). The building-to-land ratio and floor-area-to-land ratio of each section are shown in Table 2.

Gwangbok Street housing complex is a mid-sized new town that was planned in a unique way, without either a land-use plan or a systematic circulation plan. The street system is totally dependent on Gwangbok Street; access roads to each apartment building are cul-de-sacs. This means the planning of the housing estate was different from conventional planning. Instead, in addition to service facilities, various programmes were inserted to boast of the achievements of Kim's family. For example, special education facilities of a militaristic character, such as Mangyongdae Children's Palace and Kang Pan-sok Revolutionary School, were included. This meant a transition from the equality-based educational system that had existed under Kim Il-sung to the elite educational system required by Kim Jong-il's military-first strategy. At the centre of Gwangbok Street is the Pyongyang Circus Theatre. In North Korea circus is a genre of literary art and enjoys a similar status to literature, film, drama, art, and dance.[20] Kim Jong-il sought to revitalise North Korean circus in the context of theatre, drama, gymnastics, and artistic performances. Another notable feature is Gwangbok Department Store, considered one of North Korea's three major department stores (along with Pyongyang Department Stores No. 1 and No. 2), at the entrance to Gwangbok Street. The planning of Gwangbok Street thus took into account not only its actual residents but users from various classes, including the upper class and foreigners; this made it a mid-sized city. In design of individual residential buildings, priority was given to cityscapes and diversity of building forms (elliptical, hexagonal, and polygonal) arranged in a free formation.

Planning method
Kim Jong-il's aesthetics evidently played an important role in the planning of Gwangbok Street New Town. However, since the new town is a place where hundreds of thousands of people live, Kim Jong-il's aesthetic idea need to be examined from diverse perspectives. North Korean architects and planners used their expertise to support Kim Jong-il's ideas. In the process they needed to substantially change the existing planning method. In the Kim Il-sung era, the partition of urban space and the arrangement of service facilities had been dependent on a hierarchical system.[21] At that time, prioritising economic feasibility, the North Korean government had placed cities into five categories – 'special city', 'large city 1', 'large city 2', 'mid-sized city', and 'small city' – in accordance with population size and urban character. For each group, the hierarchical structure had been further subdivided into four levels: residential groups, microdistricts (*jutaek soguyeok*), residential districts (*jutaek guyeok*), and cities. Under this hierarchical system 'a large city consists of three levels (microdistrict, residential district, large city), a mid-sized city of two levels (microdistrict, city), and a small city of one level (a city centre coinciding with the centre of the microdistrict)'.[22] The microdistrict approach had played a crucial role in determining the basic size, building layout, and services infrastructure of an urban block. Because it satisfied communities' social requirements and facilitated mass-produced urban housing, the North Korean regime had enthusiastically adapted this approach to

No.	Area (ha)	Population	Households	Building-to-Land Ratio (%)	Floor Area Ratio (%)	Blocks
①	32	16,119	3,980	4.8	76.0	
②	27	17,780	4,390	9.1	83.6	
③	15	23,693	5,850	12.3	138.3	
④	79	12,798	3,160	5.5	39.9	
⑤	59	2,592	640	7.2	38.1	
⑥	39	20,615	5,090	10.1	100.6	
⑦	46	14,903	3,680	7.1	71.7	
⑧	52	26,285	6,490	9.0	107.7	
⑨	67	7,775	1,920	6.6	56.8	
Total	416	142,560	35,200	8.0	79.2	Total Floor Area: 330ha Density: 342.7(person/ha)

The building-to-land ratio and the floor-area-to-land ratio for each block in Gwangbok Street (Table 2).

Source: Li, Hyeon-deok, and Li, Hyeon-bok, 1990; Kim, 1987; redrawn by the authors

fit its own reality.²³ Planning of residential districts had expanded the treatment of the microdistrict as a self-contained unit, using it on the urban scale for effective distribution of service amenities and to correctly calculate usage cycles for services and economy in self-management activities.²⁴,²⁵ The rise of Kim Jong-il brought the rejection of this hierarchical system and its replacement with his aesthetic principle.

The subdivision of the site into smaller areas in Gwangbok Street depends on an approach which is markedly different from the microdistrict approach. The first stage of the new town consists of nine districts, 33 apartment buildings, public buildings, and convenience service facilities, etc. connected by a single 100-metre-wide, six-kilometre-long arterial road serving a suburban area completely independent of the centre of Pyongyang. The access roads inside the complex do not follow a regular layout. Instead, houses and service networks are located relatively freely around main roads. The nine districts are not subdivided to form independent blocks. They do not serve as units of urban space as the microdistrict does. In terms of their size, population, building layout, building-to-land ratio, and floor-area-to-land ratio (see Table 2), there is no consistent principle permeating the design of these districts.²⁶ This means that it is difficult to say that the existing microdistrict planning approach was applied to the Gwangbok complex. Instead, a greater role was played by the clustering of diverse buildings and views of them from close up, mid-range, and long distance. In terms of services infrastructure, this housing estate includes educational facilities, such as kindergartens and elementary, middle, and high schools, as well as all types of amenity, such as restaurants, shops selling rationed food, a rice factory, a laundry facility, etc. However, the numbers and size of these amenities were not calculated based on pedestrian distances or intensity of use by residents. Instead, the most important factor was visual contrast with the high-rise towers on Gwangbok Street. The services infrastructure mainly occupies three-storey buildings stretching horizontally along Gwangbok Street; small horizontal windows and pilotis

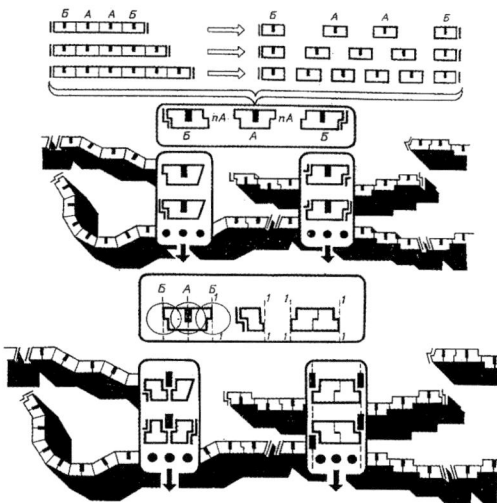

Diagrams the Soviet ILG-600 housing estate.
Source: Meuser, P. and Zadorin, D., 2016

reinforce this design concept. Furthermore, consistent consideration was not taken of residents' usage cycles in existing residential districts. Instead, priority was given to aesthetic considerations, such as impressive building form and the desire to embellish the capital's cityscape as the gateway to the southwest of Pyongyang.²⁷ Large service facilities were deployed without much thought for residents' usage cycles.

Building types

Residential buildings from the era of Kim Jong-il are clearly distinguishable from those of the previous era. Gwangbok Street and Tongil Street, in particular, adopt non-repetitive form as a reflection of Kim Jong-il's aesthetic principles. To comply with these principles, North Korean architects made two changes to existing prefabrication methods. The first was to create a tower-type building with a completely new unit plan to match. The second was to deploy long, linear buildings by transforming the existing unit plans and using prefabrication. The latter buildings served as a kind of background for the high-rise towers. Similar transformations of the unit plan and building forms had already emerged

Building plans and unit plans for the Soviet ILG-600 housing estate.
Source: Meuser, P. and Zadorin, D., 2016

in Soviet apartment housing in the late 1960s, and it seems that North Korea imported the necessary assembly technology in the 1970s. Urban housing in the era of Kim Jong-il was clearly influenced by the Soviet Union. This is evident from comparison of the Soviet ILG-600 residential complex shown in Philipp Meuser's book on Soviet mass housing with Gwangbok Street.[28]

Although mass-produced dwellings in the Khrushchev era contributed to addressing the Soviet Union's chronic housing shortage, this monotonous standardised urban housing not only led to a dramatic deterioration in the quality of urban landscapes but also failed to satisfy residents' diverse needs. Aware of this problem, on 28 May 1969 the Central Committee of the Soviet Communist Party passed an act (the Plan for Improving the Quality of Residential and Urban Construction (SNiP II-.1-71)) in a bid to shift the focus of Soviet housing policy from quantity to quality. The existing housing policy, whose rationale was based entirely on cost-cutting on the urban scale, was no longer considered appropriate. In particular, Soviet planners were responding to two social changes. One was the divorce laws passed in the early 1960s; the other, new statistical data on how the Soviet family was organised. It was clear that existing housing types could not take care of residents' needs. Additionally, as use of household appliances such as dry cleaners and refrigerators increased and demand for private space intensified, Soviet planners attempted to diversify housing types and adapt the prefabrication method. In North Korea, on the other hand, architectural forms did not derive from changing social needs as in the Soviet Union. As argued above, the driving forces were Kim Jong-il's theory of architectural aesthetics and the emphasis on diversity and three-dimensionality. Once Kim Jong-il had determined the overall direction for planning, the role of North Korean architects was to explore new construction technology that could overcome the limitations of the existing monotonous prefabrication techniques and allow for more diverse assembly. The various building types under Kim Jong-il were more closely related to construction technology than anything else. They came in two categories: a transformed method of prefabrication applied to linear buildings, and an integral construction method called 'the slip-form method', which was applied to high-rise towers.

Linear buildings with staircase-access unit plans
After the declaration of the ceasefire in 1953, the reconstruction of North Korean cities began with active support from socialist brother countries, including the Soviet Union, China, East Germany, and Poland. In this process a number of modern housing types were introduced, and norms were established for standard minimum housing. During the era of Kim Il-sung, two types of building plan were mainly used: the staircase-access type (*sektsjiashik*), imported from the Soviet Union, and the single-corridor-access type (*oeryangshik*), which was adopted following its use by East German architects during the reconstruction of Hamhŭng. Additionally, from 1961 forwards, the combination of these two types led to the creation of a third type: 8-to-12-storey apartment buildings.[29] This pattern changed, however, because the single-corridor-access type, which had been the most popular type in the era of Kim Il-sung, was too rigid to accommodate Kim Jung-il's new aesthetic. The staircase-access type with 2, 3, or 4 dwelling units on a staircase now became the dominant type. When the building layout was based on the staircase-access type, the interior space could be arranged more freely, even if there was an increase in the number of rooms. An additional advantage of this type was that slight changes in the unit floor plans could produce changes in the building shape. The original idea for this came from the Soviet Union. In the Soviet Union in the 1970s, after Khrushchev's retirement in 1964, Soviet architects discussed diversity of form based on the staircase-access-type layout for construction of third-generation housing. Such new methods could strain the existing prefabrication system. Theoretically, however, this was a transitional stage that would lead to a completely open design process. After the 1970s, Soviet architects devised various new building forms by developing existing prefabrication methods. Buildings became curved or bent as opposed to rectilinear; sometimes, they were even shaped like stacks of Tetris blocks. As the assembly system developed, along with housing equipment, the height of buildings increased from five to nine or 16 storeys, with a maximum of 37 storeys.[30]

In North Korea similar methods were applied for the first time in the mid-1980s to apartment buildings on Gwangbok Street. These linear buildings were 10–16 metres wide, but as much as 200–300 metres long. Containing 10–19 unit modules, they could be as massive as a great wall.[31] The building plan for Gwangbok Street features 16 different types of house, including shapes that are linear, bent, stepped, curved, etc. In spite of these buildings' complex shapes, their unit modules were simple. Based on a rectangular standardised floor plan, they had one or both oblique sides. For example, in bent buildings, a rectangular plan and a trapezoid plan were used to create seven types of unit. In the case of a curved building plan, various curvatures were possible by varying the oblique angle of the trapezoidal unit plan. The use of such methods on Gwangbok Street shows that under the influence of Soviet socialist housing North Korean architects were able to explore the visual consequences of following Kim's aesthetic principle of *hyeongseong*. Building designs were drawn up taking into account aesthetic aspects rather than inhabitants' needs.

A close look at each of the unit plans for Gwangbok Street reveals that, although the building shapes become gradually more diverse and the buildings taller, the basic unit module remained substantially unchanged. The basis for Gwangbok Street is an orthogonal system with a 3000/3600-millimetre module.[32] This orthogonal unit module was a constant since most apartment buildings were planned based on a prefabrication construction method that used the existing large wooden sliding walls.

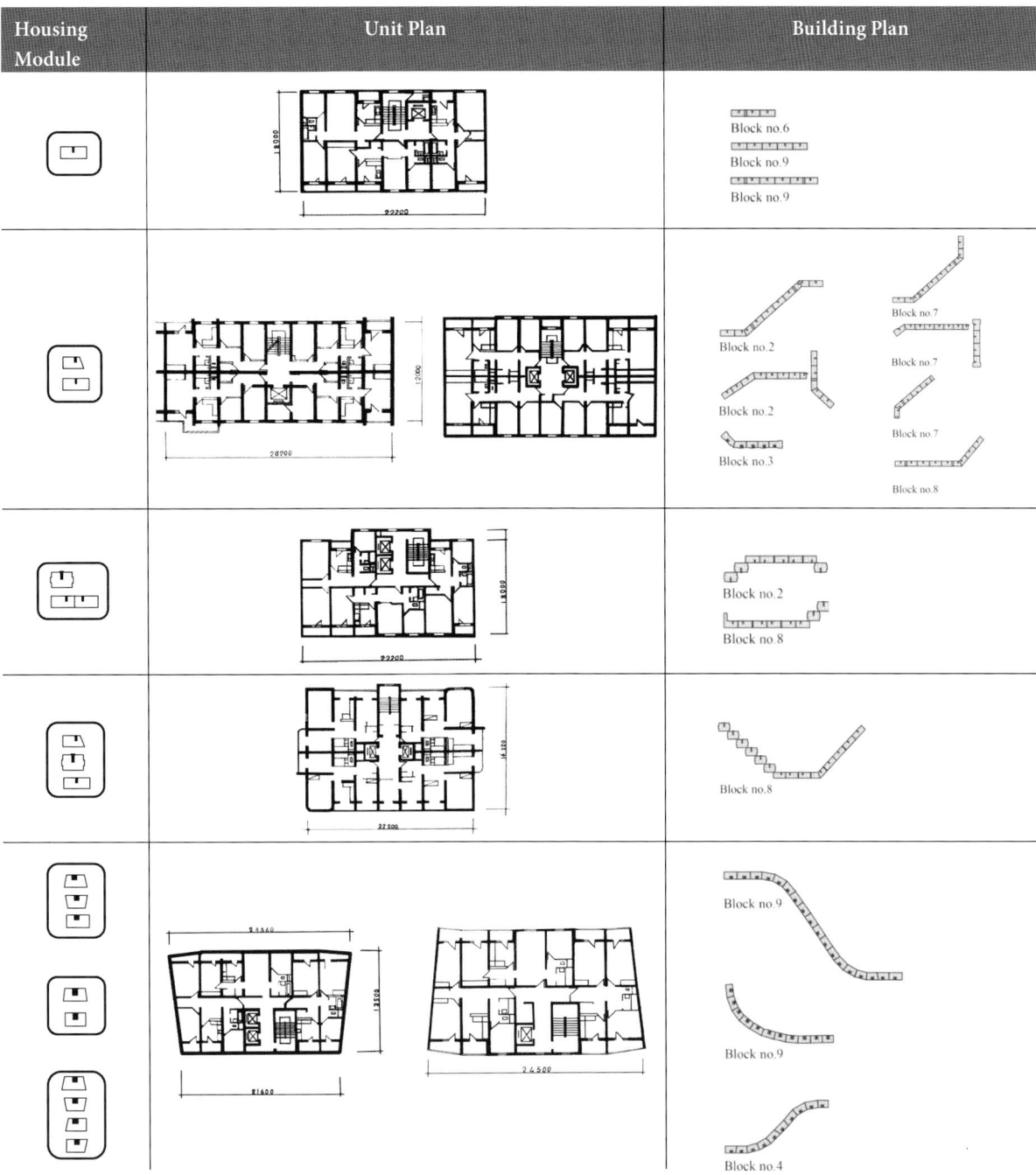

Building plans and unit plans for Gwangbok Street.
Source: Li, Hyeon-deok, and Li, Hyeon-bok, 1987, redrawn by the authors.

Prefabricated panels for housing construction.
Source: Meuser, Philipp, vol.2, 2012, pp.206-7

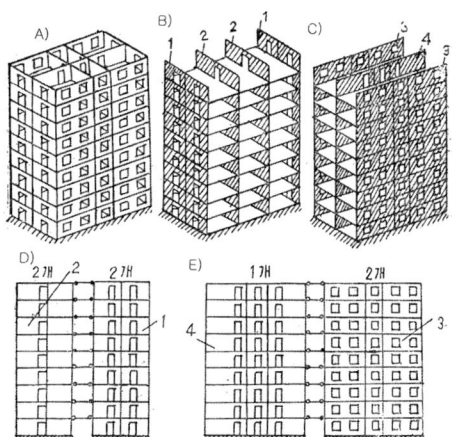

A: grid-supporting structural system,
B: horizontally-supporting(garojiji) structural system
C: vertically-supporting(serojiji) structural system

Structural diagram showing large-panel assembly.
Source: Choi, Won-hun, 1991

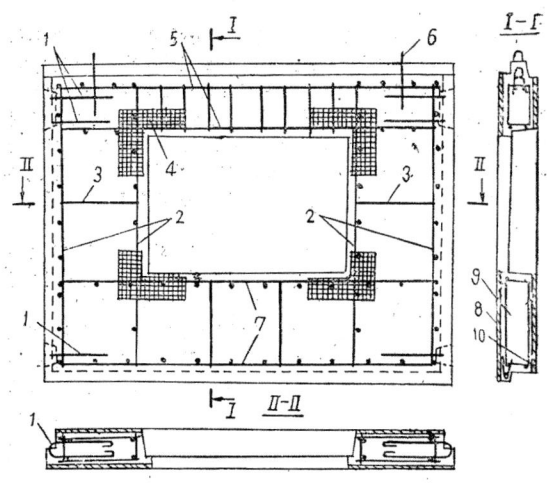

Positioning of rebar in large panels.
Source: Choi, Won-hun, 1991

In North Korea prefabrication technology dates to 1953. Soviet prefabrication technology was first introduced to North Korea with the aid of experts from socialist countries such as the Soviet Union, Germany, and Poland and of North Koreans returning after studying architecture at the Soviet Academy of Architecture. Until this point, masonry had been the main construction method in North Korea. Prefabrication technology developed in three phases. First, came a method for joining standardised blocks: second, a method was developed for assembling large panels for use in walls, floors, and ceilings; third, there was a method for assembling prefabricated housing units on site.[33] Unlike the Soviet Union, which preferred the third of these methods, North Korea adopted the production and assembly of large panels as its main construction method. This reflected the capabilities of the North Korean construction industry, which did not possess the tower cranes needed to lift prefabricated housing units. When the construction boom of the 1960s led to advances in the prefabrication method, China's National Construction Committee of China sent a delegation to take a close look at the prefabrication system in Pyongyang in 1975. At this time, Pyongyang had eight prefabrication factories, including the Pyeongcheon-ri Factory and the Dongpyeongyang Factory (located approximately eight and ten kilometres from Pyongyang respectively). The eight factories were able to supply prefabricated components to housing construction sites all over Pyongyang. According to the report published by the Chinese delegation, the use of prefabricated large wall panels was very common in North Korean housing construction at this time. All residential buildings of fewer than 12 storeys used large panels in their construction; the panels comprised about 80% to 90% of a building's total wall surface. The development of large-panel prefabrication technology enabled an increase in the height of residential buildings to 20–30 storeys.

Another development at this time was unification of structural systems. Three structural systems emerged that went hand in hand with the panel-assembly method: a horizontally supporting structural system (*garojiji*), a vertically supporting structural system (*serojiji*), and a grid structural system.[34] North Korea's architects used various systems between 1957 and 1958, but gradually the horizontal structural system became the most common; as a result, in around 1959–1960, the basic structural module was standardised to a width of 3000 millimetres. Use of the horizontally supporting structural system meant that it was possible to reduce the consumption of steel and the number of types of prefabricated component. However, since the wall width was determined at the factory,[35] floor plans using this system were less flexible than those based on a vertically supporting structural system. In other words, since the three-metre-wide wall was a recurrent element, room size had to adhere to the basic module. On the other hand, if the wall width were increased to 360 and the span to 570 centimetres, a building's size could be proportionally enlarged. Suggested in a proposal by state-run institutes, this idea was never realised.

The linear buildings on Gwangbok Street were thus of the staircase-accessed type. However, to make buildings with a bent or curved shape, the edge of the unit plan needed to be oblique. Furthermore, it was necessary to make curved balconies of a linear shape. North Korean architects and engineers devised ways to create various building types though slight changes in the prefabricated method. A serious problem, however, was that such assembly methods could not be applied to buildings of more than 25 storeys and building forms could not easily be modified much beyond the basic linear shape.[36] Thus the most important challenge facing North Korean architects during the Kim Jong-il era was to overcome such limitations of structural system and design and realise an appropriate street *hyeongseong* (formation) through exploration of the three aesthetic concepts of unity, diversity, and three-dimensionality. The tower type of building became popular as a means of solving these difficulties.

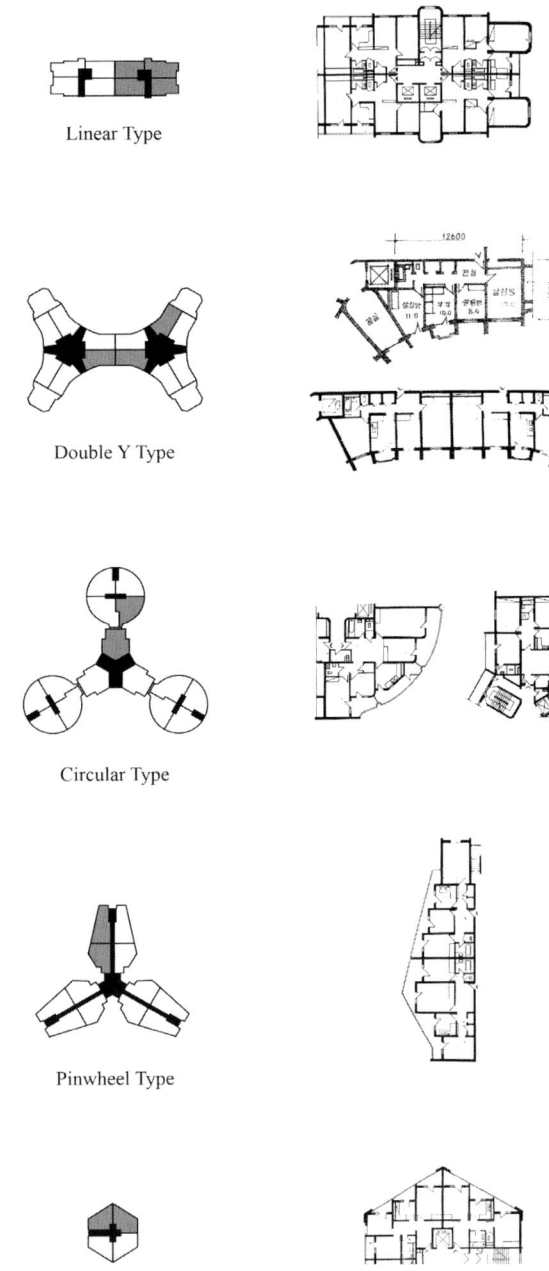

Building plans and unit plans for tower-type housing in Gwangbok New Town.
Source: Li, Hyeon-deok, and Li, Hyeon-bok, 1987, redrawn by the authors.

High-rise towers

Towers more than 40 storeys high first appeared on the Gyeongheung Street housing estate in the early 1980s. The buildings on Gyeongheung Street are 41 storeys high with a radial plan and are approximately 37.7 metres long and wide – larger than the towers previously erected on Changgwang Street. The high-rise towers on Gwangbok Street are of five shapes: linear, double Y, circular, pinwheel, and hexagonal. Regardless of shape, they are also bulky, about 60 to 80 metres high. Their architects followed Kim's instructions in paying attention to visual effects. In these buildings the units are not accessed from a corridor as in residential buildings in the era of Kim Il-sung. Instead, units are bundled together around a core containing the stair hall and elevator. The units are combined in diverse patterns in which the module is rotated, mirrored, or inverted vertically or horizontally.

The units had the same number of rooms (usually three or four) per household but different interior layouts.[37] These differences occurred because the design process prioritised the building's exterior form. Another important factor was that this residential complex was first used for foreign participants in the Pyongyang Festival, leading to the creation of an ante-room that was much wider than in previous prefabricated housing. Depending on the situation, the ante-room could be a separate room or for use as a living room. It was only in 2005 that living rooms began to appear in earnest in floor plans for North Korean apartments.

In addition to diversity of unit plans, in the Kim Jong Il era residential towers became taller. North Korean architects faced difficulties in designing these buildings using the existing structural basis. At this time, the Juche ideology led to minimisation of exchange with foreign countries. Following the collapse of the Soviet Union, North Korea turned into an island. North Korean architects therefore came up with new ways to overcome the technological limitations that confronted them. First, they increased the thickness of the walls of the large panels to improve their structural performance. In a typical large-panel building the thickness of the wall panel was set to about 200 millimetres based on a building height of 20 storeys. In the Soviet Union, wall panels were usually between 140 and 180 millimetres thick, and external walls were usually around 300 millimetres thick.[38] In North Korea, however, high-rise buildings had walls that were 300 to 400 millimetres and sometimes as much as 750 millimetres thick. Increasing the thickness of the wall in this way, despite the inefficiency of such a structural system, made it possible to increase the number of storeys. Second, in addition to the prefabricated-construction method, extensive use was made of an integrated method called 'slip forming'. Introduced in North Korea in the late 1960s, this method involves pouring concrete into continuously moving formwork. When the concrete reaches the point where it can stand on its own, the formwork is slid upwards, new rebar is assembled, and fresh concrete is poured.[39]

The slip-forming method does not use prefabricated materials. Instead, if the formwork is assembled in a rational way, a variety of unit plans and architectural forms can be realised.[40] This method was partially used for the rounded corners of the outer walls on Gyeongheung Street and for the round balconies in apartments at South Sinuiju;[41] on Gwangbok Street, however, it was used to build the entire exterior walls and the verandas that give these buildings their architectural form. This technology enabled the construction of the cylindrical, three-winged, and four-winged towers on this housing estate. The slip-forming method was also used to join large panels instead of the use of vertical welding joints, taking advantage of unskilled workers on the site.[42] However, such methods were merely a temporary measure to mobilise unskilled workers across the country without the need for proper professional skills. During the manufacturing of the concrete, workers had to carry the aggregate to the central mixing area in carts. The concrete, which was transported to the construction site using ordinary trucks without ReMiCon machines, had to be carried by the workers directly to where it was needed. In the process many workers died as they were crossing between high-rise apartments..[43]

Conclusion

The cost of large-scale construction carried out in North Korea from 1980 to 1996 was 1.6 times greater than the country's GNP in 1995. It is estimated that 27.4% of this amount was spent on housing construction.[44] As a result, the era of Kim Jong-Il saw the emergence of large-scale housing complexes and new cityscapes. This was a period during which North Korean architects and planners followed Kim Jong-il's aesthetic principles and gave him technological advice. Whereas under Kim Il-sung large cities in North Korea had filled with monotonous residential complexes and dreary concrete buildings, under Kim Jong-il the city was embroidered throughout with atypical buildings. Photo collections published for propaganda purposes include pictures of these various types of building and portray a visually harmonious urban appearance. Gwangbok New Town is a good illustration of characteristics that appeared in residential complexes and urban planning during the Kim Jong-il era.

There has never in modern times been intervention on such a scale by a political leader in the planning of large housing estates or such a speedy change of cityscape from monotonous to spectacular. However, it cannot be denied that this approach led to numerous serious problems. First, this kind of planning ignored how inhabitants wanted to live. We know from defectors who used to live in residential complexes on Gwangbok Street that they were exposed to many discomforts in their daily lives. The intermittence of the electricity supply made for unreliable operation of the elevators, water supply, and hygiene facilities in the high-rise towers. This situation was not anticipated at an early stage. There are also serious defects in these buildings' state of preservation due to the speed at which they were erected and their builders' lack of professionalism. The pursuit of so-called 'Pyongyang speed' led to many students and soldiers being mobilised on construction sites; it was within their capabilities to construct five-storey apartment buildings using the prefabrication method. However, when building height increased to as much as 50 storeys on the large housing estates built under Kim Jong-il, this presented a structural problem. An attempt was made to solve the problem not by technological innovation but by merely increasing the thickness of the walls; this meant that the façades of the residential buildings are load-bearing, resulting in an unattractive proportion of window to wall surface.

Even if this is not something that is visible in the photo collections, the emphasis on visual effects at the expense of consideration for distribution of the population resulted in the creation of an ambiguous external space around the residential buildings. Today's satellite photos show that unidentified small buildings encroach on this external space in a disorderly manner. Finally, the biggest limitation of such projects is that public works realised without thought for economic viability have dealt the North Korean economy a serious blow. Since the third seven-year plan (1987–1993), which involved construction of large-scale housing and urban projects, North Korea's economic growth rate has been negative, leading eventually to the country's most difficult period of suffering, the Arduous March.

1. Kim Jong-il's five revolutionary operas are: *Sea of Blood*, *The Flower Girl*, *Tell O'The Forest*, *A True Daughter of the Party*, and *The Song of Mount Kumgang*.
2. See Kim, Mina and Jung, Inha, 'The Planning of Microdistricts', pp. 199–223.
3. Songdowon Street in Wonsan, Sapo Street in Hamheung, Namcheonjin Street in Chonjin, Yeokjeon Street in Sinuiju, Yuriseon Street in Nampo, Cheongnyeon Street in Kyesong, Kanggeon Street in Sariwon, Donghaeju Street in Haeju, and Joongsim Street in Gangkye-si are all examples. Li Hwa-seon(a) (Pyongyang, 1989), p. 306.
4. Jeon Man-gil, 'Jeonhwanui sibaljeom', p. 6.
5. Kim, Jong-il, (Pyongyang, 1991), p. 128.
6. Ibid., p. 129.
7. Cha, Cha-yeong 'Cheollima georiui', p. 49.
8. Ibid., p. 49.
9. Kim, Jong-il (Pyongyang, 1991), p. 112.
10. *Baekgwasajeonchulpansa* (Pyongyang, 1995), p. 558.
11. Li, Sang-cheol, 'Namsinuijue geonseoldoego', pp. 86–87.
12. Li Hwa-seon(a) (Pyongyang, 1989), p. 345.
13. First, arrange tall buildings so that they overlap each other. Second, place tall buildings on high slopes. Third, place tall buildings at the main entrances to residential complexes.
14. Kim, Jong-il (Pyongyang, 1991), p. 122.
15. Heo, Jae-su, 'Saero iltteoseoneun', p. 20.
16. Kim, Yeong-bok, 'Deouk saeropgo', pp. 66–67.
17. Li Hwa-seon(a) (Pyongyang. 1989), p. 319.
18. Ibid., p. 319.
19. Kim, Bong-ho, '5mansedae sallimjim', p. 38.
20. Kim, Mi-jin, 'Bukan gyoyeui giwonwa', p. 237.
21. Nam Il, 'Sae hwangyeong-e jeokeunghage', pp. 2–13.
22. Rah, In-won, 'Hapnijeogin dosisaenghwaldanwichegyewa', p. 41.
23. Kim, Mina and Jung, Inha, 'The planning of microdistricts', p. 199.
24. Kim, Mina and Jung, Inha, 'The planning of microdistricts', p. 20.
25. Rah, In-won, "Hapnijeogin dosisaenghwaldanwichegyewa", p. 42.
26. The residential area of each small district was calculated three-dimensionally based on the floor plans of the residential buildings in individual small districts, and the number of households and the size of the population in each small district were calculated. In addition, with respect to calculations of population size, we have referred to material indicating that the average household size in Pyongyang in 1993 was estimated as 4.05 (Kim, Doo-seop, et al., *Bukan inguwa ingu*, p. 208.)
27. Kwon, Yeong-tae, 'Urisik georiui tto', p. 2.
28. Meuser, Philipp and Zadorin, Dimitry (Berlin, 2015), p. 297.
29. For details see Shin, Gun-soo, and Jung, Inha, 'Appropriating the Socialist Way', pp. 159–180.
30. Ruble, Blair, A. (Cambridge, 1993), p. 240.
31. With respect to such residential buildings, North Korean planners thought that they should be situated far from the road, should maintain the natural undulations and mountain landscape of Mangyeongdae that spreads out like a folding screen with the River Taedong in the background, and should house harmonious arrangements of large, varied, and modern apartments (Joseon Central News Agency, 'Dangui ryeongdomite', p. 3.)
32. See the figure in Li, Hyeon-deok, and Li, Hyeon-bok (Pyongyang, 1987), pp. 52–66.
33. Guknip Geonseol Chulpansa (Pyongyang, 1962), pp. 69, 104, 110.
34. Choi, Won-hun (Pyongyang, 1991), p. 62.
35. Li Hwa-seon(a) (Pyongyang, 1989), p. 131.
36. Choi, Won-hun (Pyongyang, 1991), p. 61.
37. It has been argued that the introduction of apartments with more than three rooms built by the state came after Changgwang Street. 'It would be good,' said Kim Jong-il during construction of Changgwang Street, 'if the units in the apartments of Changgwang Street could have three rooms... the grandparents can use one room; the children, another; and the parents, the third.' (Li, 'Sae segie bitbalchineun, p. 41.)
38. For large-panel buildings, see Meuser, Philipp and Zadorin, Dimitry (Berlin, 2015), pp. 160–441.
39. Choi, Won-hun and Kim, Jun-gil (Pyongyang, 1991), p. 126.
40. Li Hwa-seon (Pyongyang, 1989), Changgwang Street p. 220.
41. Li, Sang-cheol, 'Namsinuijue geonseoldoego', pp. 86–87.
42. From an interview with the North Korean architect In-sook Jang on 3 March 2018.
43. Ibid.
44. Jo, Hyeon-sik, 'Bukanui gakjong daegyumo', pp. 92–94.

Gwangbok Street, Pyongyang (2005).
Source: Philipp Meuser

Gwangbok Street, Pyongyang (2005).
Source: Philipp Meuser

Gwangbok Street, Pyongyang (2005).
Source: Philipp Meuser

7. Planning of Gwangbok Street New Town in Pyongyang

Gwangbok Street, Pyongyang (2010).
Source: Philipp Meuser

Gwangbok Street, Pyongyang (2010).
Source: Philipp Meuser

여덟

The Development of the Housing Market and its Influence on Apartment Unit Plans

Inha Jung

North Korea entered a period of prolonged hardship following the death of Kim Il-sung in July 1994. In the 1990s North Korean society suffered a barrage of domestic and international crises and a sharp decline in quality of life caused by a combination of political, economic, and environmental factors. Most obviously, as the socialist bloc collapsed, its economic benefits disappeared, making it very difficult for North Korea to procure foreign currency for international transactions (payment in cash was necessary in all trade, even with socialist counties). North Korea's volume of international trade grew steadily until the mid-1990s, with over 50 percent of the country's GNP dependent on foreign trade. However, this plunged to just 19 percent in 1996,[1] leading to serious problems in terms of energy consumption and food supply. In response, North Korea sought to maintain self-sufficiency in energy. Although anthracite is produced domestically, the country does not possess its own oil resources, making it dependent on imports. The dismantling of the socialist bloc in the 1990s brought a halt to North Korea's oil imports, resulting in severe energy shortages. These crises were exacerbated by successive environmental disasters, including 1.2 million tonnes of hail damage in 1994, 1.9 million tonnes of flood damage in 1995, the largest flood in 60 years in 1996, and more than two million tonnes of the worst drought damage in a century in 1997.[2] In just four years these natural disasters led to a dramatic drop in crop yields, disrupting the food rationing system and causing the starvation of 500,000 to 600,000 people.[3] Nevertheless, US-led capitalist countries continued to block North Korea, driving its system of governance into crisis.

In response, the North Korean regime abolished the planned economy that had sustained post-war North Korean society and introduced a new economic system: a partial market economy. This change had an enormous impact on North Korean society. A real estate market was established and began to develop; the impact of the new economic system was particularly noticeable in this sector. This chapter explores the emergence of a new class of capitalists known as *donju* in the North Korean market in the 2000s, and their impact on apartment unit plans. To this end, I shall examine architectural drawings for apartment houses built by *donju*. My analysis differs from those in previous studies, which were primarily based on the testimony of North Korean defectors. While North Korean defectors provide vivid accounts of life in North Korea, their claims regarding architectural design may lack accuracy: the defectors are usually not experts in architecture or urban design. By contrast, architectural drawings reveal with great clarity the changes that have occurred in North Korean housing since the 2000s.

The apartments built by *donju* deviate from accepted socialist ideology by prioritising commercial value in the real estate market. Architectural drawings for these apartments reveal the hidden desires of North Koreans who have been oppressed by the North Korean regime. Accordingly, this chapter's aim is threefold. The first is to identify changes in the concept of the family in unit plans in apartment houses built by *donju*. While the relationship between ideology and family in North Korean society has been observed in a variety of ways, apartments built by *donju* reveal a new aspect of this dynamic. The second is to elucidate the influence of South Korean pop culture – i.e. the so-called Korean Wave (*hallu*) – which was secretly spread in North Korean marketplaces from the early 2000s forwards. Since South Korean dramas and movies depict the lifestyle of South Koreans, they have naturally affected North Korean domestic culture too. The third aim is to clarify how *donju* apartments responded to the energy shortage after the introduction of international sanctions against North Korea's development of nuclear technology.

The Emergence of North Korea's Housing Market and the *Donju*

Numerous studies have explored the key features of post-socialist cities. In the 1990s, following the fall of communism, urban fabric and land use changed as the housing sector became progressively marketised. The same is true for North Korea. Although the North Korean regime continues to promote the socialist revolutionary spirit, North Korean society shows clear signs of marketisation. However, since North Korea has not introduced a fully capitalist economy as other communist countries have, it may be debated whether North Korean cities remain socialist in nature or have been converted to post-socialist cities.[4] In this respect there are valuable insights to be gained from looking at apartment buildings erected by *donju*, who have played an important role in the marketisation of the North Korean economy.

The collapse of the socialist bloc in the 1990s plunged North Korea into an unprecedented economic crisis. According to estimates by the Bank of Korea, the country saw its GDP drop by a whopping 30 percent, with negative growth for nine consecutive years from 1990 to 1998. The economic crisis completely undermined North Korea's planned economy, with sharp declines in production across almost all industries. These difficulties were further compounded by a severe shortage of raw materials, which led to the collapse of the production and supply chain. Scope for construction of new housing was greatly reduced.[5] The period between 1995 and 1997 became known as the 'Arduous March' or the 'March of Suffering' (*Gonanui Haenggun*); it brought the collapse of the central planning system and the suspension of the state system for distribution and supply.

The collapse of the planned economy had a huge impact on the everyday lives of North Koreans. First, poor food distribution resulted in residents flocking to early-stage markets called *jangmadang* to procure food. These markets were originally created for the exchange of agricultural products grown in private gardens in rural areas. However, due to severe food shortages in the mid-1990s, many residents turned to *jangmadang* for their daily necessities, including the food they needed to survive. Such markets grew rapidly, becoming a vital part of the North Korean economy. Income from marketplaces surged to ten times what was earned in factories and cooperative farms; the weight of economic activity shifted to the marketplaces. According to the testimony of North Korean defectors, many North Koreans had two jobs: one officially assigned to them by the Party, the other in a private business operated by the *donju*. Significantly, few people actually performed their official jobs, even choosing to pay a certain sum in penalties each month so that they could continue working for private businesses run by the *donju* instead.

The development of a market led to the formation and differentiation of a merchant class. Early *donju* accumulated capital in the marketplace and then gradually expanded and multiplied their capital through investment and employment. The capitalism of the *donju* takes the form of investment of capital and hiring workers to increase assets. However, North Korea's legal and institutional mechanisms remain insufficient for such activities. Nevertheless, as the market expanded, so did the *donju*, leading to a subdivision of their roles. First, they subdivided into retailers and wholesalers. A second subdivision was between specialist merchants dealing only with certain items and general merchants dealing with a wide range of items.[6] Today, *donju* have expanded their activities to include moneylending, construction, overseas investment, transportation, and finance. They are also said to be involved in foreign trade, making enormous amounts of money by transferring foreign trade permits from state agencies and paying a certain percentage of their profits to the state and the Party. According to a survey of North Korean defectors in 2015, the proportion of state-run companies invested in or directly operated by the *donju* amounted to 64.1 percent of restaurants, 56.2 percent of shops, 26.2 percent of local industrial plants, and 21.7 percent of national industrial plants.[7] The *donju* also entered the profitable housing-construction sector, where they have carried out a variety of projects.

Uncertain how to respond to the growth of the *donju* and the market, the North Korean regime frequently alternates policies – oscillating between curbing the market and allowing it to continue growing. When Kim Jong-il pushed for the 7.1 economic reform in January 2002, he recognised the significance of the market and initiated a change of policy to legalise clandestine parts of it. Farmers' markets were accordingly legalised and expanded to general markets in March 2003. At the same time, however, the regime prohibited adult women under the age of 40 from engaging in trade, controlled market transactions, and began cracking down on private businesses. In 2009 the government attempted to abolish the general markets and to implement currency reform in a surprising bid to reduce trading of goods in markets. When the knock-on effects of this move threatened the livelihoods of common residents, in 2010 the regime returned the market's status as a legal entity. Meanwhile, the *donju* continued to operate, outmanoeuvring the government's attempts to control the market without technological innovation.

The *Donju* in the Housing Sector

The *donju* have become indispensable in various kinds of housing-construction project. North Korea's housing supply was hit hard by the collapse of the planned economy. Under the latter, North Korea's housing construction system had been centralised, with the state controlling all processes from planning, implementation, and evaluation to allocation. The government announced the quantity of housing to be built each year; completed new housing was allocated free of charge. The government's ultimate goal was to supply each household with a home. However, housing-construction projects did not always meet their targets, and a severe housing shortage took shape. The sluggish tempo of housing construction at this time is attributable to North Korea's economic system, which, with an eye on inter-Korean confrontation, was focused on military-industrial production. The difficulties with housing were further compounded by a lack of expertise and efficiency. Given the state's monopoly on construction projects, students and soldiers were frequently mobilised so as to complete construction as speedily as possible.

The housing shortage worsened as North Korea's baby-boomer generation reached marriageable age in the 1980s. Although demand for housing surged, the North Korean government took no active steps to meet it. Apartment complexes constructed in the 1980s were incapable of mitigating the housing shortage: Kim Jong-il, who orchestrated all urban planning, prioritised the visual impact made by residential buildings on the cityscape over consideration of people's real needs.[8] North Korea was consequently only able to supply approximately 65 percent of housing needed before the start of the Arduous March.[9] The housing shortage was responsible for two to three households having to live together in a single home; acquiring an apartment-use permit typically took four to five years even when a citizen had been allocated a new job. According to North Korean defectors, cohabitation by several families in a single apartment was common in large cities such as Pyongyang, and residential conditions continued to deteriorate over time.

Prior to the economic crisis, the North Korean regime prohibited housing sales between individuals. However, this principle was undermined by the suspension of housing construction and worsening housing shortages in the 1990s. The development of a free market led to the population becoming more mobile. The result was that demand for new housing emerged in areas to which people moved and empty homes appeared in areas which they left; empty homes and illegal trading started soon thereafter. Wealthy people who made their fortune in the market moved into new apartments in a quest for better living conditions. Real-estate deals were made through professional brokers, with the cost usually settled in US dollars or Chinese yuan. While cracking down on private housing transactions, public agencies have tended to overlook clandestine trading activities. As there is no private land ownership in North Korea, the object of these transactions is the 'home-use permit'. Housing sales in North Korea are for this reason technically defined as 'the illegal sale of home-use rights.'[10] Initially, most housing sales were conducted in local cities, as opposed to in the capital, Pyongyang, where the food rationing system remained partially in force. Housing transactions began occurring in Pyongyang, however, from 2000 forwards. Today, as the real estate market expands, emergent capitalists are building new apartments to sell.

The marketisation of the North Korean economy has had a significant impact on the way housing is constructed. Prior to marketisation, standard plans were drawn up by state-run design institutes and distributed to construction sites en masse, regardless of local differences. However, the involvement of the *donju* in construction projects has led to marked changes to conventional construction methods. The *donju* have taken advantage of soaring demand for housing and North Koreans' desire to buy decent homes, often in collaboration with officials in the Party and the administration. Indeed, the *donju* and the North Korean ruling elites are closely connected. Without the support of the latter, the *donju* would be unable to conduct their business: the construction of apartments is a highly complicated process. The elite and the *donju* maintain symbiotic relationships in grey areas, operating in the space between the legal and illegal. Hong Sung-won identifies three types of relationships between the *donju* and the ruling elite with respect to construction of housing. In the first type of relationship all funds and construction materials for construction of an apartment building are guaranteed by the state. In this case, the *donju* act as a catalyst for construction. If the construction project is successfully completed, the *donju* are rewarded with apartments. In the second type of relationship, the state's public investment is combined with private investment by *donju*. In the third type all construction is financed by private investment by *donju*. In all cases the *donju* utilise the national system for prerequisites such as building design, construction machinery, and electric power.

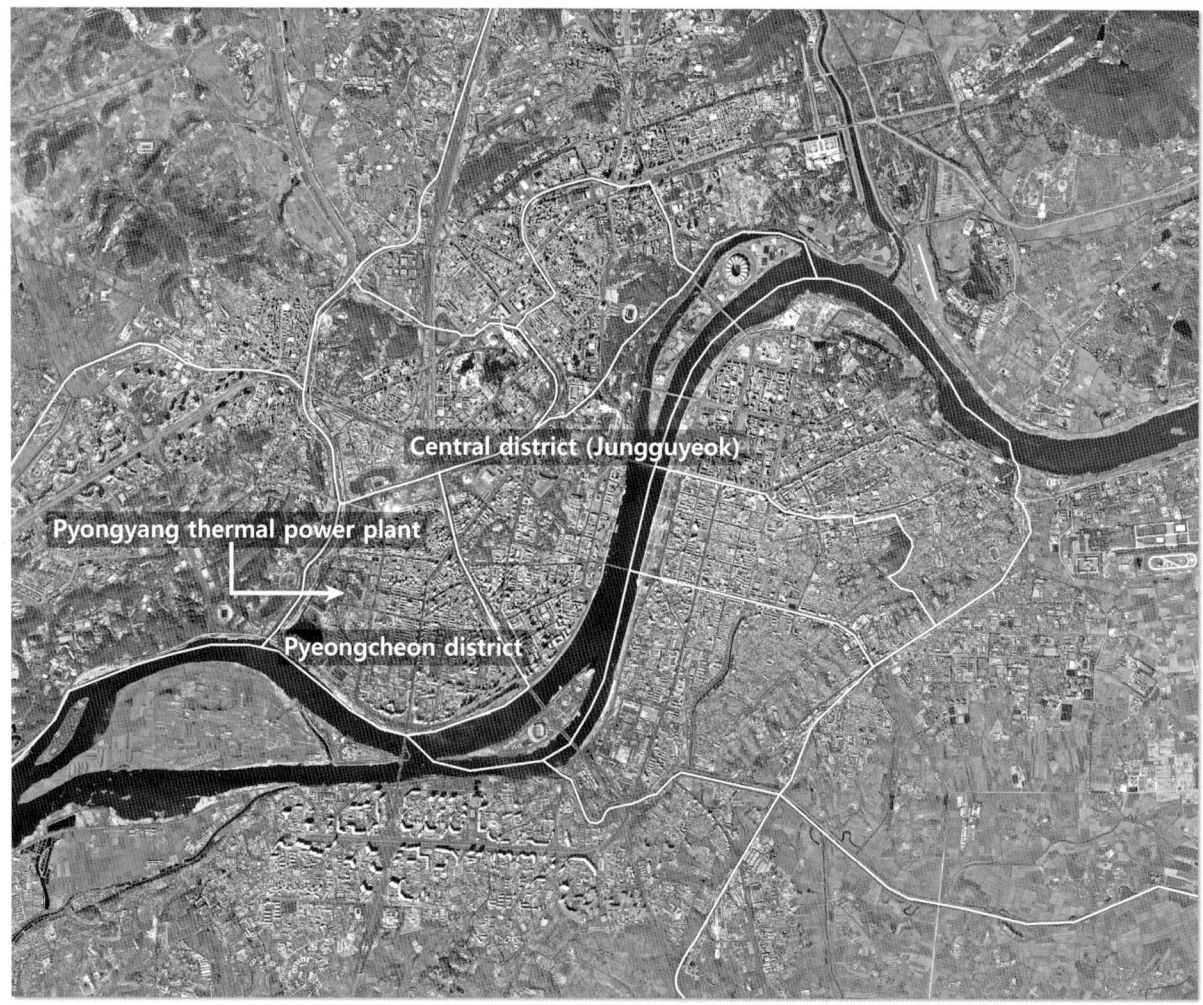

Comparison of two maps of Pyongyang from the 2000s and 2010s: the red dots indicate new buildings constructed during this period.
Source: The National Geographic Information Service

It is unclear what proportion of apartments in North Korea have been built by donju. According to a survey of North Korean defectors, housing construction by private investors is increasing in large cities such as Pyongyang, Pyongsong, Sinuiju, Nampo, Hamhŭng, and Chongjin, as well as in small local cities like Suncheon and Wonsan.[11] Maps produced by the National Geographic Information Service permit a more accurate assessment, particularly since they show the locations of apartments built by *donju* in Pyongyang. More specifically, comparison of maps of Pyongyang in the 2000s and 2010s, the peak of the *donju*'s activities, reveals that approximately 200 high-rise buildings were constructed over this ten-year period, including three large-scale, state-led apartment complexes: Mansudae Apartment Complex (2012; 14 buildings), Mirae Science Street Apartment Complex (2015; 19 buildings), and Ryomyong Street Apartment Complex (2017; 44 buildings). Apart from these large complexes, most high-rise buildings were constructed individually. Additionally, more than 70 of the 120 individual buildings constructed during this period were located in the central district and Pyeongcheon district.

There are several reasons for the concentration of *donju* buildings in these areas. Most notably, the Pyongyang thermal power plant situated in Pyeongcheon district provides these two districts with a stable supply of electricity. As electricity is essential for the operation of various facilities in high-rise apartments, a stable electricity supply is crucial to being able to sell the apartments in a building at a high price. This is why many buildings have been constructed around the Pyongyang thermal power plant, which uses anthracite coal to generate electricity. Moreover, many buildings have been erected along the River Daedong. Together with a stable electricity supply, river views have played an important role in determining real-estate prices. With the exception of in Central and Pyeongcheon districts, no noteworthy construction occurred during this period; no construction was carried out in the new towns of the Kim Jong-il era, such as Munsu Street, Gwangbok Street, and Tongil Street. The poor living conditions in these areas make them unattractive for investment by *donju*.

Apartments in *Donju* Buildings and the Concept of Family

Interestingly, unit plans for apartments in *donju* buildings reveal recent changes in North Korea's family system. The family has been regarded as a key part of social reform since the founding of the North Korean government. At first, the North Korean regime tried to dismantle the traditional family system which had long dominated East Asian society. This attempt was in line with socialist ideology. Many socialists, including Marx and Engels, were anti-family. The socialist view of the family is based on Engels' *The Origin of the Family, Private Property, and the State* (1884). Engels believed that bourgeois monogamy came into being with the emergence of the system of private property. In this case, marriage between men and women was based on economic interest, with men, who held economic power, unilaterally oppressing women, who did not. Engels thus believed that the first class conflict was between men and women and that true socialist revolution could eliminate these power-based relationships by transforming inheritable wealth into social wealth. This idea appeared in the *Communist Manifesto* (1848), in which Marx and Engels write, 'On what foundation is the present family, the bourgeois family, based? On capital, private gain. In its completely developed form, this family exists only among the bourgeoisie.' According to Marx and Engels, abolishing the family would be relatively easy once bourgeois property was abolished – after all, 'The bourgeois family will vanish as a matter of course when its complement vanishes, and both will vanish with the vanishing of capital.'[12]

This idea had a significant impact on traditional concepts of the family based on blood or marriage. As individual families were no longer the main economic unit in society in socialist countries, housework became a social industry, and child rearing and education were considered public issues. With the establishment of a socialist system after the 1917 Russian Revolution, Soviet revolutionaries opposed the bourgeois concept of 'housing as private space.' They sought to re-establish the public/private distinction socially and use spatial design to promote the socialist ideology at home. In this respect, they believed that the private sphere in a bourgeois dwelling could contaminate the proletariat at any time; its elimination was therefore necessary. Various policies relating to the separation of the public/private spheres were discussed in the first decade after the Revolution; there was a desire to eradicate 'private life' in socialist housing. Everything that was not connected to the state or the group was considered counter-revolutionary – a sentiment primarily expressed in its dominance over private space.[13] As we see from the *dom-kommuna* (commune house), which was introduced in the 1920s, the Soviet government attempted to minimise individual private spaces and expand state-provided communal facilities (e.g., toilets, bathrooms, restaurants, and kitchens).

In the 1960s North Korea tried to establish a proper relationship between family and society by revolutionising the family. This revolution, the North Korean regime believed, would socialise the family – the basic unit of society. The initiative began with Kim Il-sung's speech 'On the Mother's Mission in Child Education' in November 1961; its principles were subsequently systemised in his speech 'On the Revolutionising of Women and Their Transformation into the Labour Class' in October 1971. 'Family revolution' in this sense can be interpreted in two ways: as the revolution of the parents on the one hand, and as the revolution of the children on the other. Women are at the centre of the revolution of the family: the focus is on the mother, whose goal is to cultivate and socialise her children. While the family remained an important unit of society, relationships between men and women and parents and children changed in accordance with socialist ideology.[14] This idea was also applied to the mass construction of apartments in North Korea in the 1960s. The North Korean regime similarly sought to reduce private space and push women from the home out into the workplace. These apartments accordingly lacked family rooms or living rooms for family gatherings; all that they provided was individual sleeping rooms, while the bathroom was commonly shared by households on the same floor. However, to completely dismantle the family and liberate women proved impossible.

This situation changed in the 1980s, when the ante-room expanded significantly in size and the emphasis switched to the family. In this respect, changes in the concept of the family were reflected in the unit plan for the typical apartment. During this period, Kim Jong-il, designated the official successor of Kim Il-sung, strengthened his position. In order to elicit loyalty from the North Korean people, he legitimised the hereditary succession of power from his father by advancing the idea of the 'socialist large family.' In a 1986 article, 'On Some of the Issues Raised in the Juche Ideology,' he declared,

Society is defined as a living organism comprising the leader, the Party, and the public, and their relationship is assumed to be a communal destiny, dominated by a leader. In accordance with the 'Socialist large family', there is a life-giving leader in a society or a state just as family relationships revolve around the head of a family.

This argument sought to overcome crises of legitimacy arising from hereditary succession. It put less emphasis on socialist principles in family policy, leading to the partial revival of traditional family ethics. In the 1980s the proportion of extended families comprising more than three generations had decreased, while the proportion of nuclear families had increased. Large families comprising three generations were now a common type of household, while approximately 31.5 percent of households were nuclear families. Nuclear families now consisted of 3.02 people on average, while large families comprised 4.42 people. In the case of Pyongyang, approximately 36.9 percent of households were nuclear families – approximately 5.4 percent higher than the national average (the remaining indicators for Pyongyang are similar to national averages). Under these circumstances, the North Korean government enacted the Family Act in October 1990. This introduced a new concept of family-based welfare including the implementation of two policies: a family-support system and a guardian system. Prior to this act, the state had been primarily responsible for raising children; the Family Act shifted this responsibility to the family. The law also recognised inheritance of private property.[15] This made familism (the emphasis on family) more concrete. This phenomenon was also reflected in the typical apartment floor plan.

The 1980s saw an increase in the number of rooms in North Korean apartments. Most apartments built in the 1960s had had two rooms. Apartments with a relatively large number of rooms were advantageous during the housing shortage: they allowed for the cohabitation of several households. As the number of rooms increased, so did the floor area of the ante-room connecting them. By the mid-1980s the ante-room occupied about 15 percent of the entire area. It served as both a communal space and a passageway.

The significance of familism grew in the mid-1990s, when North Korea faced a period of overwhelming crisis. Specifically, the collapse of the socialist planned economy meant that the North Korean government could no longer distribute food to citizens, forcing people to search desperately for ways to procure food themselves. As a result, families, not the state, now played the key role. In other words, families began filling the vacuum left by the state. The North Korean regime's emphasis on familism was intended to cover the structural flaws revealed by the economic crisis. In particular, women became the main players in overcoming the crisis, a move which has helped to dissipate the strong dissatisfaction directed towards the nation's leader. In the process of fulfilling this role the family system has also changed. The types of production activity engaged in by families vary depending on their economic conditions, deepening the economic differences between families.[16] In this regard, the newly emerged familism of this period can be seen as a revival of traditional Confucian ideology. This trend has led to the strengthening of family-centred space in apartment housing, with the emergence of living rooms linked to this social change. It is no coincidence that the communal living room emerged in apartments in *donju* buildings.

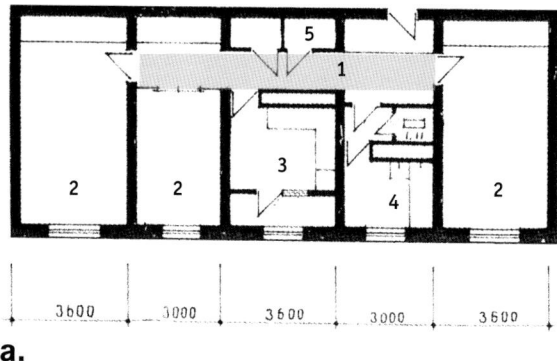

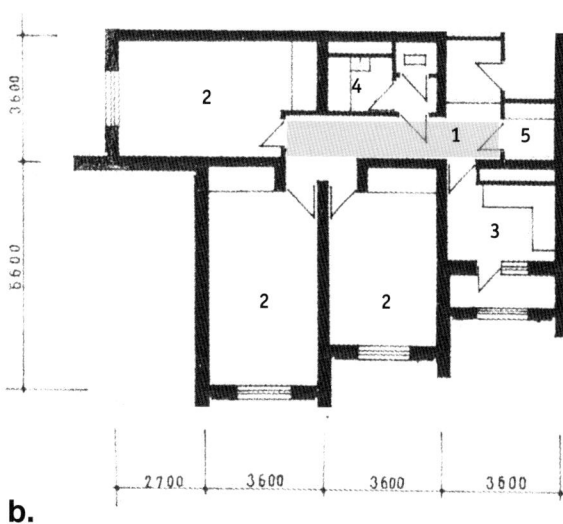

The corridor type of ante-room: a) unit plan in a Y-shaped Changgwang Street apartment b) unit plan in an H-shaped Changgwang Street apartment (1. ante-room; 2. bedroom; 3. kitchen; 4. sanitary room; 5. storage).
Source: Lee, Hyeon-deok, Lee, Hyeon-bok, 1987

Changes in Unit Plans:
From the Ante-room to the Living Room

The *donju*'s entry into the housing sector brought numerous changes in the layouts of North Korean apartments. The *donju* were typically involved in designing apartments in the buildings they erected and sometimes asked for specific elements of interior design reflecting their target audience's preferences. North Korean apartment prices vary in accordance with diverse factors, including their interior layout. As Lee Chul explains,

> *Pyongyang's apartments before 2000 generally had no living rooms; instead, there were ante-rooms next to the entrance. Some households with more than three rooms converted one room into a living room, but in the 2000s a communal space for dining together and watching TV was added to the layout. According to North Korean defectors, the price of new homes has risen significantly because practically designed living rooms are now conveniently connected to individual rooms, large bathrooms, and kitchens. Apartments with this kind of internal layout cost more than 50,000 USD on average.*[17]

This claim can be verified by comparing unit plans published in North Korean architectural magazines for North Korean apartments in the 1980s and the 2000s. Rooted in the emergence of the *donju* and the marketisation of housing, three differences are immediately apparent. First, most of the 1980s apartments had an ante-room (*jeonsil*), a special kind of space connecting the apartment entrance to various rooms. By contrast, apartments built in the 2000s had a communal living room (*gongdong salimbang*) located in the middle of the interior space. The shift from the ante-room to communal living rooms is closely linked to socio-economic changes that have occurred in North Korea since the 1990s. Second, the newer apartments have larger sanitary spaces. Apartments built in the 1980s typically comprised two or three rooms, one of which included a bathroom. By comparison, apartments built in the 2000s typically had two bathrooms, including an en-suite bathroom connected to the master bedroom. This change reflects user convenience. Third, apartments in North Korea have encountered difficulties due to the unstable energy supply or lack of electricity; this has rendered many of the appliances and equipment inoperable. The *donju* have made attempts to solve these issues to increase the commercial value of their apartments.

One of the most remarkable changes in the North Korean apartments built in the 2000s was the disappearance of the ante-room and the emergence of a communal living room. The ante-room first emerged in North Korean apartments in the 1960s. Kim Su-young has traced it to two origins: traditional folklore houses in Hamgyeong Province and Soviet design practices. In arguing that the emergence of the North Korean ante-room was influenced by traditional houses in Hamgyeong Province, Kim Su-young noted that 'the ante-room and *jeongjugan* are similar in that they are located closest to the entrance, adjacent to the kitchen, and at the centre of the inner space.'[18] Folklore houses in Hamgyeong Province possess a unique structure compared to houses in other regions: a double-layered layout comprising four rooms, with the *jeongjugan* located between two bedrooms and the kitchen. In terms of position, the *jeongjugan* is similar to the *hiroma* in Japanese folklore houses. However, unlike in the *hiroma*, the heat generated by the furnace of the Korean *ondol* flows under the *jeongjugan*. Hamgyeong Province is a mountainous area with a rugged topography. Days are short and incredibly cold, especially during winter. The region's harsh winters encourage people to spend most of their time inside their houses; the result is that the *jeongjugan* is a highly useful, multipurpose space – used for cooking, dining, indoor work, sleeping, and family gatherings. For this reason, this space is relatively undifferentiated.[19] Given the similar function of the ante-room in North Korean apartments, the *jeongjungan* is a likely precursor of this modern space.

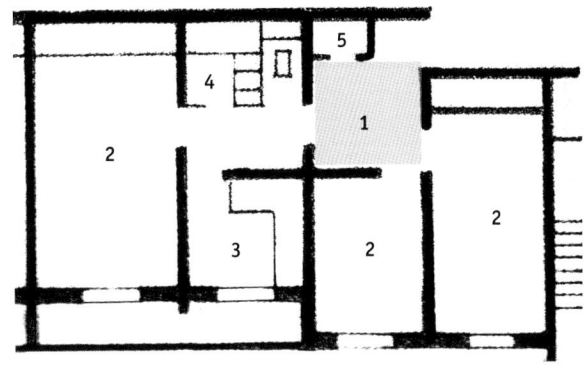

a.

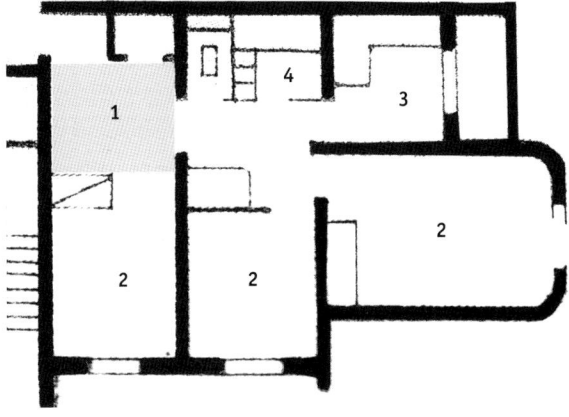

b.

The hall type of ante-room: a, b) unit plans for Gwangbok Street Apartment (1. ante-room; 2. bedroom; 3. kitchen; 4. sanitary room; 5. storage).
Source: Lee, Hyeon-deok, 1990

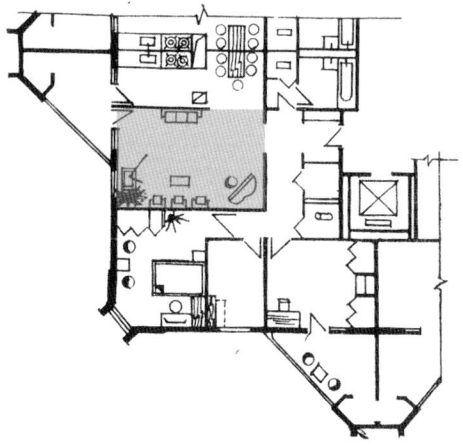

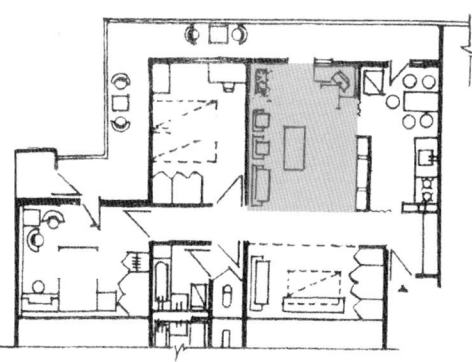

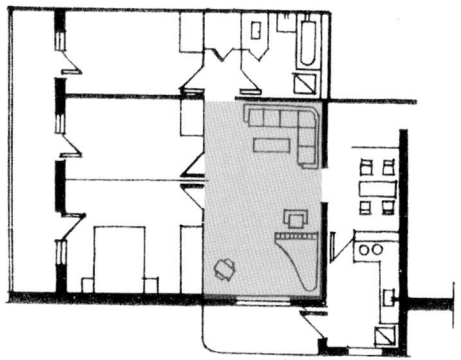

Three unit plans for high-rise apartments: 1, 2, 3.
Source: Joseon Geonchuk, January 1994

Kim Su-young also argued that the ante-room was influenced by Soviet standard designs.[20] This argument is unconvincing. In the 1960s North Korean apartments largely comprised two types: single-corridor-access apartments (*oerangsik*) and staircase-access apartments (*sekjiasik*). The former came from the Soviet Union, while the latter type was imported from East Germany. Since the ante-room was present in both types, it is unlikely to have been significantly influenced by Soviet housing designs. On the contrary, it emerged as the unit plans imported from abroad were localised. Initially, the ante-room was a small space located between the kitchen and a bedroom. It gradually expanded and acquired multi-functionality. In the 1960s most North Korean apartment layouts were designed to suit the *Existenzminimum* concept: the ante-room was the only place in which the family could gather. In this respect, the ante-room came to reflect North Koreans' lifestyle in the 1960s.

However, the size of the ante-room subsequently increased significantly, as did the number of rooms in the apartment. Two types of ante-room are to be seen in North Korean apartments built in the 1980s: namely, a corridor type and a hall-style type. In the early 1980s the first type of ante-room, which served as a kind of passageway, accounted for approximately 15 percent of the apartment's total floor area.[21] This corridor-type ante-room is typical of apartment complexes in Changgwang Street and Gyeongheung Street. It was popular due to the predominance of tower buildings on these estates, where a typical floor comprised four to six households gathered around the elevator hall – making a long corridor the most suitable design. However, in the mid-1980s the ante-room was connected to the kitchen and served as a kind of hall, resulting in a three percent increase in total area. Approximately 51.3 percent of the apartment complexes in Buksae Street, Gwangbok Street, Bonghwa Street, and South Shinju opted for this type of ante-room.[22] In most of these cases bedrooms, kitchens, and bathrooms were positioned around the hall. Compared to the corridor type, the hall type of ante-room significantly reduced an apartment's circulation space; instead, it was connected to the kitchen to create communal space for family gatherings.²³

However, the ante-room is almost absent from apartments built in the 2000s; such ante-rooms as there are are significantly reduced in size. Essentially, the ante-room has here been replaced by a communal living room (*gongdong sallimbang*) at the centre of the apartment. While some of the apartments on Gwangbok Street, designed in the mid-1980s, have similar spaces, they were called reception rooms (*eungjeopsils*) and have a spatial role that differs from the role of the living room. The North Korean media officially confirmed the existence of a communal living room in 1994. The January 1994 issue of the North Korean architectural magazine *Joseon Architecture* was the first to examine three proposals for apartment layouts. It contains the following characterisation of the political leader's design approach:

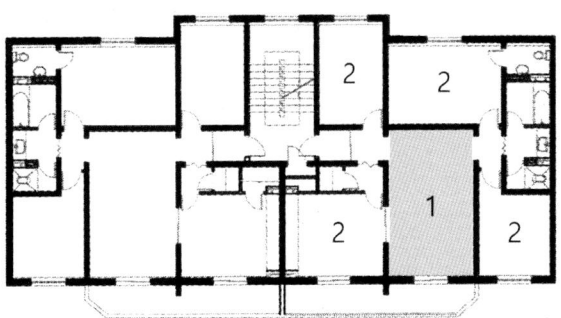

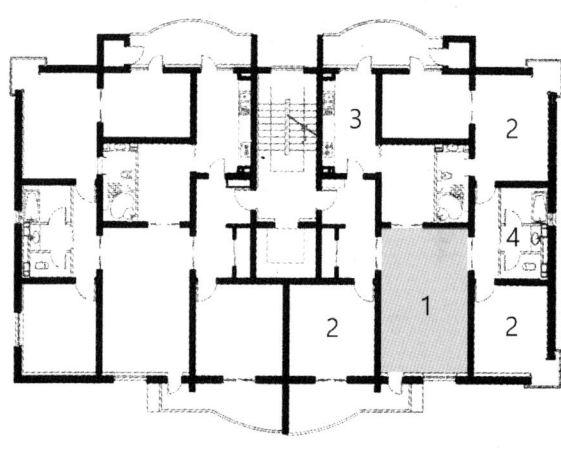

As society develops and the people's material and cultural lives become richer, their demands and orientation toward better living conditions become higher. Considering the people's direction and demands, Comrade Kim Jong-il has stated that the home interior needs to be designed in a completely different way from in the past, with a large living room connecting the bedrooms and dining room. In line with this design approach to new homes, we have created new home designs that allow us to put the living room at the centre and place bedrooms, kitchens, and auxiliary rooms around it to transform the interior space.

The January 1994 issue of *Joseon Architecture* presented three proposals for high-rise apartments. All three plans placed the living room at the centre of the interior space, with the other rooms around it – reflecting the enduring influence of the hall-like ante-rooms of the 1980s. This layout was typical of unit plans in North Korea after 2000; the unit plans of the Mansudae apartment complex in Pyongyang are similar. In this regard, the proposals may be regarded as a standard arrangement of the time.

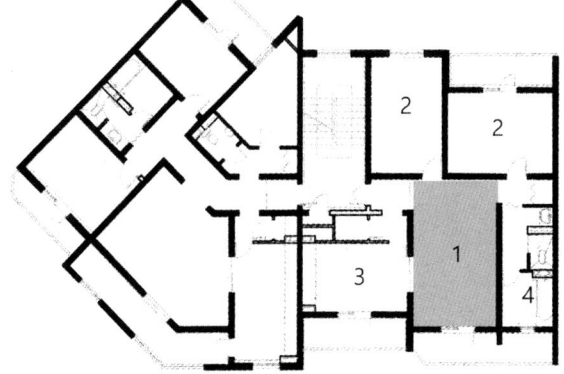

Unit plans for the Mansudae apartment complex, Pyongyang (1. living room; 2. bedroom; 3. kitchen; 4. sanitary room; 5. storage).
Source: Joseon Geonchuk, February 2010)

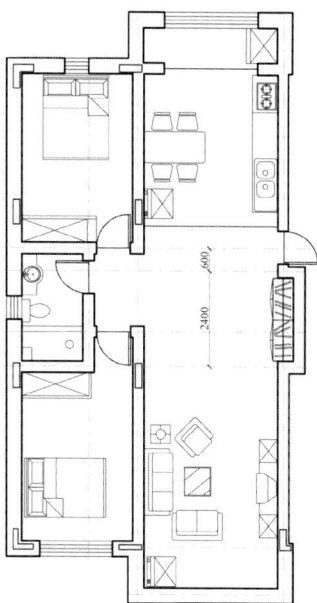

Unit plan for Namsan-dong apartment building, Raseon.
Source: Son, Jae-jun, 2015

North Korean unit plans are strikingly different to those of South Korean apartments. Although traditional South Korean houses did not possess a 'living room', this space emerged as an important feature following modernisation. Architectural historians have identified two possible origins of the South Korean living room. The first theory is that the living room became a feature of modern Korean housing when the courtyard merged with the *daecheong* – a wooden floor running between the master bedroom and the opposite bedroom – of the traditional house. A 1960s spec house appears to support this claim. A second argument sees the living room as an adaptation of the living room in western-style houses, which were imported in the colonial period, to the Korean lifestyle, creating a unique hall-style space. Some architectural historians believe that traditional and western-style houses in South Korea have interacted with each other since the 1960s.

After a layout incorporating a living room had become established in spec houses, it was subsequently adopted as a unit plan for high-rise apartments and multi-household houses as large cities in South Korea expanded and densified.[24] In this respect, apartment design in South Korea differs from in other East Asian countries. Nonetheless, the living rooms in the three proposals published in the January 1994 issue of *Joseon Architecture* show a markedly different arrangement to those of South Korea. The kitchen is situated on the south side together with the living room; there is a half-wall between the living room and the kitchen to provide a degree of spatial separation and connection simultaneously; and the dining room is attached to the kitchen instead of occupying a separate space. In comparison, in South Korean apartments, the living room is usually placed between two bedrooms, while the kitchen is situated on the north side; additionally, there is no separation between the living room and the kitchen. The relationship between the kitchen and dining area is shaped by a cooking culture that requires frequent movement between the kitchen counter and the dining table.

North Korean apartments also differ from their Chinese counterparts. Although the layouts of Chinese apartments vary widely depending on size and region, the kitchen is typically independent of and spatially separated from other rooms. This spatial layout appears to reflect the Chinese diet. More specifically, as Chinese cooking uses a large amount of oil, the kitchen is placed in a separate room to facilitate ventilation and minimise the spread of smells and residue to adjacent rooms. Although the layout of a North Korean apartment is similar to its Chinese counterpart insofar as the kitchen is located on the south side together with the living room, North Korean kitchens are not separate spaces.[25] Chinese apartments also tend to separate the dining room from the kitchen. 'In China,' write Kim Sung-kyu and Kim Kyung-bae, 'the dining room and the living room are considered social and reception spaces. Many parts of domestic culture such as entertaining guests, eating meals, and sharing social activities with family members take place in the dining room. This is part of traditional custom.'[26]

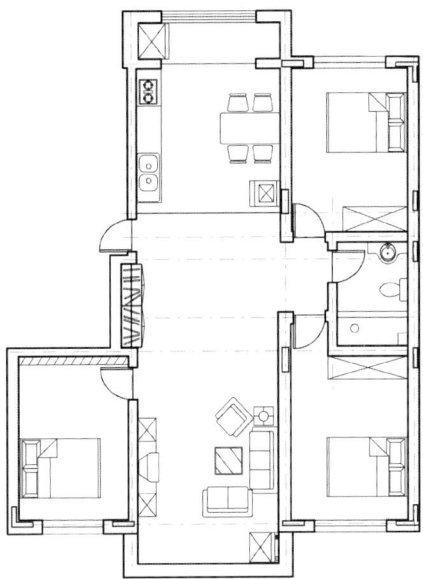

Unit plan for Namsan-dong apartment building, Raseon.
Source: Son, Jae-jun, 2015

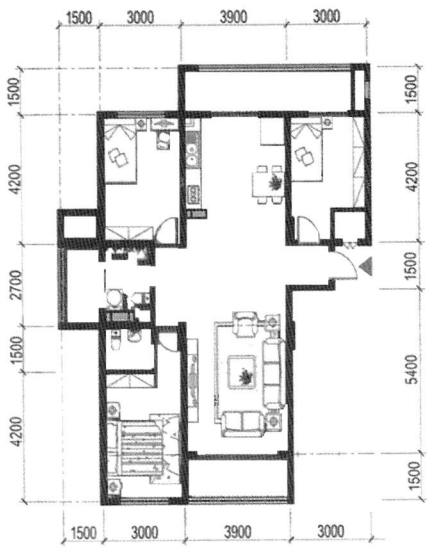

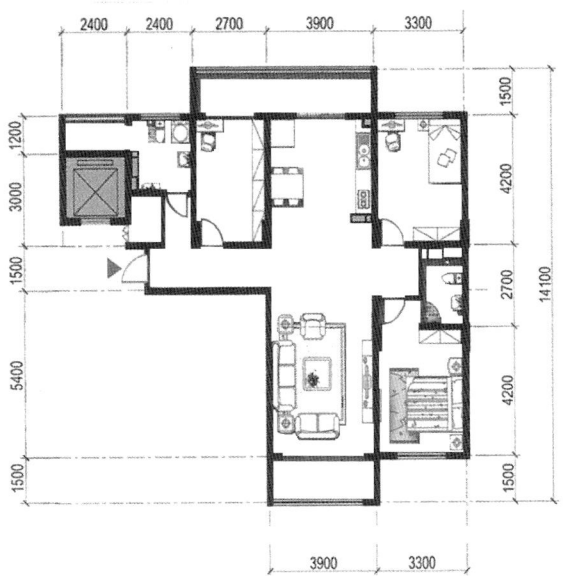

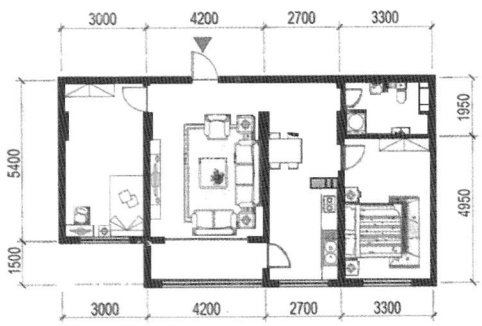

Unit plan for Anhwa-dong apartment building, Raseon.
Source: Son, Jae-jun, 2015

The layouts of North Korean apartments presented in the January 1994 issue of *Joseon Architecture* differ from those of China and South Korea in terms of the relationship between the living room and the kitchen, the location of the kitchen, and the relationship between the kitchen and the dining room. However, two apartment buildings in Raseon reveal the emergence of a new trend since the 2010s. Located in Namsan-dong at the centre of Raseon, one apartment building is 15 storeys high and has four apartments on each floor, with two apartments sharing a staircase on each floor. This building employs two unit plans: one for a two-room apartment with a floor area of 83.88 m²; the other for a three-room apartment with an area of 108 m². The Chinese architects Raseon Geonseong Development Limited completed the building in 2014 in cooperation with Raseon Architectural and Urban Design Institute.[27] The other building is located in Anhwa-dong, Raseon and is 20 storeys high with three apartments per floor. It was designed by architects at Pyongyang Architectural College and developed by Raseon Heungwon Company.

Built by the *donju*, these two apartment buildings use unit plans that differ from those in the three proposals presented in 1994. Their unit plans provide for a similar relationship between the living room and kitchen to that seen in South Korean apartments. However, no concrete evidence exists to explain this connection. The design may have been influenced by South Korean domestic culture, disseminated via South Korean pop culture. These floor plans were developed at about the same time as the master bedroom with en-suite bathroom became popular. Until the 2000s, North Korean apartments had typically had just one sanitation space subdivided into three elements: washbasin, toilet, and bath/shower. These elements were subsequently assigned to separate spaces. From the 2000s, the sanitary facilities were placed in one room, and another bathroom was created for the master bedroom – as in South Korean apartments. Apartments in *donju* buildings thus appear to have been influenced by South Korean trends since 2010, probably as a result of South Korean pop culture.

The selling of apartments to individual buyers also affected their interior design. In the case of new apartment buildings erected by the *donju*, apartments were transferred to buyers without interior decoration. The buyers then purchased the decorative finishes for their apartments, including the bathrooms. Materials were purchased at shops in North Korea in accordance with the buyers' personal taste. Alternatively, the buyers ordered materials through relatives living in China. Apartments thus reflect the individual taste of their owners. Some owners choose an interior similar to those seen in widely circulated South Korean videos. This explains why the interiors of *donju* apartments increasingly resemble apartments in South Korea.

Energy Shortages and Apartment Life

Changes in North Korean apartments since the 2000s are also closely linked to the energy shortage caused by international sanctions and the *donju*'s response to this issue. In 2006 the United Nations Security Council adopted nine major sanctions resolutions on North Korea in response to the country's pursuit and testing of nuclear weapons. The UN limited North Korea's imports of crude oil and refined-petroleum products to 500,000 barrels per year; banned the export of food, machinery, and electrical equipment; and called for the repatriation of all North Korean nationals earning income abroad within 24 months. International sanctions left North Korea facing a severe energy shortage. North Korea's electric-power generation relies heavily on coal- and water-generated power, which the country can produce on its own. Specifically, hydroelectric power generation accounted for more than 60 percent of overall electricity generation. International sanctions rendered imports of oil and natural gas unstable, preventing the development of large thermal power plants. North Korea has also encountered challenges transporting electricity, resulting in severe energy shortages. A recent UN report estimated that North Korea was able to satisfy just 39 percent of electricity demand in 2019, with rural areas only able to afford three to four hours' electricity a day. As a result of such energy shortages, most appliances installed in apartments cannot be used effectively.

A comparison of energy consumption in North and South Korea reveals that South Korea consumed 9.3 times more energy and 15.8 times more electricity per person than North Korea in 2012. In terms of individual energy consumption, one North Korean consumes 30 percent of the global average (141 countries) and 13 percent of the OECD average in energy, and 22 percent of the global average and 8 percent of the OECD average in electricity.[28] To resolve the deficit of power, the North Korean government is seeking to diversify its power production. According to the World Small Hydropower Development Report 2019, published by the United Nations

Industrial Development Organisation (UNIDO) and the International Center on Small Hydropower (ICSHP), North Korea had a hydropower generation capacity of at least 83.2 MW in 2017 – nearly three times higher than their 33 MW capacity in 2016. By contrast with ordinary waterpower, small hydropower refers is small devices installed in rivers, streams, and brooks and able to generate up to 10 MW of electricity.

Since Kim Jong-un took power in 2011, North Korea has actively encouraged the use of solar energy by enacting related laws and establishing research institutes. The use of solar energy to supplement everyday life is becoming increasingly commonplace.[29] In 2013 in order to regulate the development and use of renewable energy, the regime passed the Renewable Energies Act. In 2014 the government released the 'Mid-term and Long-term Development Plan for Natural Energies,' intended to expand the capacity of renewable-energy power facilities to five million kW by 2044. Completed in 2015, the Ryeomyong Street Apartments Complex is fitted with a variety of eco-friendly technologies, making it 'an exhibition centre for green technology.' According to David Von Hippel, a researcher at the Nautilus Institute in the US, 'Although solar energy accounts for only 0.1 percent of North Korea's total electricity production, it is benefitting the everyday lives of ordinary people. Solar energy is not sufficient to operate factories or office buildings, but it is helpful for charging phones in ordinary homes and lighting at night.' Von Hippel and Hayes have estimated that in 2014 approximately 100,000 households in North Korea were using solar panels.[30]

This severe energy shortage has caused great inconvenience to residents living in apartments. This is particularly so in the numerous high-rise apartment buildings – typically more than 30 storeys high – built to create a unique urban landscape during the era of Kim Jong-il. According to many North Korean defectors, insufficient electricity supply renders the elevators in such complexes inoperable, forcing residents to use the stairs. Heating is also a serious problem. Indeed, rumour has it that some residents set up tents in their apartments during the winter months due to the lack of hot water in heating pipes. In response to the indefinite periods of limited water supply, the entire family is mobilised to receive water rations whenever they are available. In response to the lack of water, excrement is often wrapped in plastic and discarded.

The *donju* have had to address these problems in order to sell apartments on the market. The supply of electricity, water, and heat (including hot water) has become one of the most important criteria for determining housing prices. Location is paramount to satisfying these needs in North Korea. For instance, according to Lee Chul, a three-room apartment in Oseong-dong, Central District, Pyongyang, cost approximately USD 45,000 in 2005 because this area had reliable access to various types of energy supply. Location and infrastructure shape pricing, resulting in wide variations in value. The Buksae Street apartments in Moranbong District, for instance, sold for over USD 30,000 each, apartments in Munsu Street Apartments in Daedonggang District and Munheungdong Apartments in Dongdaewon District cost less than USD 30,000, while apartments on Gwangbok Street in Mangyongdae District went for approximately USD 25,000.[31]

To increase the commercial attractiveness of apartments, the *donju* have focused on providing the facilities necessary to improve quality of life. For instance, *donju* apartments are fitted with a relatively large water tank in the bathroom to ensure a steady water supply. Installing such tanks has led to an increase in the size of the sanitation room in apartments. In addition to helping residents cope with water shortages, the provision of such tanks has encouraged the popularity of flush toilets in Pyongyang.[32] The *donju* have also attempted to solve the heating problem independently of the authorities by installing natural-circulation boilers. The growing popularity of natural-circulation boilers in North Korea is hardly surprising given their ability to heat a large room with a small amount of coal and without carbon monoxide emissions. These boilers use pressed and processed *altan* – a small, oval-shaped piece of coal – as their primary heating material. The carbon monoxide which is incompletely burned during combustion of the coal is converted into carbonated gas and burns completely in contact with air. Accordingly, natural-circulation boilers reduce both the potential for carbon monoxide poisoning and the amount of coal required to heat an apartment. 'It takes a third less coal to heat a room than used to be the case,' say the experts, 'and the combustion efficiency of the *altan* and the thermal efficiency of the boiler are so good that a single boiler can heat many rooms at the same time.' Moulded *altan* is also easier to transport and store, good for burning, and less harmful to the surrounding environment. In order to install such boilers, apartments require a separate space for storing *altan* on the veranda. The Namsandong apartment building in Raseon provides such a storage space near the veranda. As *altan* is used as fuel to supply the hot water needed for heating in the building, its transport and storage are important factors in designing the building's layout. Apartment balconies are therefore typically 1.2 m x 3.6 m – large enough to store approximately three days' worth of *altan*. Installing personal inspection devices on balconies can also facilitate transportation of coal.[33]

A recent pamphlet advertising the Raseon Anhwadong apartment building captures the problems facing North Korean apartments and the solutions found to address them. In this respect, apartment developers have promoted two advantages: the provision of boilers to supply hot water and heating, and the allocation of self-activated generators to ensure a consistent supply of electricity. The pamphlet lists 11 advantages that place this apartment building above others, including high ceilings, wide rooms, large triple-glazed windows, conveniently placed washrooms, structural safety, pleasant outer spaces, customised interior designs, and high-quality appliances. The pamphlet also emphasises that the building's elevator is always operational, regardless of electricity supply (the building has its own generator). This building's well-insulated outer walls guarantee an indoor temperature of 20 °C in winter.

1. Kim Eun-young (Seoul, 2001), p. 81.
2. Ibid, p. 77.
3. There are different estimates of the number of deaths in North Korea between 1994 and 1998. Wikipedia cites the researcher Andrei Lankov in support of the view that both the high and low ends of these estimates are inaccurate (Lankov, Andrei (Oxford, 2015), p. 81). In 2001 and 2007 independent groups of researchers estimated that between 600,000 and 1 million people, or 3 to 5 percent of the pre-crisis population, died due to starvation and hunger-related illness (Goodkind, Daniel and West, Loraine, 'The North Korean Famine and Its Demographic Impact'; Haggard, Stephen and Noland, Marcus, (New York, 2007), pp. 72–76. Andrew Natsios and others estimated 2–3 million deaths (Natsios, Andrew, *The Politics of Famine in North Korea, Special Report*, (Washington, D.C.: United States Institute of Peace, 2 August 1999)). According to research by the US Census Bureau in 2011, the likely range of excess deaths between 1993 and 2000 was between 500,000 and 600,000, and there was a total of 600,000 to 1,000,000 excess deaths from the year 1993 to the year 2008 (Spoorenberg, Thomas and Schwekendiek, Daniel, 'Demographic Changes in North Korea: 1993–2008', *Population and Development Review*, vol. 38, no.1, 2012, pp. 133–158); doi:10.1111/j.1728-4457.2012.00475.x. accessed 25 October 2021.
4. For this controversy, see Em, Pavel P. and Ward, Peter, 'City profile: Is Pyongyang a Post-socialist City?', *Cities*, vol. 108, 2021.
5. Yang, Moon-Soo (Seoul, 2013), p. 20.
6. Kim, Jiksu, *Donjuui Hyeongseonggwajeonge*, p. 25.
7. Lee Je-hun, *82cheung apart buk yeomyeonggeori*.
8. Hong Sung-Won, *Bukhan jutaeksijangui hyeongseonggwa*, p. 19.
9. Joung, Eun-lee, *Bukhan budongsansijangui*, p. 292.
10. Ibid., p. 292.
11. Hong Sung-Won, *Bukhan jutaeksijangui hyeongseonggwa*, p. 26.
12. Karl Marx and Frederick Engels (Moscow, 1969), p. 24.
13. Ki Kye-hyeong, 'Soviet sidae chogiui', p. 260.
14. Park, Hyun-seon, Ph.D. Dissertation thesis, 1998, p. 97.
15. Ibid., p. 97.
16. Park, Hyun-seon (Seoul, 2003), p. 367.
17. Lee, Chul, 'Bukhanui jutaengmaemae gwanhan yeongu', p. 70.
18. Kim Su-young, 'Bukhan gongdongjugeo', p. 7.
19. Cho, Sung-ki (Seoul, 2006), p. 300.
20. Kim Su-young, 'Bukhan gongdongjugeo', p. 7.
21. Park Ju-yeon, dissertation thesis for a master's degree, 2002, p. 48.
22. Ibid., p. 56.
23. Unknown, 'Saeroun hyeongsikui', p. 55.
24. Jung, Inha (Honolulu, 2013), p. 71.
25. Kim Sung-kyu, and Kim, Kyung-Bae, 'Hangukgwa junggukui apart', p. 58.
26. Ibid, p. 57.
27. Son, Jae-jun, dissertation thesis for a master's degree, 2015, p. 38.
28. Yu, Sang-Gyun and Choi, Joo Young, 'Miganchamyeoleul tonghan', pp. 151–163.
29. Kim, Min-kwan, *Bukhanui taeyanggwang energy*, p. 20.
30. Von Hippel, David F. and Hayes, Peter, 'Energy Insecurity in the DPRK' (Nautilus Institute for Security and Sustainability).
31. Lee, Chul. 'Bukhanui jutaengmaemae gwanhan yeongu', p. 64.
32. Ibid., p. 29.
33. Son Jae-Jun, *Bukhan gocheung sallimjip namsan18hodongui*, p. 45.

Mirae Science Street Apartment Complex, Pyongyang.
Source: dreamstime/Frenta

Mirae Science Street apartment complex, Pyongyang.
Source: dreamstime/Frenta

Mansudae apartment complex, Pyongyang.
Source: dreamstime/Boggy

8. The Development of the Housing Market and its Influence on Apartment Unit Plans

Mansudae apartment complex, Pyongyang.
Source: *dreamstime/Frenta*

참고문헌

Bibliography

A

Abramov, L., 'Vosstanovlenie i rekonstruktsiyagor odaPkhen'yana', *Arkhitektura SSSR*, January 1955, pp. 31–37.

An, Ryang-ok, 'Daetaryeong mobeom jutaek guhoek jojik-e daehayeo' (On the Organisation of Daetaryeong Model Microdistrict), *Geonchukgwa Geonseol* (Architecture and Construction), vol. 21, no. 2, Feb. 1959, pp. 7–11.

An, Ryang-ok., 'Dong Pyongyang jungangbu jutaek guhoek seolgyeeseo eodeun gyeongheom' (An experience from the site planning of the central place of East Pyongyang), *Geonchukgwa Geonseol* (Architecture and Construction), vol. 19, no. 12, Dec. 1958, pp. 23–26.

Armstrong, Charles K., '"Fraternal Socialism": The International Reconstruction of North Korea, 1953–1962', *Cold War History*, vol. 5, no. 2, May 2005, pp. 161–187.

Armstrong, Charles K., 'The Destruction and Reconstruction of North Korea, 1950–1960', *The Asia-Pacific Journal/Japan Focus*, vol. 7, 16 March 2009.

Armstrong, Charles K., *Tyranny of the Weak: North Korea and the World, 1950–1992* (Ithaca: Cornell University Press, 2013).

B

Baek, Jungi, 'Soryeonui hanbando anjeonghwa jeongchaekui giwongwa jeongae' (The Origin and Development of the Soviet Union's Korean Peninsula Stabilisation Policy), 'Hangukgwa russia gwangye pyeonggawa jeonmang' (Assessment of and Prospect for the Relationship Between Korean and Russia), in Suh, Dae-sook (eds.), *Hangukgwa Russia Gwankye Pyeonggagwa Jeonmang* (Evaluation of and Prospects for the Korea-Russia Relationship), (Changwon: Gyeongnam daehaggyo geukdongmunje yeonguso (The Institute for Far Eastern Studies Kyungnam University), 2001), pp. 165–207.

Baek, Wan-gi, 'Pyongyangsi jutaek soguyeokseoui sangeopmang pochie daehayeo'(On the Disposition of Commercial Networks in the Microdistrict of Pyongyang)' *Geonchukgwa geonseol* (Architecture and Construction), vol. 16, no. 4, Sep. 1958, pp. 28–29.

Baekgwasajeonchulpansa, Joseon daebaekgwasajeon 1 (Encyclopedia of North Korea 1) (Pyongyang: Baekgwasajeonchulpansa, 1995)

Bater, James. H., *The Soviet City: Ideal and Reality* (Beverly Hills: Sage Publications, 1980).

Bauhaus Dessau Archives, Erläuterungsberichte für den Wohnkomplexe der Baujahre 1956/1957 in Hamhung Komplex 3, Hamhung Komplex 1, Hungnam Komplex Rjusongri, Hungnam Komplex Rjuhungri (I_010014_D), 1956.

Bauhaus Dessau Archives, Für den Entwurf von Wohnkomplexen und den Entwurf wirtschaftlicher Aufbau- und Teilbebauungspläne in der VDR KOREA (I_10015_D), 1956.

Berg, Auri C., *Reform in the time of Stalin: Nikita Khruschchev and the Fate of the Russian Peasantry* (Toronto: University of Toronto, 2012).

Bundesarchiv Berlin-Lichterfelde, Bericht Über die Durchführung des Beschlusses des Präsidiums des Ministerrates über die Hilfe der Deutschen Demokratischen Republik beim Aufbau der Stadt Hamhung in der Koreanischen Volksdemokratischen Republik (DC20-1326),1955.

Bundesarchiv Berlin-Lichterfelde, Jahresabschlußbericht der Deutschen Arbeitsgruppe Hamhung für das Jahr 1958 (DC20-1326), 1959.

C

Cha, Cha-yeong, 'Cheollima georiui geonchukhyeongseongsang teukjinge daehayeo'(On the Characteristics of the Architectural Design of Cheollima Street), *Joseon Geonchuk* (Joseon Architecture), vol. 26, no. 1, 1994, pp. 49–51.

Cha, Jiade, Gao, Chengzeng, Xie, Ruosong, 'Chaoxian nongcun jumin dian guihua sheji (Planning of North Korea's Countryside)', *Jianzhu xuebao* (architectural journal), no. 3, 1978, pp. 16–19.

Cha, Munseok and Kim, Ji-hyeong, *Bukhan-ui gongjang mich nodongsiltae bunseok* (Analysis of North Korea's Factories and Actual Labour Situation) (Seoul: Hanguknochongjungangyeonguwon the Federation of Korean Trade Union Research Center, 2008).

Cho, Sung-hun, 'Bukhan-ui dosibaldal yeongu', (A Study of Urban Development in North Korea), *Guksagwan nonchong* (Treatises on Korean History), vol. 70, October 1996, pp. 207–242.

Cho, Sung-ki, *Hangukui minga* (The Korean Folklore House), (Seoul, Hanul Academy, 2006).

Choi, Chun-yeol, 'Bangsedae biyulgwa geonseollyang gyesane daehan uigyeon' (An Opinion Regarding How to Calculate the Ratio of Room Numbers in a Household), *Geonchukgwa Geonseol* (Architecture and Construction), vol. 114, no. 11, 1966, p. 31.

Choi, Won-hun, *Dol mit daehyeongbyeokpangujoui seolgye* (Design of Stone and Large-panel Construction) (Pyongyang: Gongeopjonghapchulpansa, 1991).

Choi, Won-hun and Kim, Jun-gil, *Kongkeuriteu cheomgamulgwa geu riyong* (Concrete Admixtures and Their Use) (Pyongyang: Gongeopjonghapchulpansa, 1991).

Choi, Yeong-pyo, 'Bukhanui haggyogyoyukjedoui byeoncheongwa gujo' (The Transformation and Structure of North Korea's Educational System), in Bukhanyeonguhakhoe (The Korean Association of North Korean Studies), *Bukhanui gyoyukgwa gwahakgisul* (North Korea's Education, Science, and Technology) (Seoul: Kyungin Publishing Co, 2006).

Collins, Robert, *Marked for Life, Songbun North Korea's Social Classification System* (Washington: The Committee for Human Rights in North Korea, 2012).

Communings, Bruce, *Korea's Place in the Sun: A Modern History* (New York : W. Norton, 2005).

D

Day, Andrew,'The Rise and Fall of Stalinist Architecture', in James Cracraft and Daniel Rowland (eds), *Architectures of Russian Identity; 1500 to the Present*, (Ithaca, NY: Cornell University Press, 2003).

E

Editorial, 'Nongchon munhwa jutaek geonseol' (Construction of rural cultural housing), *Rodongsinmun*, 8 December 1961.

Elden, Stuart and Crampton, Jeremy W., *Space, Knowledge and Power: Foucault and Geography* (Hampshire: Ashgate Publishing Limited, 2007).

Em, Pavel P. and Ward, Peter, 'City profile: Is Pyongyang a Post-socialist City?', *Cities*, vol. 108, 2021, <https://doi.org/10.1016/j.cities.2020.102950>, accessed 21 October 2021.

F

Foot, Rosemary, *A Substitute for Victory: The Politics of Peacemaking at the Korean Armistice Talks*, (Ithaca: Cornell University Press, 1990).

G

Gang, Chunmo, 'Dosigyehoekeseo sangeopmangui hamnijeok pochi' (The Rational Disposition of Commercial Networks in Urban Planning), *Geonchukgwa geonseol* (Architecture and Construction), May 1961: 24.

Gang, Jiyeon, *'Uli inminban: nunmullo sseun talbukmin sugi* (Our People's Unit: a Defector's Memoir Written in Tears)', *Wolgan Bukhan* (Monthly North Korea), no. 516, 2014, pp. 158–165.

Geonseol daehak geonchukhak gangjwa (architecture class at costruction college), 'Gocheung jutaekseolgyeeseo jegidoeneun myeot gagi munje' (Some Problems Arising in High-rise Housing Design), *Geonchukgwa Geonseol* (Architecture and Construction), vol. 32, no. 1, January 1960, pp. 23–26.

Geertz, Clifford, Negara, *The Theatre State in Nineteenth-Century Bali* (Princeton, NJ: Princeton University Press, 1981).

Goodkind, Daniel and West, Loraine, 'The North Korean Famine and its Demographic Impact,' *Population and Development Review*, vol.27, no. 2, June 2001, pp. 219–238.

Gukgageonseolwiwonhoe dosigyehoegguk (National Construction Committee, Urban Planning Bureau), 'Dosigyehoek bumuneseo 3wol jeonwonhoeui gyeoljeonggwa susang dongjiui gyosi gwancheoleul wihayeo'(For the Accomplishment of the Instruction of the Prime Minister and the Decision of the Plenary Session in March on Urbanism) in *Geonchukgwa geonseol* (Architecture and Construction), vol. 48, no. 5, May 1961, pp. 21–22.

Guknip Geonseol Chulpansa, Joripjageobui gigyehwa (Mechanisation of Assembly Operation), (Pyongyang: Guknipgeonseolchulpansa, 1962).

Gukgageonseol wiwonhoe jungang seolgye yeonguso dosigyehoeksil (National Construction Committee, Central Design Institute Urban Planning Bereau), 'Dosi gyehoekeseo soguyeok seolgyee daehan myeot gaji uigyeon (Several Opinions on Microdistricts in Urban Planning)' in *Geonchukgwa geonseol* (Architecture and Construction), vol. 55, no. 12, December 1961, pp. 19–23.

Gwon, Seonga, 'Bukhanui gyoyuggwajeong jeongchaek' (North Korea's Educational Policy), in Bukhan yeonguhakoe (The Korean Association of North Korean Studies)(eds.) in *Bukhanui gyoyukgwa gwahakgisul* (North Korea's Education, Science, and Technology), (Seoul: Kyung-in Publishing Co, 2006), pp. 253–296.

Gyeonggongeopseong Seolgye Yeonguso (Light Industry Design Institute), 'Onsu ondol nanbang bangbeobe daehayeo' (On the Ondol System of Warm Water Heating) in *Geonchukgwa Geonseol* (Architecture and Construction), vol. 2, no. 2, April 1958, pp. 32–33.

H

Haggard, Stephen and Noland, Marcus, *Famine in North Korea: Markets, Aid, and Reform* (New York: Columbia University Press, 2007).

Hain, Simone, 'Von der Geschichte beauftragt, Zeichen zu setzen. Zum Monumentalitätsverständnis in der DDR am Beispiel der Gestaltung der Hauptstadt Berlin', in R. Schneider, W. Wang (eds) *Moderne Architektur in Deutschland 1900 bis 2000. Macht und Monument*, (Stuttgart: Gerd Hatje, 1998).

Hamhŭngsi dosiseolgyeyeonguso (Hamhŭng Urban Design Institute), 'Hamnijeogin ondol pyeongmyeondeul (Rational Ondol Plans)' in *Geonchukgwa Geonseol* (Architecture and Construction), vol. 113, no. 10, Oct. 1966, p. 3.

Hamhŭngsi dosiseolgyeyeonguso dosigyehoeksil (Hamhŭngsi Urban Design Institute Urban Planning Bureau), 'Soguyeokgyehoekeun dosi chonggyehoekui ilbulo doeyeoya handa'(The Planning of Microdistricts Should Be Part of Overall Urban Planning) in *Geonchukgwa geonseolv* (Architecture and Construction), vol. 60, no. 5, May 1962, pp. 17–19.

Han, Beom-jik and Li, Bok-u, *Joseoneseoui geonseol* (Construction in North Korea) (Pyongyang: Oegunkmunjonghap chulpansa, 1991).

Han, Jong-ok, *'Sinposi jungsimbuui geonchuk hyeongseong(Architectural formation of the urban center of Sinpo City)'* in *Geonchukgwa Geonseol* (Architecture and Construction), Feb., (1965) pp. 25–27.

Harris, Steven E., *Communism on Tomorrow Street: Mass Housing and Everyday Life after Stalin* (Washington, DC, Woodrow Wilson Center Press, 2013).

Heo, Jae-su, 'Saero iltteoseoneun suncheonyeokgeori geonchukyeongseong' (Architectural Design of New Suncheon Station Street) in *Joseon Geonchuk* (Joseon Architecture), vol. 17, no. 4, 1991, pp. 20–21.

Hong Sung-Won, 'Bukhan jutaeksijangui hyeongseonggwa baljeone gwanhan yeongu' (A Study of the Formation and Development of the Housing Market in North Korea: Based upon Construction and Sales of Apartments), University of North Korean Studies, dissertation thesis for master's degree, 2014.

Hong, Young-sun, *Cold War Germany, the Third World, and the Global Humanitarian Regime* (New York: Cambridge University Press, 2015).

Hou, L., Sheng, Y., Stanek, L., Gzowska, A., Bujas, P., 'Zhongbo jiaoliu beijing xia de quyu guihua shiyan yu yingxiang (Experiments and Influences of Regional Planning under the Background of China-Poland Exchange)' in *Guihuazhi* (Planner), vol. 19, no. 35, 2019, pp. 83–85.

Hunter, Helen-Louise, *Kim Il-sung's North Korea* (Connecticut: Greenwood Publishing Group, 1999).

Hwang, Ae-ri, 'Bukhan-ui yeoseong nodongjeongchaek: 1950nyeondaewa 1990nyeondae bigyo bunseok'(North Korea's Policy of Labour Women: A Comparative Analysis of the 1950s and the 1990s), dissertation thesis for master's degree, Ewha Women's University, 2000.

I

Ikonnikov, Andrey, *L'architecture russe de la période soviétique* (Paris : Edt. Pierre Mardaga, 1990).

IUA Inquiry, Moscow (1958), 'The Proceedings of North Korea in the Fifth Congress of the International Union of Architects', Bauhaus Dessau Archives, I 010299 D.

J

Jeon, Man-gil, 'Itjimothal Namsanjae (Unforgettable Namsan Hill)' in *Joseon Geonchuk* (Joseon Architecture), vol. 24, no. 3, 1993, pp. 5–10.

Jeon, Man-gil, 'Jeonhwanui Sibaljeom' (The Starting Point of the Turnaround) in *Joseon Geonchuk* (Joseon Architecture), vol. 25, no. 4, 1993, pp. 4–7

Jeon, Seok-dam, 'Joseon Nodongdangui Yeongdohae Jeonhu Sahoejuui Geonseoleseo Joseon Inmini dalseonghan Seonggwawa Geuuiui' (The Significance of North Korean People's Achievements in Post-war Socialist Construction under the Leadership of the Joseon Workers' Party" in *Ryeoksa nonmunjip 4* (Historical Treatises 4): Socialist Construction (Pyongyang: Gwahakwon chulpansa, 1960).

Jeong, Myeong-geun, 'Wonsansi haeangeori geonchuk hyeongseonge daehayeo' (On the Architectural Formation of Wonsan's Beach Street area) in *Geonchukgwa Geonseol* (Architecture and Construction), vol. 93, no .2, February 1965, pp. 46–48.

Jeong, Yeong-cheol, 'Bukhanui sahoetongjewa jojiksaenghwal' (North Korea's Social Control and Community Life) in Bukhan yeonguhakhoe (The Korean Association of North Korean Studies) (eds.), *Bukhan-ui sahoe* (North Korea's Society), (Seoul: Kyung-in Publishing Co, 2006), pp. 109–164.

Jing, Xie and Wu Deng, 'Socialist Architecture in Mao's Model Village: A Case Study of Qinyong Village in Ningbo' in *The Journal of Architecture*, vol. 22, no. 2, March 2017, pp. 293–327.

Jo, Hyeon-sik, 'Bukhanui gakjong daegyumo geonseolgongsaga gyeongjee michineun yeonghyang bunseok ' (Analysis of the Effects of Various Large-scale Projects on North Korea's Economy) in *Bukhan* (North Korea), no. 10, 1996, pp. 92–94.

Joo, Nam-Chul, *Hanguk geonchuksa (History of Korean architecture)* (Seoul, Korea University Press, 2006).

Joseon Central News Agency (eds.), *Joseon jungang yeongam 1954–1955* ('The Yearbook of Joseon Central 1954–1955) (Pyongyang: Joseon Central News Agency, 1954).

Joseon Central News Agency (eds), *Joseon jungang yeongam* (The Yearbook of Joseon Central), (Pyongyang: Joseon Central News Agency, 1958).

Joseon Central News Agency (eds), *Joseon jungang yeongam* (The Yearbook of Joseon Central), (Pyongyang: Joseon Central News Agency, 1959).

Joseon Central News Agency (eds), *Joseon jungang yeongam* (The Yearbook of Joseon Central) (Pyongyang: Joseon Central News Agency, 1961).

Joseon Central News Agency (eds), *Joseon jungang yeongam* (The Yearbook of Joseon Central) (Pyongyang: Joseon Central News Agency, 1971).

Joseon Central News Agency, 'Nongeop hyeopdong johap gyeongyeong wiwonhoeleul jojikhal de gwanhayeo' ('On the Organisation of Management Committee of Agricultural Cooperatives'] in Joseon Central News Agency (eds.), *Joseon jungang yeongam* (The Yearbook of Joseon Central), 1962.

Joseon Central News Agency, 'Chongsan nongeop hyeopdong johapui munhwa jutaek geonseol-e chaksu' (Commencement of the Construction of Cultural Houses in the Chongsan-Ri Agricultural Cooperative), *Rodongsinmun*, 18 April 1961.

Joseon Central News Agency, 'Geunlojadeului saenghwaleul sahoejuui geonseoljadabge munhwa wisaengjeokeulo gaeseonhaja! (Let's Improve Living Conditions for Workers as Builders of Socialism in a Cultured and Hygienic Manner)' in *Rodongsimmun*, 27 Dec. 1958.

Joseon Central News Agency, 'Dosi gyeongyeong saeobeul gaeseon ganghwahal de gwanhan naegag gyeoljeong chaetaek (The Adoption of the Cabinet's Decision on the Improvement of Urban Management Projects)' in *Rodongsinmun*, 17 December 1958.

Joseon Central News Agency, 'Gungnae sangeobeul gaeseon ganghwahal dc gwanhan naegak gyeoljeong chaetaek' (The Adoption of the Cabinet's Decision on the Improvement of Domestic Commerce) in *Rodongsinmun*, 17 July 1958.

Joseon Central News Agency, 'Jeollyakayeo iman sedaeui jutaegeul deo geonseolhal geoseul gyeoru' (The Resolution to Construct More Than 20,000 Households by Economising) in *Rodongsinmun*, 18 February 1958. .

Joseon Central News Agency, 'Dangui ryeongdomite geochanghago ungjanghwaryeohage iltteoseoneun gwangbokgeori' (The Magnificent Construction of Gwangbok New Town under the Guidance of the Party) in *Rodongsinmun*, 23 June 1987.

Joung, Eun-lee, 'Bukhan budongsansijangui baljeone gwanhan bunseok (Analysis of Development of the North Korean Real Estate Market - Focusing on Illegal Trade in the Right to Use a House-)' in *The Journal of Northeast Asian Economic Studies*, vol. 27, no. 1, March 2015, pp. 289–328.

Jung, Inha, 'Sahoejuui dosi Pyongyang (Socialist City Pyongyang)' in *Landscape Architecture Korea*, vol. 373, May 2019, pp. 16–21.

Jung, Inha, *Architecture and Urbanism in Modern Korea* (Honolulu: University of Hawaii Press, 2013).

Jungang pyojunseolgye yeonguso (Central Standard Design Institute), 'Dosihyeong pyojunjutaek (Standard Plan for Urban Housing)' in *Geonchukgwa Geonseol* (Architecture and Construction), vol. 56, no. 1, January 1962, pp. 25–26.

Jungang pyojunseolgye yeonguso (Central Standard Design Institute), 'Nongchon munhwa jutaek geonseoleul ganghwahagi wihayeo' (For the Improvement of Rural Cultural Housing) in *Geonchukgwa Geonseol*, vol. 56, no. 1, January 1962, pp. 11–15.

Jungangseolgye yeonguso dosigyehoeksil (National Construction Committee, Central Design Institute, Urban Planning Bureau).'Dosi jubyeonui gyeongsajiwa gureungjidaeeseo hamnijeogin soguyeok jojik'(The Rational Organisation of Microdistricts on Sloping Land and in Hilly Areas Around the Urban Fringe) in *Geonchukgwa Geonseol* (Architecture and Construction), vol. 57, no. 2, Feb. 1962, pp. 5–9.

'Jungang pyojunseolgye yeonguso in *Geonchukgwa geonseol*, 12, 1964.

Jungang pyojunseolgye yeonguso (Central Standard Design Institute), 'Geonmurui dayangseong bojanggwa jutaekmagam seksiia jojige daehan uigyeon' (An Opinion on Guarantees of Building Diversity and Housing Finishing, and the Organisation of the *Sektsiia* Plan)' in *Geonchukgwa Geonseol* (Architecture and Construction), vol. 108, no. 5, May 1966, pp. 47–48.

K

Kang, Myeong-suk, 'Hanilhabbangijeon ilbonindeurui Pyongyang chimtu' (The Japanese Invasion of Pyongyang Before the Annexation Treaty between Korea and Japan) in *Gugsagwannonchong*, vol. 107, 2005. <http://db.history.go.kr/download.do?levelId=kn_107_0060&fileName=kn_107_0060.pdf> accessed 22 October 2021.

Ki Kye-hyeong, 'Soviet sidae chogiui ilsangsaenghwalgwa Kommunalka gongganui seonggyeok' (Everyday Life in Early Soviet Russia: the Kommunalka between the Public and the Private Sphere) in *Seoyangsaron* (The Western History Review), vol. 98, 2008, pp. 255–281.

Kim, Bong-su,'74ho sibeomjutaeksoguyeokgyehoek' (The Draft Plan for Model Microdistrict no. 74)' in *Geonchukgwa geonseol* (Architecture and Construction), vol. 123, no. 8, Aug. 1967, pp. 29–33.

Kim, Bong-ho, '5mansedae sallimjim geonseolgwa jeonmang' (The Construction and Vision of a 50,000-household Apartments Complex. Questions and Answers: A meeting with Chief of Staff Kim, Bong-ho of the Capital Construction Command) in *Chollima*, vol. 378, Nov. 1990, pp. 38–40.

Kim Byeong-heon, 'Hwanghaebugdo jigu nongchon burak gyehoek jakseong-eseo eodeun myeot gaji gyeongheom' (Some Experiences from the Rural Village Planning for North Hwanghae Province)' in *Geonchukgwa Geonseol* (Architecture and Construction), vol. 106, no. 3, March 1966, pp. 22–23.

Kim Byung-ik, '60man dongui nongchon munhwa jutaek geonseol saeobui seonggwajeok bojangeul wihayeo (For the Successful Construction of 60,000 Rural Cultural Houses)' in *Rodongsinmun*, 20 December 1961.

Kim Cheol-su, 'Gunsojaeji gyehoek'['Planning of 'Gun (County) Seat'] in *Geonchukgwa Geonseol, Geonchukgwa Geonseol* (Architecture and Construction), vol. 77, no. 10, Oct. 1963, pp. 33–35.

Kim Cheol-su, 'Gunsojaeji gyehoek (Planning of the *gun* (county) capital] in *Geonchukgwa Geonseol, Geonchukgwa Geonseol* (Architecture and Construction), vol. 78, no.11, Nov. 1963, pp. 39–40.

Kim, Cheol-su, 'Bulmyeorui hyeongmyeongsajeok giri jeonhal seonbong hyeongmyeong sajeokji' (Seonbong Revolutionary Historical Site Which Delivers Immortal Revolutionary Spirit) in *Joseon Geonchuk* (Joseon Architecture), vol. 19, no. 2, 1992, pp. 25–34.

Kim Dae-nyun, Rhee, Kee Choon, Lee Ki Young, Rhee Eun Young, Yi Soon Hyung, Park Young Sook, Choi Younshil, 'Bukhan juminui jugeosiltaewa jugeohaengdonge gwanhan yeongu (A Study of the Housing Life Situations of North Koreans and Their Housing Behaviours Based on Interviews and an Empirical Survey with Defectors)' in *Journal of Korean Home Management Association*, vol. 17, no. 4, Dec. 1999, pp. 221–238.

Kim, Doo-seop, Choi, Min-ja, Jeon, Gwang-hui, Lee, Sam-sick and Kim, Hyung-suk, 'Bukan inguwa ingu senseoseu' (North Korean Population and Population Census) (Seoul: Tonggyecheong, 2011).

Kim Eun-young, 'Sahoejuuigwon bunggooe daehan bukhanui insikgwa daeeung (North Korea's Attitude Toward and Perception of the Collapse of the Socialist Bloc)', Ewha Women's University, dissertation thesis for master's degree, 2001.

Kim, Eung-sang, *Juche geonseol ryeoksaui galpireul deodeumeo* (In Search of Juche Construction History), (Pyongyang: Joseon rodongdang chulpansa, 1998).

Kim, Gwang-yun, 'Nongchon burak gyehoek bangdo' (Planning Method for Rural Villages) in *Geonchukgwa Geonseol* (Architecture and Construction), vol. 56, no. 1, January 1962, pp. 16–18.

Kim, Hana, 'Iljegangjeomgi malgi Chongjinui sigajigyehoek' (Urban Planning of Chongjin in the Late Japanese Colonial Era) in *Proceedings of the Korean Association of Architectural History Autumn Conference*, November 2010, pp. 289–291.

Kim, Il-sung, 'Jeonguk geonchukga mit geonseolja heouieseo hasin Kim Il-sung wonsuui yeonseol' (President Kim Il-sung's Speech at the National Conference of Architects and Builders) in *Geonchukgwa Geonseol* (Architecture and Construction), no. 2, May 1956, pp. 1–7.

Kim, Il-sung, 'Nongchon munhwa jutaekeul daedaejeogeuro geonseolhal ep gwanhayeo' (On Mass Construction of Rural Cultural Housing) in *Joseon jungangnyeongam* (Annuals of North Korea) (Pyongyang: Joseon jungangtongsinsa, 1962).

Kim Il-sung, 'Joseon Rodongdang je4cha daehoeeseo han jungang wiwonhoe saeop chonghwa bogo' (Report of the Central Committee's Review of National Projects at the Fourth Congress of the Labour Party) in *Joseon jungangnyeongam* (Annuals of North Korea) (Pyongyang: Joseon jungangtongsinsa, 1962).

Kim Il-sung, 'Sinnyeonsa' ('New Year's Address'), 1 January 1962, in *Joseon jungangnyeongam* (Annuals of North Korea) (Pyongyang: Joseon jungangtongsinsa, 1963).

Kim Il-sung, 'Ulinala sahoejuui nongchon munjee gwanhan teje' (Theses on the Socialist Rural Question in Our Country) in *Joseon jungangnyeongam* (Annuals of North Korea) (Pyongyang: Joseon jungangtongsinsa,1965).

Kim Il-sung, *Jeojakjip 6* (Works 6) (Pyongyang: Joseon Rodongdangchulpansa, 1980).

Kim Il-sung, 'Ulinala sahoejuui nongchon munjee gwanhan teje' (Theses on the Socialist Rural Question in Our Country) in *Joseon jungangnyeongam* (Annuals of North Korea) (Pyongyang: Joseon jungangtongsinsa, 1965).

Kim Il-sung, *Jeojakjip 6* (Works 6) (Pyongyang: Joseon Rodongdangchulpansa, 1980).

Kim Il-sung, '*Jeojakjip 10* (Works 10) (Pyongyang: Joseon rodongdangchulpansa, 1982).

Kim Il-sung(a), 'Geonseorui jireul nopigi wihayeo' (For the Improvement of Construction Quality) (25 December 1958) in Kim Il-sung, *Jeonjip 22* (Complete Works 22) (Pyongyang: Joseonnodongdang chulpanbu, 1998), p. 516.

Kim Il-sung(b), 'Gibon geonseoleul jeongsanghwahagi wihayeo' (For the Normalisation of Basic Construction) (1 January 1964), in Kim Il -sung, *Jeonjip 32* (Complete Works 32) (Pyongyang, Joseon rodongdang chulpansa, 1998).

Kim Il-sung, 'Sinnyeonsa' (New Year's Address), (1 January 1963) in Kim Il-sung, *Jeonjip 30* (Complete Works 30) (Pyongyang, Joseon rodongdangchulpansa, 2000).

Kim, Jeong-Hui, *Dosi geonseol* (Urban Construction) (Pyongyang: Joseon Minjujuui-Inmin Gonghwaguk Gwahakwon, 1953).

Kim, Jeong-hui, 'Pyongyangsi Kim Il-sung gwangjanui geonchukjeok guseonge daehayeo' (On the Architectural Composition of Kim Il-Sung Square in Pyongyang) in *Geonchukgwa Geonseol* (Architecture and Construction), no. 2, May 1956, pp. 25–31.

Kim, Jiksu, 'Donjuui hyeongseonggwajeonge gwanhan yeongu' (A Study of the Formation of Donju), University of North Korean Studies, dissertation thesis for master's degree, 2012.

Kim Jin-hyeong, *Sajineuloboneun hangukchogi seongyo 90 jangmyeon – gamligyopyeon* (Korea's Early Missions as Seen in Photos) (Seoul: Jinheung, 2006).

Kim Jong-deuk, 'Josso chinseon nongeop hyeopdong johap burak guseong-eseo eodeun gyeongheom' (Lessons Learned from Village Planning for Choseon-Soviet Goodwill Agricultural Cooperative) in *Geonchukgwa Geonseol*(Architecture and Construction), vol. 15, no. 8, 1958, pp. 42–44.

Kim, Jong-suck, 'Polish Aid for North Korea during the Korean War', *East European & Balkan Studies*, vol. 38, no. 6, 2014, pp. 161–179.

Kim, Jong-il, *Geonchuk yesullon* (On the Art of Architecture) (Pyongyang: Joseonroodongdang chulpansa, 1991).

Kim, Jong-un, '*Sahoejuui nongchontejeui gichileul nopi deulgo nongeopsaengsan-eseo hyeoksineul ileukija*' (Let's Achieve Innovation of Agricultural Production, Holding High the Banner of the Socialist Rural Theses), (Pyongyang, Joseon rodongdang chulpansa, 2014).

Kim Gwang-yun, 'Nongchon saengsan jiyeok gyehoeke daehan uigyeon' (An Opinion on Planning of Agricultural Production Region) in *Geonchukgwa Geonseol* (Architecture and Construction), vol. 88, no .9, Sep. 1964, pp. 10–15.

Kim Gwang-yun, 'Seohaean pyeongjidae nongchon bulagui haplijeok saenghwaldanwi jojik' (Organisation of Rational Living Units in Rural Villages on the West Coast Plain Area) in *Geonchukgwa Geonseol*, 1 (1966), pp. 32–35.

Kim, Mi-jin, 'Bukhan gyoyeui giwongwa hyeongtae yeongu' (A Study on the Origin and Types of Gyoye in North Korea) in *Dongasia munhwa yeongu* (Journal of East Asian Cultures), vol. 62, 2015, pp. 229–252.

Kim, Mina, Bukhanui jutaeksoguyeoke gwanhan yeongu (A Study on the Planning of Microdistricts in Post-War North Korea), Hanyang University, Ph.D. dissertation thesis, 2018.

Kim, Mina and Jung, Inha, 'The Planning of Microdistricts in Post-war North Korea: Space, Power, and Everyday Life' in *Planning Perspectives*, vol. 32, no.2, 2017, pp. 199–223.

Kim Min-kwan, 'Bukhanui taeyanggwang energy hwalyonghyeonghwanggwa jeonmang' (Current Status of and Prospects for Utilisation of Solar Energy in North Korea), Weekly KDB Report, 24 July 2017.

Kim Myun, 'Dokil guklipmunseobogwanso sojang jaryoleul donghaeseobon bukhangwa gudongdokui gyeongje hyeopryeok (Economic Cooperation between North Korea and East Germany, Seen from the Documents of the German Federal Archives)', *North Korean Studies Review*, vol. 7, no. 1, 2003, pp. 83–105.

Kim, Myun, 'Gudongdokui dae bukhan sahoejuui geonseoljiwon' (A Study of East German Assistance to North Korea in the 1950s) in *Hanguk dongbuka nonchong* (Northeast Asia Studies) vol. 34, no. 1, 2005, pp. 351–374.

Kim Myun, 'Bimilmunseolo bon gudongdok Hamhŭngsigeonseol project: jeonhu sahoejuuidosigeonseol-ui saeloun model' (The Hamhŭng Construction Project as Seen in Classified Documents from the German Democratic Republic) in *Minjok21*, vol. 51, June 2005, pp. 94–99.

Kim, Nam-sub., 'Khrushchevui jutaek jeongchaekgwa soryeonsahoe-ui ilsang' (Housing Policy under Khrushchev and Soviet Everyday Life) in *Reosiayeongu* (Russian Studies), vol. 20, no. 1, 2010, pp. 215–244.

Kim Ryong-chul, 'Nongchon burak gyehoekeseo daeji jojiksang jegidoeneun myeot gaji munje' (Some Issues Relating to Site Planning in the Rural Village Plan) in *Geonchukgwa Geonseol* (Architecture and Construction), vol. 76, no. 9, 1963, pp. 51–52.

Kim Su-young, 'Bukhan gongdongjugeo pyeongmyeoneso natananeun jeonsilui giwon mit byeonhwayangsange gwanhan yeongu' (A Study on the Origin and Transformation of the Entrance Space in the Collective Housing Plan in North Korea) in *Journal of the Architectural Institute of Korea Planning and Design*, vol. 33, no. 7, July 2017, pp. 3–12.

Kim, Suk-ja, 'Ganggyesiui bokgu geonseol gyehoek' (The Reconstruction Plan for Ganggye) in *Rodongsinmun*, 21 March 1954.

Kim, Suk-ja, 'Sariwonsiui bokgu geonseol jeonmang' (The Outlook for Reconstruction of Sariwon) in *Rodongsinmun*, 22 March 1954.

Kim, Suk-ja. 'Bokgu geonseoldoeneun Namposiui jeonmang' (The Outlook for Reconstructed Nampo) in *Rodongsinmun*, 23 March 1954.

Kim, Sunkwan. 'Namposi-ui juyo garo hyeongseong gyehoek-e daehan iyagileul deuleumyeo' (Listening to the Story of the Formation of Arterial Streets in Nampo City) in *Geonchukgwa Geonseol* (Architecture and Construction), vol. 84, no. 5, May 1964, pp. 24–27.

Kim Sung-kyu, and Kim, Kyung-Bae, 'Hangukgwa junggukui apart pyeongmyeonggyehoek teukseonggwa jusaenghwal munhwaui gwangye yeongu' (A Study of the Relationship between the Apartment Floor Plan and Housing Culture in Korea and China) in *Journal of The Urban Design Institute of Korea*, vol. 17, no. 5, Oct. 2016, pp. 49–62.

Kim Tae-ro, 'Nongchonmaeul gyehoekeseo jutaekeul eotteotge anchineun geosi joeunga' (The Best Way to Lay Out Houses in Rural Village Planning) in *Geonchukgwa Geonseol*, no. 2, Feb. 1967, pp. 33–35.

Kim Taewoo, 'Limited War, Unlimited Targets: US Air Force bombing of North Korea during the Korean War, 1950–1953' in *Critical Asian Studies*, vol. 44, no. 3, Sep. 2012, pp. 467–492.

Kim, U-ho., 'Soguyeok jojikeseoui geonchuk mildoe daehayeo' (On Architectural Density in the Microdistrict), *Geonchukgwa geonseol*, vol. 16, no. 9, Sep. 1958, pp. 37–40.

Kim, Yeong-bok, 'Deouk saeropgo ungjanghage geonseoldoen chollima geori' (Newly Constructed Chollima Street) in *Joseon Geonchuk* (Joseon Architecture), vol. 10, no. 1, 1990, pp. 65–68.

Kim, Yeong-bok, 'Munsudong gwangjang mit juyogarogeonchuk gyehoek (Architectural Planning for Munsudong Square and its Principal Road) in *Geonchuggwa Geonseol* (Architecture and Construction), vol. 97, no. 6, June 1965, pp. 23–24.

Kim, Young-Jae, Jang, Bo-hye, and Han, Dong-soo, 'Saheojuui gukgaui nongchon-hurake gwanhan yeongu (A Study of the Rural Community Plan of Socialist Nations – Focused on the Site Planning of the Chinese Commune and the North Korean Collective Farm) in *Journal of the Architectural Institute of Korea Planning and Design*, vol. 16, no. 9, Sep. 2000, pp. 115–126.

Kim, Young-hoon, 'Bukhan nongeopnongchonui byeonhwa' (Changes in North Korea's Agricultural Countryside)', *KREI (Korean Rural Economic Institute) Quarterly Bukhan Nongeop Donghyang* (North Korea's Agricultural Trend), vol. 12, no. 3, Oct. 2010, pp. 3–17.

Korea Institute for National Unification, *2009 North Korea Overview* (Seoul: Dahae Media, 2009).

Kwon, Heonik and Chung, Byung-Ho, *Geukjang gukga Bukhan* (North Korea: Beyond Charismatic Politics) (Seoul: Changbi Publisher, 2013).

Kwon Tai-Joon, 'Iljesidaeui dosihwa' (Urbanisation in the Japanese Colonial Period) in *Hanguk-ui sahoewa munhwa* (Korean Society and Culture) no. 11, January 1990.

Kwon, Yeong-tae, 'Urisik georiui tto hanaui hullyunghan bonbogi' (Another Excellent Example of Our Style Street) in *Joseon Geonchuk* (Joseon Architecture), vol. 10, no. 4, 1990, pp. 2–6.

L

Lankov, Andrei, *The Real North Korea: Life and Politics in the Failed Stalinist Utopia* (Oxford: Oxford University Press, 2015).

Lee, Chul, 'Bukanui jutaekmaemae gwanhan yeongu: gyeongjenan ihu pyeongyangeul jungsimeuro'(A Study on the Housing Market in North Korea: Focusing on Pyongyang since the Arduous March), University of North Korean Studies, dissertation thesis for master's degree, 2017.

Lee, Hang-gu, 'Bukhanui naemak 28: bukhan-ui jutaek'(The Inside Story of North Korea 28: Housing) in *Bukhan Monthly*, vol. 98, 1980, pp. 254–257.

Lee Je-hun, '82cheung apart buk yeomyeonggeori 1nyeongmane wangong… bigyeoleun donju' (The Completion of an 82-storey Apartment Building in Ryomoyong Street in Just One Year… The Secret of Success is *Donju*)', Hankyoreh, 27 January 2019. <http://www.hani.co.kr/arti/PRINT/880026.html>, accessed 25 October 2021.

Lee, Kyo-duk and Gong Seon-ja, '1950nyeondae bukhan jeongsee daehan ilbon oemuseongui insik' (The Japanese Foreign Ministry's Perception of North Korea's Situation in the 1950s) in Cho Han-bum (eds.), *Haeoejaryoro bon bukhanchejeui hyeongseonggwa baljeon* (The Formation and Development of the North Korean System as Seen from Overseas Data) (Seoul: Seonin, 2006).

Lee, Wang-kee, O Young-sik, 'Bukhanui nongcho maeulbaechi mit jugeogyhoeke gwanhan yeongu' (A Study on the Rural Settlement and Rural Housing Planning in North Korea) in *Journal of the Korean Institute of Rural Architecture*, vol. 1, no. 2, 1999, pp. 133–144.

Lee, Wang-kee, 'Bukhangeonchuk tto hanaui uri moseop'(North Korea's Architecture: Another Version of Ourselves) (Seoul: Seoul Forum, 2000).

Levi, Nicolas, 'Zarys Historii Stosunków Między Polską a Koreańską Republiką Ludowo-Demokratyczną (1948–1974) in *Kwartalnik Historyczny*, vol. 124, no, 4, 2017, pp. 733–752.

Li Hwa-seon(a), *Joseon geonchuksa 2* (History of Joseon architecture 2) (Pyongyang: Gwahakbaekgwasajeon jonghab chulpansa, 1989, reedited, Seoul: Baleon, 1993).

Li Hwa-seon(b),'*Joseon geonchuksa 3* (History of Joseon Architecture 3) (Pyongyang, Gwahak baekgwasajeon jonghab chulpansa, 1989, reedited, Seoul: Baleon, 1993).

Li, Hyeon-deok, and Li, Hyeon-bok, Daehwacheop, *Juche geonchkui daehwawon 1 (Great Album-Great Garden of Juche Architecture 1)* (Pyongyang: Munye chulpansa, 1987).

Li, Hyeon-deok, Daehwacheop- *Juche geonchukui daehwawon 3* (Great Album-Great Garden of Juche Architecture 3) (Pyongyang: Munye chulpansa, 1990).

Li, Hyeong, 'Sae segie bitbalchineun hyangdoui taeyang' (A Leading Sun of the New Century) in *Chollima*, vol. 315, no. 8, August 1985, pp. 41–42.

Li, Hyo-su, 'Dosi gyehoekeseo pyojun seolgyee uihan jutaek guhoek seolgyeleul jiljeokeuro bojanghagi wihan daechaek' (A Measure to Qualitatively Guarantee Housing Section Design through Standardised Design in Urban Planning) in *Geonchukgwa Geonseol* (Architecture and Construction), vol. 17, no. 10, Oct. 1958, pp. 7–9.

Li, Hyo-sun, 'Geunrojadeului saenghwaleul munhwa wisaengjeokeuro gaeseonhal de daehayeo (On Cultural and Hygienic Improvement of Workers' Living) in *Rodongsinmun*, 27 December 1958.

Li, Sang-cheol, 'Namsinuijue geonseoldoego inneun sallimjipdeul' (Housing Constructed in South Sinuiju) in *Joseon Geonchuk* (Joseon Architecture), vol. 11, no. 2, 1990, pp. 86–87.

Li, Sun-gwon and Baek, Wan-gi., *Jutaek soguyeokgyehoek*' (The Planning of the Microdistrict) (Pyongyang: Guklipgeonseol chulpansa, 1963)

Li, Sun-gwon, 'Pyojun seolgyee uihan jutaek guhoek geonchukui haprijeok bangbeope daehayeo' (On the Rational Method of Housing Section Construction through Standardised Design) in *Geonchukgwa Geonseol* (Architecture and Construction), vol. 15, no. 8, Aug. 1958, pp. 19–22.

Lim Ki-beom, *Ulisig nongchon munje haegyeolui bichnaneun gyeongheom* (Glorious Experiences in Our Own Way of Solving Rural Problems]' (Pyongyang, Nongeop chulpansa, 1992).

Lu, Duanfang, *Remaking Chinese Urban Form: Modernity, Scarcity and Space* (Abingdon: Routledge, 2006).

M

Marx, Karl and Engels, Frederick, 'Manifesto of the Communist Party (Translated by Samuel Moore in cooperation with Frederick Engels, 1888)' in Marx/Engels, *Selected Works, Vol. One*, Progress Publishers, Moscow, 1969, pp. 98–137.

Meuser, Philipp (eds), *Architectural and Cultural Guide Pyongyang, 2 vols.*, (Berlin: DOM publishers, 2012).

Meuser, Philipp and Zadorin, Dimitrij, *Towards a Typology of Soviet Mass Housing: Prefabrication in the USSR, 1955–1991*' (Berlin: DOM publishers, 2015).

N

Nam, Il, 'Sae hwangyeonge jeokeunghage geonseol saeopeul gaeseon ganghwahal de daehayeo jeonguk geonseolja daehoeeseo han naegak bususangimyeo gukga geonseol wiwonhoe wiwonjangin Nam Il dongjiui bogo' (The Report of Nam Il, Vice Prime Minister and Chief of the National Construction Committee, at the National Builders' Congress on the Improvement of Construction Projects for a New Environment) in *Geonchukgwa Geonseol* (Architecture and Construction), vol. 47, no. 4, April 1961, pp. 2–13.

Natsios, Andrew, 'The Politics of Famine in North Korea, Special Report', (Washington, D.C.: United States Institute of Peace, 2 August 1999)

Nove, Alec, *An Economic History of the USSR*. (Harmondsworth, Penguin, 1972).

O

O, Ik-geun, 'Ttohanaui hyeoksin tongbang panel jutaekgeonseol' (Another Innovation: Tonbang Panel Housing Construction) in *Rodongsinmun*, 22 June 1958.

Oh, Dae-yeong and Ha, Gyeong-ho, *Dangui yeongdomite changjakgeonlibdoen daeginyeombideului sasang yesulseong*' (The Ideas and Artistic Values of Monuments Created under the Party's Guidance) (Pyongyang: Joseon misulchulpansa, 1989).

Oh, Gyu-tae, 'Bokgu geonseoldoeneun Wonsansiui jeonmang' (The Outlook of Reconstructed Wonsan) in *Rodongsinmun*, 24 March 1954.

P

Pai, Hyung-min, and Cho, Minsuk (eds.), *A Crow's Eye View: The Korean Peninsula* (Seoul: Archilife, 2014).

Pallot, Judith, 'Living in the Soviet countryside' in Willam Craft and Blair A. Ruble (eds.), *Russian Housing in the Modern Age: Design and Social History* (Washington, DC: Woodrow Wilson Center Press, 1993).

Park, Dong-min, 'The General Plan for the Reconstruction of Pyongyang and the Role of Kim Jung-hee: Myths and History' in *Journal of the Architectural Historian*, vol. 27, no. 2, 2018, pp. 125–138.

Park, Geum-cheol, 'Gibon geonseol saeopeul gaeseonhal de daehayeo Joseon nodongdang jungang wiwonhoe 10wol jeonwon hoeuieseo han Park Geumcheol dongjiui bogo' (The Report of Park Geumcheol at the Plenary Session of the Central Committee of the Korean Workers' Party in October on the Improvement of Basic Construction Projects) in *Rodongsinmun*, 19 October 1957.

Park, Hyun-seon, *Hyeondae bukhansahoewa gajok* (Contemporary North Korean Society and Family) (Seoul: Hanul Academy, 2003).

Park, Hyun-seon, 'Hyeondae Bukhanui gajokjedoe gwanhan yeongu ' (North Korea's Family System), Ewha Women's University, Ph.D. dissertation thesis, 1998.

Park, Im-tae, 'Nongchon geonseoleseo geodun seonggwawa gwaeop' (Achievements and Tasks in Rural Construction) in *Geonchukgwa Geonseol* (Architecture and Construction), vol. 16, no. 4, Sep. 1958, pp. 21–24.

Park, Jong-chol, and Jeoung, Eun-lee, 'Hangukjeonjaeng ihu Bukhanjaegeoneul wihan dongeurope saheojuui gukgaui wonjoe daehan geomto' (East European Socialist Countries' Aid for Reconstruction of North Korea after the Korean War), *CEESOK Journal of Korean Studies*, vol. 15, 2014, pp. 49–73.

Park, Ju-yeon, 'A Study of the Compositional Character of the Layout of Urban Apartments in North Korea', Sunmoon University, dissertation thesis for master's degree, 2002.

Park, Sehoon, Kim, Taehwan, Kim, Seongsu, Song, Jieun, 'Bukhan dosigyehoek mit dosigaebal siltae bunseokgwa jeongchaekgwaje' (Urban Planning and Development Practices in North Korea: Urban Consequences of Informal Market) (Anyang: KRIHS, 2016).

Park, Soo-heon, 'Stalin chejewa soryeonsahoe' (Soviet Society Under Stalin) in *Reosiayeongu* (Russian Studies) vol. 7, Dec. 1997, pp. 263–296.

Park, Young-ja. 'Bukhanui yeoseong nodongjeongchaek: nodong gyegeuphwawa supyeongjeok, sujigjeok wigyeleul jungsimeulo' (North Korea's Policy for Women's Labour: Focusing on the Labour Class and its Horizontal and Vertical Hierarchies) in Bukhanyeongukoe (The Korean Association of North Korean Studies) (eds.), *Bukhan-ui yeoseong-gwa gajok* (Women and Family in North Korea), (Seoul: Kyungin Publishing, 2006), pp. 129–165.

Ptichnikova, Galina and Antyufeev, Aleksey, 'Architecture of Stalingrad: The Image of the Hero City using the Language of "Stalinist Empire Style"', E3S Web of Conferences 33, 2018. < https://doi.org/10.1051/e3sconf/20183301046> accessed 22 October 2021.

Pyonganbukdo dosiseolgye yeonguso (Rural Village Design Division of Pyongbuk Province Urban Design Institute), 'Nongchon burak gyehoek seolgyewa jutaek daeji jeonglieseo goryeohal myeoch gaji munje' (Some Issues to Consider in Rural Village Planning and the Development of Housing Sites) in *Geonchukgwa Geonseol* (Architecture and Construction), vol. 57, no. 2, Feb.1962, pp. 10–11.

Pyongyangsi dosigeonseol yeonguso (Pyongyang Urban Construction Institute), 'Dosihyeong oerangsik jutaekseolgye' (Single-corridor-access Urban Housing Design) in *Geonchukgwa Geonseol* (Architecture and Construction), vol. 57, no. 2, February 1962, p. 25.

Pyongyang dosigyehoek yeonguso nongchon burak gyehoek seolgyesil (Pyongyang Urban Design Institute, Rural Village Design Division), 'Nongchonmaeul gyehoekeseo mukkeumsik jutaek baechi bangbeop' (Methods for Clustering Houses in Rural Planning), *Geonchukgwa Geonseol* (Architecture and Construction), vol. 120, no. 5, May 1967, pp. 22–24.

Pyongyang geonseoljeonsa pyeonchanwiwonhoe (The Committee for Writing the History of the Construction of Pyongyang) (eds.), *Pyongyang geonseoljeonsa 2* (The Whole Story of the Construction of Pyongyang 2)', (Pyongyang, Gwahak baekgwasajeon jonghabchulpansa, 1997).

Püschel, Konrad, *Wege eines Bauhäuslers* (Dessau: Anhaltische Verlagsgesellschaft mbH, 1997).

R

Rah, In-won, 'Hapnijeogin dosisaenghwaldanwichegyewa soguyeok seoljeonge daehan myeot gaji munje'(A Few Issues Relating to Rational Urban Living Units and the Microdistrict) in *Geonchukgwa geonseol* (Architecture and Construction), vol. 120, no. 5, May 1965, pp. 41–42.

Rolf, Jenni, 'Learning from Moscow: Planning Principles of the 1935 General Plan for Reconstruction and its Political Relevance,' <http://www.raumbureau.ch/files/Learning_from_Moscow.pdf>, accessed 19 March 2015.

Ruble, Blair, A., *Russian Housing in the Modern Age: Design and Social History* (Cambridge: Cambridge University Press, 1993).

Rüdiger, Frank, *Die DDR und Nordkorea: Der Wiederaufbau der Stadt Hamhung von 1954–1962.* (Aachen: Shaker Verlag, 1996).

S

Schneider, R., and Wang, W. (eds), *Moderne Architektur in Deutschland 1900 bis 2000. Macht und Monument* (Stuttgart: Gerd Hatje, 1998).

Seo, Dong-man, *Bukjoseon yeongu*(*North Korea Studies*) (Paju, Changbi Publishers, 2010).

Shen, Zhihua and Xia, Yafeng, 'China and the Post-War Reconstruction of North Korea, 1953–1961. North Korea International Documentation project Pater Series n.4', Woodrow Wilson International Center for Scholars, May 2012.

Shim, J., Lee, H., Min, W., 'Iljegangjeomgi Chongjinui Paengchanggwa jeongeori eoeop' (The Expansion of Chongjin and its Sardine Fishery during the Japanese Colonial Era) in *The Journal of History and Practical Thought Studies*, vol. 63, July 2017, pp. 133–177.

Shin, Dong-sam, 'Die Planung des Wiederaufbaus der Städte Hamhung und Hungnam in Nordkorea durch die DAG-Städtebaubrigade der DDR von 1955–1962', dissertation, Hafen City Universität Hamburg, 2016.

Shin, Dong-sam, *Hamhŭngsiwa Hungnamsiui dosigyehoek* (The Urban Planning of Hamhung and Hungnam) (Seoul: Nonhyung, 2019).

Shin, Gun-soo, and Jung, Inha, 'Appropriating the Socialist Way of Life: the Emergence of Mass Housing in Post-war North Korea' in *The Journal of Architecture*, 2 (2016).

Shin, Sun-gyeong, 'Jutaek geonseolui joriphwaeseo eodeun seonggwawa gyeongheom (Achievements and Experience in Prefabrication of Housing Construction) in *Geonchukgwa Geonseol* (Architecture and Construction), vol. 9, no. 2, April 1958, pp. 6–8.

Smith, Mark B., *Property of Communists* (Illinois: Northern Illinois University Press, 2010).

Son Jae-Jun, 'Bukhan gocheung sallimjip namsan18hodongui gongchk teukseonge gwanhan yeongu' (A Study on the Architectural Characteristics of North Korea's High-Rise Apartment Building Namsan 18Hodong)', Inha University, dissertation thesis for master's degree, 2015.

Song, Kue-jin, 'Hangyeongseon buseolgwa Gilhoeseon jongdanhang gyeoljeongi jiyeokgyeongjee kkichin yeonghyang' (The Impact of the Construction of the Hamgyeong Railway on Local Economies) in *Hanguksahakbo* (The Journal for the Study of Korean History)', vol. 57, Nov. 2014, pp. 325–358.

State Committee of Civil Engineering and Architecture., *Principles of Town Planning in the Soviet Union II,* reprint of the 1967 edition, (Hawaii: University Press of the Pacific Honolulu, 2004).

Strumilin, S., 'Family and Community in the Society of the Future' in *Soviet Review*, no. 2 , 1961, pp. 3–29.

Suh Dae-Sook, *Kim Il Sung: The North Korean Leader* (New York: Columbia University Press, 1988).

T

Tanigawa, Ryuichi and Kuznetsov, Dmitry, 'North Korea's Urban planner Kim Jeong-hui: An elucidation and Analysis of his Career before the Korean Armistice (1953)', *Journal of Architecture and Planning*, AIJ, vol. 86, no. 781, March 2021, pp. 1103–1113.

Tomita, Hideo and Ishii, Masato, 'The Influence of Hannes Meyer and the Bauhaus Brigade on 1930s Soviet Architecture', *The Journal of Asian Architecture and Building Engineering*, vol. 13, no. 1, January 2014, pp. 49–56.

Tomita, Hideo, 'Wohnkomplexe in 1930s USSR and 1950s North Korea by an East German Architect', Proceedings of the 11th ISAIA, Sept.20–23, 2016, Miyagi, Japan, pp. 2288–2292.

U

Unknown, *Joseon geonchuk geonseolui 10nyeon* (Ten Years of North Korea's Architecture and Construction) (Pyongyang: Guklipgeonseol chulpansa, 1958).

Unknown, *Joripjageopui gigyehwa* (Mechanisation of Assembly Operation) (Pyongyang, Gungnipgeonseolchulpansa, 1962).

Unknown, 'Botongbeolui oneulgwa naeil' (The Today and Tomorrow of Botongbeol) in *Geonchukgwa Geonseol* (Architecture and Construction), vol. 63, no. 8, Aug. 1962.

Unknown, 'Deouk aleumdawojineun uri nongchon maeul' (Our Rural Villages Which Keep Getting More Beautiful) in *Chollima*, vol. 65, no. 2, 1964, p. 118.

Unknown, 'Junggongsik junghyeong block-e uihan nongchon munhwa jutaek-ui jolipsik geonseol' (Construction of Rural Cultural Houses Using Large Chinese Blocks) in *Geonchukgwa Geonseol* (Architecture and Construction), vol. 87, no. 9, Sep.1964, p. 20.

Unknown, 'Tongbang jutaek seolgye sian' in *Geonchukgwa Geonseol* (Architecture and Construction), vol. 83, no. 4, April 1964, p. 20.

Unknown, 'Saeroun hyeongsikui salimjip (Sian)' (New Types of Apartments (Proposals)), *Joseon Architecture*, vol. 26, no. 1, January 1994, pp. 55–56.

V

Van Ree, Erik, 'The Limits of Juche: North Korea's Dependence on Soviet Industrial Aid, 1953–76' in *The Journal of Communist Studies*, vol. 5, no. 1, 1989, pp. 50–73.

Von Hippel, David F. and Hayes, Peter, 'Energy Insecurity in the DPRK: Linkages to Regional Energy Security and the Nuclear Weapons Issue, NAPSNet special report, Nautilus Institute for Security and Sustainability', 3 January 2018. <https://nautilus.org/napsnet/napsnet-special-reports/energy-insecurity-in-the-dprk-linkages-to-regional-energy-security-and-the-nuclear-weapons-issue/> accessed 22 October 2021.

W

Weathersby, Kathryn, 'Dependence and Mistrust: North Korea's Relations with Moscow and the Evolution of Juche' (Washington DC: US–Korea Institute at SAIS, Working Paper Series, WP 08-08, December 2008).

Wu, Hung, *Remaking Beijing: Tiananmen Square and the Creation of a Political Space* (Chicago: University of Chicago Press, 2005).

Y

Yang, Jin-young, 'Gyeongpan jolipsik nongchon jutaek sigong' ('Construction of Rural Houses Prefabricated Using Light Concrete Plates') in *Geonchukgwa Geonseol* (Architecture and Construction), vol. 88, no. 9, Sep. 1964, pp. 18–19.

Yang, Moon-soo, '*Bukhanui gyehoekgyeongjewa sijanghwa hyeonsang* (North Korea's Planned Economy and Marketisation) (Seoul: National Institute for Unification Education, 2013).

Yim, Dong-woo, 'Pyongyangui dosigyehoek' (Urban Planning of Pyongyang) in *Reading the City of Pyongyang, Journal of Environmental Studies*, < https://s-space.snu.ac.kr/bitstream/10371/92359/1/06_%EC%9E%84%EB%8F%99%EC%9A%B0.pdf> accessed 22 October 2021.

Yim Dong-woo, *Pyongyang, and Pyongyang After-Urban Transformation in Program, Scale, Structure* (Paju: Hyohyeong, 2011)

Yim, Dong-woo, 'Bukhanjuyodosiui gonggangujowa diagram' (Urban Structure and Diagrams of North Korea's Major Cities) in Ko Yu-hwan et al. (eds.) *Hamhŭnggwa Pyongseong* (Hamhung and Pyongseong) (Seoul: Hanul, 2014).

Yoon, Cheolgee, 'ukhancheje-eseo gyehoekgwa sahoejeok jonghab:1953~69nyeon' (The Plan and Social Synthesis in the North-Korean System: 1953–1969) in *Hangukjeongchihakoebo* (Korean Political Science Review), vol. 45, no. 1, 2011, pp. 235–263.

Yu, Sang-Gyun and Choi, Joo Young, 'Miganchamyeoleul tonghan nambuk energy hyeopryeok bangan' (Energy Cooperation on the Korean Peninsula Involving the Participation of the Private Sector) in *Journal of the Korean Planning Association*, vol. 50, no. 1, Jan. 2015, pp. 151–163.

Yun, Changbong, 'Mobeom jutaek soguyeogui geonseol gyehoeke daehayeo: Hamhŭngsi' (On the Construction of a Model Microdistrict : Hamhung City) in *Geonchukgwa geonseol* (Architecture and Construction) vol. 21, no. 2, Feb. 1959, pp. 12–15.

Yun, Changbong, 'Hamhŭngsi mobeom jutaek soguyeokui geonseol gyehoeke daehayeo' (On the Construction Plan for the Model Microdistrict in Hamhŭng) in *Geonchukgwa Geonseol* (Architecture and Construction), vol. 24, no. 5, May 1959, pp. 23–24.

Z

Zaremba, Piotr, 'Joseon dosi geonseolui baljeonwonchike daehan myeotgaji gochal' (Thoughts on the Principles of Development in the Construction of North Korean Cities) in *Geonchukgwa Geonseol* (Architecture and Construction), no. 2, May 1956, pp. 37–40.

Zaremba, Piotr, 'Metody Pracy Urbanistycznej w Korei', *Miasto*, no. 2, 1956, pp. 30–32.

Zaremba, Piotr, 'Siljejeokin dosigyehoekui munje 1' (Practical Urban Planning Problems) in *Geonseolja (*Builder), no. 5, May 1957, pp. 55–62.

Zaremba, Piotr, 'Siljejeokin dosigyehoekui munje 2' (Practical Urban Planning Problems) in *Geonseolja* (Builder), no. 6, June 1957, pp. 78–84.

Zaremba, Piotr, 'Polski Projekt Koreańskiego Miasta Czon-dżin', *Miasto*, no. 1, 1957, pp. 4–11.

Zhang, Jie and Wang, Tao, 'Housing Development in the Socialist Planned Economy from 1949 to 1978' in Lu. Junhua, Rowe. Peter G. and Zhang, Jie (eds.), *Modern Urban Housing in China* (Munich, Prestel, 2001).

Zchang Sung-Soo and Yoon Hae-Jung, '*Bukhanui jugeojeongchaekgwa geonseol siljeoke gwanhan yeongu* (On North Korea's Housing Policy and Construction Results), Jutaek Forum, 2 (2000).

Zhao, Chunlan, 'Socio-spatial Transformation in Mao's China: Settlement Planning and Residential Architecture Revisited (1950s-1970s)', PhD dissertation thesis, Catholic University of Leuven (KUL), 2007.

Zhou, Buyi, 'Bolan jianzhushi fanghua daibiaotuan dui zhongguo chenshi guihua jianzhu yishu he jianzhu jiaoyude yixie yijian' (An Opinion on Chinese Urban Planning, Architecture, and Architectural Education by Polish architects Visiting China) in *Jianzhu Xuebao*, no. 1, 1956, pp. 102-118.

Zigurds L. Zile, 'Programs and Problems of City Planning in the Soviet Union', *Washington University L. Q.*, 19, 1963, pp. 19–59.

Iconic architecture as stage set: Arirang mass gymnastics in the *1 May Stadium* in Pyongyang. *Source: Philipp Meuser (2010)*

The *Deutsche Bibliothek* lists this publication in the *Deutsche Nationalbibliografie*; detailed bibliographic data is available on the internet at *http://dnb.d-nb.de*

ISBN 978-3-86922-686-6

© 2023 by DOM publishers, Berlin
www.dom-publishers.com

This work is subject to copyright. All rights are reserved, whether the whole or part of the material is concerned, specifically the rights of translation, reprinting, recitation, broadcasting, reproduction on microfilms or in other ways, and storage or processing in data bases. Sources and owners of rights are given to the best of our knowledge; please inform us of any we may have omitted.

Korean in this book has been transliterated following the rules set out in 'Revised Romanisation of Korean', published on 7 July 2000.

Proofreading
John Nicolson

Typesetting
Shaun Yong

Printing
Master Print Super Offset, Bucharest
masterprint.ro

Acknowledgments
Chapters 3, 4, 5 of this book are based on articles already published in the following journals: Gunsoo Shin & Inha Jung (2016), 'Appropriating the Socialist Way of Life: the Emergence of Mass Housing in Post-war North Korea', *The Journal of Architecture*, 21:2; Mina Kim & Inha Jung (2017), 'The Planning of Microdistricts in Post-war North Korea: Space, Power, and Everyday Life', *Planning Perspectives*, 32:2; Gunsoo Shin & Inha Jung (2019), 'Socialising Rural Space in North Korea: Settlement Planning, Housing, and Service Networks', *The Journal of Architecture*, 24:1.